THE REPORTER'S ENVIRONMENTAL HANDBOOK

THE REPORTER'S ENVIRONMENTAL HANDBOOK

▪ THIRD EDITION ▪

BERNADETTE M. WEST

M. JANE LEWIS

MICHAEL R. GREENBERG

DAVID B. SACHSMAN

RENÉE M. ROGERS

RUTGERS UNIVERSITY PRESS

NEW BRUNSWICK, NEW JERSEY, AND LONDON

Library of Congress Cataloging-in-Publication Data
The reporter's environmental handbook / [edited by] Bernadette M. West ... [et al.].—3rd ed.
p. cm.
Includes bibliographical references and index.
ISBN 0-8135-3286-8 (cloth : alk. paper) — ISBN 0-8135-3287-6 (pbk. : alk. paper)
1. Environmental protection—Press coverage—United States—Handbooks, manuals, etc. 2. Environmental health—Reporting—United States—Handbooks, manuals, etc. I. West, Bernadette.
PN4888.E65R46 2003
070 4'493637—dc21 2002037014

British Cataloging-in-Publication information is available from the British Library.

Manufactured in the United States of America

CONTENTS

PREFACE AND ACKNOWLEDGMENTS

The rapid collapse of an Antarctic ice shelf raises fears about the impact of global warming. A salt dome in New York is mined too extensively and collapses along with the ground it was supporting, shifting the foundations of homes and ruining aquifers and farmland for miles. A plastics warehouse burns to the ground in Indiana, releasing a toxic cloud that travels for miles. Residents living near an island off of Puerto Rico that is used as a bombing range by the United States Navy have abnormally high rates of cancer and other health problems. Chernobyl . . . Three Mile Island . . . Love Canal . . . Bhopal . . . Times Beach, Missouri . . . mercury poisoning in Minamata, Japan . . . radon-contaminated homes . . . dioxin dumping in the bay. . . . These are the stories that make the front-page and nightly news headlines. Environment and health coverage is no longer relegated to the back of the paper or the tail end of the broadcast.

As the public becomes increasingly aware of and worried about the environment, editors and reporters cannot rely on a "seat-of-the-pants" approach when reporting on environmental issues. Stories must be technically accurate, responsible, objective, and balanced. The quality of reporting influences public perception, and from public perception, often, comes public policy. Yet few newspapers or broadcast stations can assign a full-time reporter to environmental stories. Faced with a fast-breaking story, even beat reporters may not have time to consult a specialist. The aim of this book is to give every reporter and editor the background needed to report these complex and controversial stories effectively.

The Reporter's Environmental Handbook was first published by the Hazardous Substance Management Research Center (HSMRC) at the New Jersey Institute of Technology (NJIT) in 1988 under the title *The Environmental Reporter's Handbook*. The book won praise from reviewers and a Special Award for Journalism from the Sigma Delta Chi Society of Professional Journalists in 1989. A second edition, published in 1995, was retitled *The Reporter's Environmental Handbook* to reflect the need of all reporters for sound background information on environmental issues. The third edition is a joint undertaking of the

University of Medicine and Dentistry of New Jersey's (UMDNJ) School of Public Health and Rutgers, The State University of New Jersey, and funded once again by the HSMRC. It has been extensively revised, enlarged, and updated.

In the fall of 2000, we surveyed the membership of the Society of Environmental Journalists and asked them what were the important environmental health issues in their communities. Most of the topics included in this edition were chosen based on what journalists told us. This edition includes seventeen new briefs and eleven revised briefs from the second edition. Briefs were prepared by experts in the field or by the editors based on interviews with experts and from information available in the field. The general information sections on finding an expert, doing background checks on a company's environmental record, and covering an environmental emergency have also been updated.

Outside reviewers for briefs were recruited from members of the HSMRC's Industrial Advisory Board and its Public Policy Division, faculty at UMDNJ and Rutgers University, representatives from the New Jersey Department of Environmental Protection, and representatives of industry and environmental organizations. All new briefs in this edition have been reviewed by at least one outside reader, and more than half have been reviewed by two or more outside readers. Some comments received were quite brief and some quite extensive. Every attempt was made to incorporate the suggestions offered by the reviewers. The revised briefs retained from the second edition were sent for outside review as well.

The authors are greatly indebted to all who helped prepare the first and second editions of the *Handbook*, including the co-editors of the first edition, David Sachsman, Liz Fuerst, and their staff, and the original group of experts who contributed briefs. In addition, we are indebted to all who helped prepare the second edition, including co-editor Peter Sandman and the experts who contributed briefs. In this third edition, we deeply appreciate the contribution of the following individuals who prepared individual briefs on selected topics: Theresa Byrd, James Detjen, Richard Fenske, Bernard Goldstein, Mark Robson, James Ross, Peter Sandman, and Michael Westendorf. For this edition, the following people provided background information for one or more briefs: Robert W. Burchell, Joanna Burger, James Florio, Natalie C. Freeman; Bernard Goldstein, J. F. Grassle, Michael Hamm, Francis Hoffman, Paul Lioy, Michele Oschner, Mark Robson, Dona Schneider, Christopher Uchrin, Daniel Wartenberg, and Junfeng Zhang.

We are also deeply grateful to the reviewers of the drafts of briefs for the third edition who gave us careful critiques of the briefs and invaluable suggestions. For this edition we are especially grateful to the following reviewers: Thomas Armstrong, ExxonMobil; Tom Atherholt, Research Scientist, Division of Science, Research and Technology (DSRT), New Jersey Department of Environmental Protection (NJDEP); Michael Aucott, Environmental Indicators Scientist, DSRT/NJDEP; Michael J. Bean, Environmental Defense Fund; Linda J. Bonanno, Research Scientist, Bureau of Risk Analysis, DSRT/NJDEP; Gary Buchanan, Research Scientist, DSRT/NJDEP; Ronald Burstein, Corporate Environmental Affairs Manager at National Starch and Chemical; James H. Higinbotham, Global Remediation, ExxonMobil; Jeffrey L. Hoffman, Research Scientist, New Jersey Geological Survey, NJDEP; Haroon Kheshgi, ExxonMobil; Thomas A. Ledoux, Research Scientist, Bureau of Risk Analysis, DSRT/NJDEP; George W. Lucier, Environmental Defense Fund; Richard H. McKee, Senior Toxicology Associate, Toxicology and Environmental Sciences Division, ExxonMobil; Michael McLinden, Research Scientist, Office of Pollution Prevention, NJDEP; Karl Muessig, New Jersey State Geologist, NJDEP; Eileen Murphy, Assistant Director, DSRT/NJDEP; Jorge L. Reyes, Environmental Scientist Trainee, Sustainability Team, Office of Environmental Planning and Science, NJDEP; Jeffrey H. Siegell, ExxonMobil; Terri Smith, Brownfield Coordinator, NJDEP; Richard M. Stapleton, author of *Lead Is a Silent Hazard* (1994); Alan H. Stern, Chief, Bureau for Risk Analysis, DSRT/NJDEP; and Bernard Tramier, Director, Strategic Direction and Evaluation of Risks, Total Fina Elf-Aquitaine.

Once again, the research and writing were funded by the HSMRC. The HSMRC has also contributed additional funds to underwrite the publication of this book. The Environmental and Occupational Health Sciences Institute (EOHSI) in Piscataway, New Jersey, provided additional support for the third edition.

We wish to acknowledge Audra Wolfe at Rutgers University Press for her thoughtful and careful editing of the manuscript. We also thank the HSMRC, its staff, and its advisory committees for their financial support and helpful advice along the way. Thanks also to Margaret Mitchell, Wendy Sheay, Jennifer Tan, and Aaron Truchil for their assistance in preparing parts of the final manuscript. The opinions expressed here—and, of course, any errors—are those of the authors alone.

GETTING STARTED

HOW TO USE THIS HANDBOOK

This book contains twenty-eight briefs on specific environmental-health issues identified by journalists in our survey as important in their communities. Each brief provides background information on the issue and discusses stakeholders, problems and approaches being used to correct the problems, and resources for additional information. In addition, the book includes four introductory chapters that are designed to provide reporters with the "how to's" of covering environmental stories regardless of topic. An additional three chapters provide general background information on environmental reporting that can be useful in understanding the challenges journalists face in covering environmental issues.

First read the chapters in the "Getting Started" section. "Handling an Environmental Emergency: A Case Study in Finding Sources" serves as a guide to covering all environmental stories through its detailed description of a reporter's movements while covering an environmental emergency. The process is roughly the same for covering an emergency and nonemergency. This chapter illustrates the who, what, where, when, and why of an environmental incident; identifies the questions to be asked and how to find the answers; and suggests ways of finding sources.

"The Language of Risk" provides a necessary perspective on what is often misunderstood and often inflated: the way we talk about the risks of exposure. To write a story accurately about an environmental topic, a reporter must be sensitive to the language of risk and hazard. One quickly learns that there are two very different ways of talking about risk: one technical and quantitative, the other nontechnical and often emotion-filled. Scientists and ordinary citizens often talk at cross-purposes about risk. Paying attention to these distinctions will give your story far greater authority and win you credibility with all of your sources and your audience. "Tracking Down a Company's Environmental Record" and "Finding an Expert" present some basic material that will assist you in locating important information for your story and help you decide if the people you will be talking with are the real experts and if the information they are offering is factual or opinion.

The next three chapters that precede the briefs provide insights with regard to the larger context in which environmental reporting occurs. "Journalists' Views of the Environment: Issues and Challenges" presents the results of the original survey of journalists regarding the environmental stories journalists believe are most important in their communities today. A shortened version is reprinted here with permission from *Risk: Health, Safety, and Environment* (12 [fall 2001]:299–310). It discusses some of the challenges a journalist may face when covering environmental issues, ranging from community misunderstanding to lack of editorial support for environmental stories. "Who Sets the Environmental Agenda?" examines the even larger issue of agenda setting and lays out the sources that help shape the public agenda through their attempts to influence the media. "Thoughts on the Future of Environmental Policy and Regulation" discusses the shift in paradigms governing environmental policy over time and what this means in terms of the types of questions journalists raise in their stories.

Once you have the overall picture, use the *Handbook* as a reference for background information and sources as each story arises. The briefs are listed alphabetically from "Air Pollution (Indoor)" to "Water Supply" and should be used like recipes in a cookbook: "Cancer and Other Disease Cluster Claims" for one story, "Children's Health (Asthma)" for the next. While each brief is self-contained, briefs on related subjects are cross-referenced when useful, for example, "Air Pollution (Indoor)," "Children's Health (Lead)," and "Children's Health (Asthma)" are cross-referenced.

Each brief begins with a short background discussion of the problem. It identifies the issues and covers who is likely to be harmed, discusses whether the risk is increasing or decreasing, and concisely describes the problems raised for communities and individuals and the approaches being used to correct these problems. Next, the brief identifies what you need to know to research the story and warns of possible pitfalls in reporting it. Finally, the brief identifies specific sources for researching your story, with websites, phone numbers, and addresses as current as we can make them. Once you have read the brief, you should have a clear idea of what kinds of data you will need to gather; what experts, activists, organizations, resources, and legislation you will need to consult; and what questions to raise.

HANDLING AN ENVIRONMENTAL EMERGENCY

A CASE STUDY IN FINDING SOURCES

This case study presents a hypothetical incident designed to illustrate how a reporter might use news sources to cover an environmental crisis on deadline. Reporters should be aware that each environmental incident poses its own set of problems and that different approaches may be indicated. One rule of thumb is that reporters should always speak to at least two experts (at least one of whom is not aligned with a vested position) to verify facts (such as consequences of toxic accidents) because scientists often get conflicting results from the same data.

A call comes into the editor's desk late Friday morning from a local resident. The caller is very upset, but he manages to explain that a large tanker truck has had an accident near a drainage ditch that runs in front of his house. He says that the truck is spilling a foul-smelling liquid into the ditch. He tells the editor he is greatly distressed about possible contamination of the community's seven public wells. The incident has occurred in the small town of East Cityville, right off the town's main intersection. The editor hands the story over to the reporter who handles that geographic beat.

The reporter telephones police headquarters and learns that a police officer is on the way to the scene of the accident. When the officer reports back to headquarters, the reporter learns that the truck bears several placards, including a red warning placard marked "flammable." The truck belongs to Move for Profit Co. It was dispatched from a chemical company in an adjacent city. The police department has decided to evacuate some residents to a nearby church.

From a call to the regional office of the state's environmental agency, the reporter learns that state emergency response personnel have been dispatched to the scene. An hour later, in a subsequent call, the agency's spokesperson tells the reporter the Move for Profit truck was carrying the pesticide chlordane. "It's one of the pesticides once used in great volume in the United States," he says. "As you know, it's what we use for termites. It's probably under all the homes in this state." He further explains that chlordane would not pose a real airborne hazard unless it is mixed with the wrong substances, which is highly unlikely. "But," he adds, "it is a suspected carcinogen and acutely toxic in high doses. High concentrations in wells would necessitate closing them. Ingestion or skin contact would lead to medical problems." The spokesperson says he is awaiting reports from agency representatives on the scene before he can determine just how serious is the East Cityville spill.

The reporter next calls the Department of Environmental Sciences at the nearby university and gets the name of a chlordane expert on the faculty. The expert suggests he contact the Society for Risk Analysis in McLean, Virginia, for an opinion on the level of risk involved with chlordane. Another call is placed to Chemtrec, an emergency information service operated by the Chemical Manufacturers Association. Chemtrec helps identify placard numbers on trucks. He also goes to the HazMat Safety website for more information on the placards on the truck.

The chlordane expert, a toxicologist, explains that the chemical vaporizes, is not soluble in water (does not dissolve), and can travel through a waterway as a slug of toxic material. In addition, he says, "It certainly is toxic if people come into direct contact with it or ingest it." The reporter asks if it is dangerous to get chlordane on your skin. The toxicologist tells him if people come into contact with chlordane and it gets onto their skin, they are very likely to be symptomatic and need medical attention.

The most common symptoms, the toxicologist reports, are those that affect the nervous system. Chlordane starts off being a depressant, he continues, but it can also be a stimulant. People have been known to go into convulsions, and in very high doses, it's fatal. The journalist asks what the danger is to the city's public well system, which is near the accident scene. The toxicologist tells him there is a concern if chlordane accumulates in the well water in substantial quantities and is ingested. If it's only present in a low dose and it's not likely to cause acute symptoms, then there may be some question as to the danger. He says there are some chronic symptoms associated with chlordane involving the liver and possibly the kidneys. The state will order the wells sealed if levels higher than expected are found, according to the toxicologist.

The reporter leaves to go to the spill site. There, he learns that the 20,000-gallon truck is spilling chlordane at a rate of 25 to 30 gallons per minute into a ditch that leads to one of East Cityville's largest streams. The municipal water authority has been notified to divert water intake from the stream. Water authority officials tell the reporter that they are advising residents not to drink or bathe in the water until the state environmental agency can finish its analysis to determine the degree of risk. In the meantime, the state police have gotten the environmental agency to divert the stream feed water around the affected areas. They believe the onrush of this water was moving the spill farther downstream.

Locating a state environmental agency official at the site, the reporter verifies that the chemical is chlordane and that it was being shipped by the King Chemical Company. King has contracted with Clean Adventure Company to help with the cleanup.

The reporter also engages a federal Environmental Protection Agency (EPA) official in conversation to find out what the federal perspective is on the spill.

Police have evacuated twenty-seven people, the reporter learns. The truck driver and a police officer who slipped and fell into the chlordane spill during his investigation have been taken to Cityville General Hospital.

The reporter calls in the latest information to his editor. Before heading back to the newsroom, he telephones the hospital's spokesperson, who tells him the truck driver has suffered a concussion and the police officer is being washed down with soapy water. Back at his desk, the reporter calls King Chemical Company and finds the president of the company evasive. After several minutes of questioning, the president will confirm only that the product in the truck is a mixture of solvents that was en route to a port for shipment overseas where it would be used for insect control. On advice of counsel, he refuses to make the truck's manifest—the cargo list—available to the reporter. Neither will he let the reporter talk to the chief company chemist.

For additional background, the reporter calls the state's poison control center, where a scientist explains that chlordane is relatively common since it was once used in termite control. However, the scientist is most concerned about the wells and the drinking water because there is an immediate hazard with the sandy soil and the stream. He explains that chlordane does not travel well in water. "It's not too soluble," he says. "We have seen it throughout the state where it is found in sediment and fish but not in the water itself. Apparently it settles down out of the water. If it did reach the water column it would be in the parts-per-billion range because of its relative insolubility. The great unknown is: What does one part per billion mean? Some limited animal testing indicates that chlordane is a potential carcinogen, and right now I don't think there is a scientist in the world who could tell you what the part-per-billion contamination rate would mean." The reporter obtains additional information from the National Pesticide Information Center at Texas Tech University.

Another reporter is dispatched to the church where evacuees have been taken. She interviews a number of residents, including several who are elderly and mothers with children. One resident complains, "I don't see why they have to use these small rural roads to bring these convoys of big trucks through here. They should be using the main highway." Another resident volunteers that there have been problems before with trucks coming down this rural road, with spills and near-spills, but never of this magnitude. The reporter makes a mental note to check this with the police and newsroom files. A third resident, active in the local chapter of the Sierra Club, tells the reporter the club has been trying to restrict chemical-laden trucks to the main highways.

The first reporter returns to the site and, confronting state environmental officials, finds out that King Chemical is now telling the state that the substance is 40 percent chlordane and 60 percent formaldehyde, a flammable solvent. The reporter consults the National Institute for Occupational Safety and Health's "Pocket Guide to Chemical Hazards" and determines that formaldehyde is an irritant that affects, skin, eyes, and the respiratory system. Officials say they are not as worried about the formaldehyde threat as they are about the chlordane.

By now, the truck has been righted and the spill stopped. The state has determined that 5,000 gallons have spilled, most of it into the ditch. The reporter mentions that the spill site is six miles from the reservoir and asks officials whether those 5,000 gallons will settle out before they reach the reservoir. State officials respond that they do not think the chlordane will travel even a quarter mile.

A water resource specialist from the state is present and tells the reporter that six dikes have been erected in the stream to contain the chlordane. But chlordane has also leaked into some duck ponds outside of East Cityville. The water resource specialist says the state fish-and-game department has rescued the ducks from the pond sites and is studying the birds. Clean Adventure Company is removing the substance from the water and putting it into a containment truck as fish-and-game officials fence off the area to keep out wildlife. Spying fish-and-game officials fencing off the area, the reporter corners them and finds out that several hundred striped bass have died in nearby ponds. The reporter wants to know how far the ponds are from the city water supply and learns that they are six miles away. Officials are emphatic that people must avoid fishing in these ponds until Clean Adventure can drain them and remove the silt and residue from the bottom and haul it away in barrels.

Back at the newsroom, the editor decides that the second reporter should contact a national environmental group for a different perspective on the chlordane spill. She contacts the National Resource Defense Council (NRDC) in New York and is told that if the chlordane gets into East Cityville's major water supply, "there is the possibility that a continuing amount of chlordane could show up in the drinking water." The NRDC says that the EPA has put out a health advisory recommending a maximum of eight parts per billion in drinking water. The reporter is told to find out what the state is doing to make sure the cleanup is effective.

The NRDC also says that it is interested in knowing what is being done to clean up the soil so that children in neighborhoods around the spill are not going to be absorbing chlordane through their skin. Once chlordane gets into the soil, it apparently remains there for a long time because it bonds with soil particles. The reporter is informed that there is no good way to get chlordane out of the soil; the contaminated earth itself must be removed. Removal experts will not have to dig far below the surface, the reporter is told, because the chemical does not move very fast or very far.

The NRDC impresses upon the reporter the seriousness of communicating the problem to her audience. "I think it is serious," an NRDC official says. "Chlordane was widely used for so long. The EPA banned it because tests done by the Food and Drug Administration found that 99 percent of the meat supply had measurable residues of chlordane or its by-products. It was also found in human tissues. Every time someone is subject to an autopsy or surgery, a little sample is taken and the government keeps a registry. They found that virtually the entire U.S. population has measurable amounts of chlordane or its metabolites. Chlordane is a carcinogen in one animal species, and that's a red flag for being a possible threat to human beings."

The reporters are on deadline now, and the story has to be written. Angles to be covered for the second day include interviewing people who were exposed and finding out how they were decontaminated, how their homes were decontaminated, what officials are advising the people who breathed the chlordane mix to do next, and how the hospital dealt with the situation. Reporters should find out when people will be allowed to return to their homes and what is being done to keep the area secure. Other questions to ask of the state environmental agency are whether a health study will be done and if monitoring wells are going to be sunk to track the underground path of the chlordane.

Concentration should be on the long-term effects on the drinking water supplies, especially in other cities that get their water supply from the East Cityville stream where the spill occurred. Reporters can contact geologists to find out if there is a large aquifer beneath the East Cityville public wells, which also might have been contaminated. Contact can also be made with private regional watershed associations, which monitor water resources and development in the East Cityville area. If there is a local epidemiologist at the university, he or she may be asked about genetic implications of long-term exposure.

The reporter should contact Clean Adventure Company to determine where the chlordane was taken after it was removed from the stream and where the water that was pumped out of the ponds will go. Questions should also be raised about the final destination of the chlordane-contaminated soil.

There could be follow-up stories on the environmental history of the principal players—Clean Adventure, Move for Profit, and King Chemical. Perhaps the state environmental agency has had problems with one of them in the past. The municipal government of East Cityville should be contacted and asked if it intends to move against King Chemical on legal grounds.

Stories about companies and institutions that have been involved in an environmental controversy can be challenging. While some may not lead very far, others can prove to be very productive, especially when the reporter considers all possible angles of the story.

THE LANGUAGE OF RISK

A fundamental question in managing any risk—and in reporting it—is figuring out how risky it is. Big risks deserve big news stories, especially if the proper authorities are ignoring them. Small risks deserve small stories or no stories at all. How do you decide which is which?

It helps to have some baseline information: about two million Americans die every year from all causes. Cigarette smoking and alcohol are the two most clearly identified risk factors. Smoking tobacco is estimated to be associated with 350,000 to 450,000 of the deaths and alcohol abuse with about 200,000. None of the risks described in these briefs approaches the seriousness of smoking or alcohol abuse.

Unfortunately, the science of risk assessment does not allow us to say precisely how many people are killed or injured by any of the risks described in these briefs. In fact, for most environmental risks, the data on risk identification, dose-response, and exposure assessment are so limited that scientists have attempted risk assessments only for cancer. About 460,000 Americans die annually from cancer, which makes cancer the second leading cause of death (heart disease kills more people than cancer; tobacco smoking is a risk factor for both). So, in many of the briefs, we draw special attention to the risks of cancer associated with each hazard.

If we look at the relative risk of cancer as a measure of "how risky" something is, the briefs fall into three groups. Indoor air pollution and exposures at work are responsible for the greatest number of cancers—though far fewer than cigarette smoking. Chemical emergencies, dioxin, water pollution, and pesticides are less important problems.

The question "how risky?" has both a technical and a nontechnical side. On the technical side, we want to know how many people are likely to be injured, made ill, or killed as the result of a given environmental health risk, or how much ecosystem damage is likely to be sustained. Scientists have come up with an assortment of methods for estimating the chances of such injury, and it's important for you, in reporting a story, to be aware of the advantages and drawbacks connected with these methods.

On the nontechnical side comes a somewhat different question: How upsetting, frightening, or enraging is the situation likely to be to the people who must endure it? Technical people sometimes argue that the nontechnical aspects of risk should play little if any role in risk policy. But even they would not like to live in a world in which, for example, coerced risks were handled the same way as voluntary risks. Just because hang gliding—a voluntary risk—is legal, should a factory emitting pollutants be permitted to impose a comparable, but involuntary, risk on its neighbors? Or, conversely, just because the factory must reduce its dimethylmeatloaf emissions below the risk level of skiing, does that mean we have to outlaw skis? Figuring out how to balance technical and nontechnical considerations is a real dilemma for risk managers and journalists alike.

A host of other thorny questions confront the risk-policy maker and the reporter trying to make sense of risk. A few examples follow.

▪ HOW SHOULD WE DEAL WITH UNCERTAINTY? ▪

The answers to technical risk questions invariably come with a lot of uncertainty attached. If we wait for definite answers, we will end up ignoring serious problems for decades, just because the research isn't definitive yet. But if we act quickly, we may well be wrong—and it may be politically impossible to back off. If we base policy decisions on our best estimate of the risk, it is as likely to be too low as too high; that is, we will offer too little protection some of the time. But if we base policy decisions on a high-side "conservative" estimate of the risk, the price we will pay for being confident that we are protecting people enough is a very high likelihood that we are overprotecting them.

▪ DOES IT MATTER WHO IS AT RISK? ▪

Although some would argue that all lives are of equal value, most risk policies treat different people's lives differently. Risk to bystanders, for example, is usually taken much more seriously than risk to employees; the underlying assumption is that work involves some risk, for which the worker is presumably paid, but innocent bystanders deserve a higher level of protection. Other distinctions are even more controversial. Juries, for example, often base damage awards on how much potential income the plaintiff has lost, thus putting a higher value on the life and health of a young professional than on the life and health of an older and less prosperous victim. Similarly, risky facilities are likelier to end up in poor neighborhoods than in rich neighborhoods—the land is cheaper, people in the neighborhood may be more desperate for the jobs, and they may be less politically able to organize an effective opposition.

▪ WHAT ABOUT THE COST OF RISK REDUCTION IN MONEY OR IN JOBS? ▪

Putting a price tag on human life is always politically and morally controversial—but not putting a price tag on human life may make sensible risk management impossible. If you are willing to spend whatever it takes, there are always more steps you can think of to "pad the world" and thus reduce risk. Some risk policies cost tens of millions of dollars for every life saved, while others cost only thousands; most would agree that it would be wiser to implement the latter policies, and, of course, money spent on the former is no longer available to spend on the latter. Similarly, most employees would rather endure small risks than lose their jobs; among other things, losing your job significantly damages your health and your family's health. On the other hand, those trying to avoid regulations often overstate their cost in money or jobs. And the discovery of a cost-effective way to prevent a particular risk usually comes after the decision to eliminate that risk, not before; if cost considerations were used to justify inaction, the cheaper solution might never be found.

▪ WHAT IF WE DON'T KNOW HOW TO REDUCE THE RISK? ▪

Basing risk-policy decisions on the size of the risk sounds sensible, but it assumes we know how to reduce any risk we like and that the only issue is which ones deserve our attention. In reality, of course, some risk-reduction technologies are well established, others are experimental, and still others don't exist at all. In some areas, it may make sense to require the "best available technology" to reduce the risk in question rather than setting a quantitative standard for tolerable risk.

We could extend this list of risk-policy problems for pages. The point is that deciding what to do about a risk isn't easy even after you have answered the technical "how risky?" question and the nontechnical "how risky?" question. Still, risk policy begins with the effort to answer these two questions.

▪ SO HOW RISKY IS IT?: THE TECHNICAL ANSWER ▪

The focus of public and regulatory concern about environmental health is usually long-term, repeated, chronic health risk. Of course, explosions, spills, and other acute risks are also matters of concern. But most (though not all) of the *Handbook* will focus on chronic risks.

Since the mid-1970s, chronic human health risks associated with chemical, biological, and physical substances have been evaluated in a multistep process called quantitative risk assessment (QRA). QRA has begun to consider impacts other than human health impacts, including those on wildlife, vegetation, and other ecological systems. Historically, however, only human health effects were considered, and the *Handbook* will therefore focus most closely on these.

QRA proceeds in four steps: (1) hazard identification—what's out there that might be dangerous? (2) dose-response assessment—how much of it will do how much harm? (3) exposure assessment—how much of it are people actually getting? and (4) aggregate risk assessment—given the three previous steps, how great is the overall risk?

▪ HAZARD IDENTIFICATION ▪

The goal of the first step in QRA, hazard identification, is to determine whether a substance can affect human health. Scientists use both human and animal studies to make this determination.

The science that tries to deduce the existence of a hazard from human data is called epidemiology. Epidemiologists may follow a particular group of people over time, noting their exposure to particular potential hazards and trying to relate this to the incidence of particular diseases. More often, epidemiologists have to work backward, noting who got sick and who stayed healthy and trying to relate this information to people's past exposures to the hazard in question.

Workers are the most studied human group because they are exposed to high concentrations of many dangerous substances. For example, the extreme hazard posed by asbestos was recognized by observing excess respiratory cancers and asbestosis among shipyard and other building-trade workers who routinely handled asbestos. Likewise, uranium mine workers were observed to have higher rates of lung cancer and underground coal miners higher rates of chronic obstructive lung diseases.

Epidemiological studies have serious limitations. Humans are exposed to so many substances that only the most dangerous ones can be picked out and identified. For instance, workers exposed to asbestos, radioactive materials, and coal dust were much more likely to manifest a health problem if they also smoked tobacco products. In other words, excess disease observed among human populations can often be explained by an exposure or preexisting condition that may be independent of the exposure to the substance in question.

Another major limitation of the vast majority of human studies is that people must contract the disease before the problem is discovered—obviously an undesirable way to learn about risk.

Furthermore, it is impossible to control human studies to the extent possible with animal studies. With animal populations, the experimenter can make sure the test animals have no relevant exposures except the one being tested. But for obvious ethical reasons, you can't "experiment" on human risk exposures—and so multiple factors always complicate the analysis. Instead of controls, epidemiologists must use statistics. They "factor out" the effects of smoking, age, and other "confounders" statistically to determine how much of the effect being observed is attributable to the risk being studied (e.g., living near an incinerator).

This method is problematic for several reasons. First, it is intrinsically unconvincing to laypeople. Scientists estimate that radon results in a certain number of lung cancer deaths annually, but they cannot say specifically which people will be affected; the number is based on a statistical calculation of excess lung cancer deaths, not on counting the bodies of radon victims. This leaves people feeling free to mistrust the number, in either direction.

Second, for a clear effect to emerge from statistical analysis, the effect has to be large, or the sample has to be large, or the effect has to be concentrated in ways that make it easy to observe. If, for example, exposure to a certain chemical kills one person in three, scientists can link the death to the exposure with a small sample, regardless of confounding factors. If it kills one person in a thousand, scientists can make the linkage only if the sample is large or if the effect is idiosyncratic. (If the chemical causes a rare disease, we will be able to see the excess incidence in people living near the plant that manufactures the chemical, but if it causes a common disease, we will miss it.) If it kills one person in a million, scientists will not be able to find it. In other words, even if a hazard is serious enough that risk managers would want to know and do something about it, it still may not be serious enough for epidemiologists to isolate its effects with confidence. Assume that dimethylmeatloaf may cause one exposed person in a thousand to get, say, pancreatic cancer. If it does, the substance is a significant carcinogen in need of control. But if only a few hundred workers and neighbors of the dimethylmeatloaf factory are exposed, no epidemiological study is going to be able to find the fraction of one cancer that would be statistically expected to result. The question is worth answering, but epidemiology won't be able to answer it. The fact that lots of other substances could also cause pancreatic cancer will only make it more difficult to find the answer using epidemiological methods.

Laboratory studies of mice, hamsters, and other animals are also used to evaluate potential human health hazards. Large quantities of the substance under investigation are introduced into the animals. Effects are observed, and then the animals are sacrificed to determine if they have developed tumors and other effects that cannot be observed otherwise. During the last decade, lower organism tests have been developed to screen substances for mutagenesis, which many scientists believe is necessary to cause cancer. Tests on lower organisms and on isolated cells are, of course, less expensive and ethically less problematic than tests on large animals.

Animal studies have significant advantages: they can be done in advance of human exposure, and they can be carefully controlled to isolate the effect under investigation. But animal studies also have important limitations. Animals are not necessarily perfect sentinels of human response to exposures. That is, humans may be affected, but animals may not be—and vice versa. In addition, in order to make animal studies timely and cost-effective, laboratory animals are bred to be highly susceptible to tumors or other health effects of concern; they are placed in controlled environments (unlike humans who are exposed to multiple substances); and they are given extremely high doses of the substance in question (and the potential impact of those doses is enhanced with solvents).

In other words, protocols used in laboratories do not resemble human exposure conditions. What we learn from an animal study is what happens when small numbers of rodents are exposed to huge quantities of one substance at a time for a short period of time. What we actually want to know is what happens when large numbers of human beings are exposed to small quantities of lots of substances at once over a long period of time. The two are, obviously, not the same.

Human studies, in brief, provide weak answers to the right questions. Animal studies provide strong answers to the wrong questions. Neither is ideal—but they're all we have.

▪ DOSE-RESPONSE ASSESSMENT ▪

It is a truism of toxicology (the study of what is or isn't poisonous) that "the dose makes the poison." Lots of substances are highly toxic at high doses but harmless or even essential at low doses. Thus, the second step in QRA, dose-response assessment, estimates the human health effects of varying amounts of exposure to the substance in question. For example, is a person exposed to 16 grams of a chemical twice as likely to develop cancer as a person exposed to 8 grams? Four times as likely as a person exposed to 4 grams? Ten thousand times as likely as a person exposed to 0.0016 grams? These are not simple questions. In their efforts to come up with answers, scientists must try to take into account the age, gender, and lifestyle of exposed populations; the intensity of the exposure (e.g., 4 grams in five seconds versus 4 grams in five years); the pattern of exposure (inhalation, skin contact, ingestion); and other factors that affect response.

Threshold—the level below which risk is absent—is an important concept in dose-response assessment. Some risks have no threshold. In Russian roulette, for example, the risk of one bullet in a six-chamber gun is one in six; expand this to a six million–chamber gun and the risk is one in six million. It is never zero, no matter how many chambers. But some risks are zero until a threshold exposure is passed. Drowning is a good example. You cannot drown standing up in a few inches of water; the risk climbs sharply as the water level rises above your head; then it levels off again (deep is deep). The dose-response curve for

Russian roulette would be a straight line running through zero. For drowning, the curve would be an S-curve, with all the increased risk between two and seven feet.

However, we do not know the dose-response curve for most chronic human health risks. This has resulted in ongoing disagreement over two huge issues. First, what is the likeliest curve? And second, given that we don't really know the shape of the curve, how conservative should we be in making assumptions about its shape?

The first question is obviously very hard to answer. Dose-response assessment is almost always hindered by a paucity of data, especially dose-response observations at low doses. As we have already discussed, risks get harder to measure when the exposures get smaller, so we usually end up measuring the dose-response relationship at high levels of exposure (in animals, extremely high levels), then extrapolating the curve downward. For example, we have data on the impact of high doses of asbestos exposure in shipyards and asbestos mines but not much data on the chronic, very low dose exposures that an office worker might encounter in a public building from a ceiling containing asbestos. Scientists frequently make educated guesses (called extrapolations) from the data they do have (on shipyards or asbestos mines) to the risk they are trying to define (asbestos in homes and offices). These extrapolations are deservedly controversial because they are grounded in uncertain science and often in unacknowledged assumptions about the trade-offs between protecting public health and spending money.

Since the first question is so hard to answer, the second question becomes critical: how cautious should the guess be? Currently, QRAs tend to make very cautious guesses—and many people who acknowledge that the "real" risk is probably lower than the risk estimate arrived at in a conventional QRA argue that this is a good thing. The "best-guess estimate," by definition, is going to be too low some of the time and too high at other times. An estimate that is almost sure not to be too low will usually be too high; many experts believe this is a better way to protect public health. Other experts, however, argue that conservative risk estimates are misleading, especially since people tend to forget they were conservative and treat them as "best-guess estimates."

Sometimes scientists find contradictory results. For example, one research group finds a major health impact while another finds no discernible impact. In such a case, still other scientists will examine the two study designs to try to determine why they reached such different results. But often no consensus emerges; the studies really disagree, and so do the experts who have looked at them. Further research may or may not resolve the problem—and meanwhile a policy decision must be made. In this very common predicament, scientists, policy-makers, journalists, and the public must all decide how to handle scientific disagreement. Once again, their answers contain implicit value judgments about the trade-offs between public health and cost.

▪ EXPOSURE ASSESSMENT ▪

Now that we "know" how much of the substance in question it takes to do harm, we obviously want to know the levels at which people are actually exposed. This is the third step in QRA, exposure assessment. Using instruments, many of which have only recently been invented, scientists try to measure how much radon is accumulating in a basement or how much chromium is found in a workplace. They multiply their measurements by the amount of time people are exposed to arrive at a total dose.

Exposure assessment has been the weakest link in risk assessment because direct measurements have rarely been available. Instead, scientists have tried to re-create exposure, which is an extremely difficult task requiring numerous assumptions to replace the missing information. A workplace exposure to asbestos, for example, might be recreated from blueprints of a facility and other information about the structure, along with some knowledge about how many times workers went into the basement where they could have come into contact with asbestos-covered pipes.

▪ AGGREGATE RISK ASSESSMENT ▪

The fourth step in QRA characterizes the aggregate risk to the total population and to various subpopulations of importance (e.g., workers, community residents). This is done by using census data and surveys to estimate where people spend their time.

In assessments of total risk, both individual risk and societal risk are important. If exposure to a certain chemical causes 1 death in 100 people each year and a total of 300 people have been exposed, it is a very serious individual risk for those 300 people but a very small overall societal risk (3 deaths a year). If exposure to the chemical causes 1 death annually in 100,000 and 250 million U.S. citizens are exposed, it is a very small individual-level risk but a fairly high societal risk (2,500 deaths a year). Risk assessors try to collect data on both kinds of risk. Policy-makers and journalists should stay alert to both.

Results of the QRA are forwarded to decision-makers who explicitly add legal, economic, political, and social considerations to the results of the scientific analyses. As we have already noted, the results of many risk assessments are highly uncertain—that is, health effects are not known within a narrow enough range to strongly guide decisions. Consequently, decision-makers usually have wide latitude to impose nonscientific decision-making criteria. For example, a multibillion-dollar asbestos removal program is under way in U.S. schools. Risk assessments do not justify removing asbestos where it is not damaged. In fact, some scientists believe that short-term risk is increased by removing undamaged asbestos. Yet tens of billions of dollars are being spent on asbestos removal, motivated by parents' concerns on behalf of their children, school officials' fear of future lawsuits, and other nontechnical factors.

Overall, supporters of QRA do not consider it a scientific panacea. They argue that some worthwhile information is usually available about hazard identification, dose-response assessment, and exposure assessment and that using this information does narrow the range of reasonable management strategies for decision-makers to consider. Often they complain that decision-makers rely too little on the available data, responding more to nontechnical factors than to the QRA. Detractors contend that the results of QRAs are so uncertain that they can often do more harm than good. Vested interests, they say, use risk assessment to try to dazzle decision-makers into managing risk without taking public viewpoints into account.

QRA is still in its infancy. The answers it offers to the technical "how risky?" question are still highly debatable. But researchers are getting better at estimating risk. The problem is that we do not seem to be getting any better at achieving a societal consensus about what should be done with the risk estimates.

▪ RISK = HAZARD + OUTRAGE: THE NONTECHNICAL ANSWER ▪

So far we have been talking about risk the way risk assessors do. To experts in risk assessment, "risk" is a multiplication of three factors:

magnitude (how bad is it when it happens), probability (how likely is it to happen), and the number of exposed people. As we have seen, measuring risk is a difficult proposition, and experts do not often agree on the outcome—but at least they agree on what they ought to measure.

Unfortunately, what the experts are busy trying to measure is not really what risk means to most people. If you took a long list of hazards and ranked them in order of expected annual mortality or likely ecosystem damage and then reordered the same list by how upsetting the various risks are to people, the correlation between the two would be very low. In other words, the risks that kill people or damage ecosystems according to the experts are completely different from the risks that upset ordinary citizens, the people who read newspapers and watch television news programs.

To understand why, let's redefine our terms. Let's take what the risk assessor means by risk—magnitude times probability times the number of people exposed—and call it hazard. And let's take what the public means by risk—all the things that people are worried about that the experts ignore—and call it outrage. This gives us a new definition of risk: Risk = Hazard + Outrage.

This redefinition suggests a new way to frame the problem of disagreements between experts and the public over risk. The experts, when they talk about risk, focus on hazard and ignore outrage, while the public focuses on outrage and ignores hazard. That low correlation, then, isn't the result of public ignorance or misperception; it is the result of a definitional dispute. In the research literature on risk communication, there are at least thirty-five variables that show up as what we are calling components of outrage. The following list of ten tend to dominate most controversies over the risks discussed in this book.

■ IS IT VOLUNTARY OR COERCED? ■

Consider two ski trips. For the first, you decide to go skiing; for the second, someone rousts you out of bed in the middle of the night, shanghais you to the top of a mountain, straps slippery sticks to the bottoms of your feet, and pushes you down the mountain. The experience on the way down the mountain is exactly the same—sliding down a mountain is sliding down a mountain. Nonetheless, the first trip is recreation, while the second is assault with a deadly weapon.

The same distinction applies to community behavior. Imagine two different scenarios for siting a controversial facility. In scenario one, a company comes into town and says: "We're going to put our dimethylmeatloaf factory here, whether you want it here or not. If you don't like it you can move." In scenario two, the company says: "We'd like to put our dimethylmeatioaf factory here, but only if you want it here. If we can negotiate mutually acceptable terms, we'll sign a contract and build the facility. If we can't agree on terms, we won't build it." A voluntary siting process like this second scenario isn't guaranteed to work, of course. A coercive process like the first scenario often fails as well; it is hard to site controversial facilities. What is guaranteed is that under the second scenario the public is going to consider dimethylmeatloaf a lot less risky than under the first scenario. The right to say "no" makes saying "maybe" a much smaller risk.

■ IS IT NATURAL OR INDUSTRIAL? ■

A natural risk is much more acceptable than a coerced risk but somewhat less acceptable than a voluntary risk. It is "God's coercion," and we are all more forgiving of God than we are of regulatory agencies or multinational corporations. A very good example is radon. In northern New Jersey, for instance, roughly 30 percent of the homes have enough radon in their basements to represent an excess lifetime lung cancer risk of somewhere between one in a hundred and three in a hundred. That's a huge risk—but most people still will not spend $20 on a charcoal canister to test for radon. If some corporation were going door-to-door putting radon in people's basements, people would test—and then they'd sue the company to pay for the monitoring, the mitigation, and the worry. But because it's God's radon, not a corporation's radon—because it's a natural risk, not an industrial risk—it generates enormously less outrage.

■ IS IT FAMILIAR OR EXOTIC? ■

The risks that people underestimate are usually familiar risks, while exotic risks provoke more outrage. A beautiful example is the Superfund cleanup. Just as they're about to reduce the hazard of a familiar waste lagoon, the outrage goes through the roof because unknown exotic technologies are introduced. They're sinking high-pressure injection wells; maybe they're bringing a rotary kiln incinerator to the site; people are walking around in moon suits. (Did you ever have anybody knock on your door in a moon suit? "Just testing your drinking water, nothing to worry about.")

■ IS IT MEMORABLE OR NOT MEMORABLE? ■

Memorable risks are the ones that linger in our minds. The best source of memorability is personal experience, but a good second-best is the news media, especially television. People who have never been to Bhopal or Chernobyl learned from those two events, via journalism, about the risks of chemical manufacturing and nuclear power, respectively. Symbolism is another important source of memorability. The symbol of chemical risks is the 55-gallon drum. The symbol of nuclear risks is the cooling tower. Closely connected to symbolism is the real, but not necessarily harmful, "signal" of risk: an odor, a flare, a particulate residue on cars and houses. These signals may actually be symptoms of something amiss, or they may be irrelevant to hazard. They nonetheless make the risk more memorable and therefore make the outrage greater.

■ IS IT DREADED OR NOT DREADED? ■

All risks are not dreaded equally. Given the same number of deaths, cancer generates more dread (and therefore more public concern, media coverage, and regulatory action) than asthma or emphysema. Contaminated water generates more dread than contaminated air; air generates more dread than food; and food generates more dread than touch. High dread is a nearly universal response to radiation and to waste.

■ IS IT KNOWABLE OR NOT KNOWABLE? ■

Knowability is really several factors taken together. The public, for example, worries much more about uncertainty than do experts. But even more frightening than uncertainty is expert disagreement, what Lois Gibbs calls "dueling Ph.D.s." One side's expert says, "I eat it for breakfast," while the other side's expert says, "even thinking about it will give you cancer." Another component of knowability is detectability. At the Three Mile Island nuclear power accident in 1979, for example, even journalists were frightened. A reporter who had been through endless wars and hurricanes and other risky situations explained that radiation and cancer are undetectable: "At least in a war, you know you haven't been hit *yet*."

▪ IS IT CONTROLLED BY ME OR BY OTHERS? ▪

Control is related to, but different than, voluntariness. Voluntariness determines who decides; control, who implements. If your spouse asks you to go to the store for groceries, the trip may not be voluntary, but you're still in control because you're driving. Driving is, in fact, a good example. Eighty-five percent of Americans consider themselves better-than-average drivers. That's a sizable optimistic bias hooked to control. Agencies and companies typically have two messages for the public in a risk controversy. The first message is, "We're in charge here. Butt out." And the second message is, "Don't worry." It is very hard to disempower people and reassure them simultaneously; the reassuring message gets lost in the outrage generated by the disempowerment.

▪ IS IT FAIR OR UNFAIR? ▪

Probably the most important component of fairness is the distribution of risks as it relates to the distribution of benefits. At a manufacturing facility, for example, the risks—whether they are large or small—are concentrated in the immediate vicinity of the plant gates. Unless local demographics are unusual, the benefits are not similarly concentrated. The people who live near major manufacturing facilities tend to be lower in income and socioeconomic status than the people who live farther away. The neighborhood accurately perceives that the risk is not fairly distributed. That makes the risk a serious outrage and that, in turn, makes it a serious risk.

■ CAN I TRUST YOU OR NOT? ■

Large numbers of people believe that major manufacturing industries are capable of endangering our health, endangering our environment, and lying to us about it—and that the government is either unable or unwilling to stop them. Trust in both industry and government is low. Moreover, people use trust as a stand-in for hazard; they may not be able to tell whether the effluent is carcinogenic, but if plant management has been evasive and untrustworthy, it seems reasonable to assume the worst.

■ IS THE PROCESS RESPONSIVE OR UNRESPONSIVE? ■

There are several components of process that are important in determining public outrage—the distinction between openness and secrecy, for example, and the distinction between courtesy and discourtesy. Companies and agencies that apologize for their misbehavior generate less outrage than those that stonewall. Sharing or confronting the cultural values of the audience is also a factor: a plant manager who coaches Little League and goes to PTA meetings has more credibility than one who commutes from out of town and sends his or her children to a private school. One of the biggest factors is whether the spokesperson for the company responsible for the risk sounds hypertechnical or concerned and responsive. Technical people, by disposition and training, don't much like dealing with "soft" issues that are all tied up in emotions and values. Ordinary citizens, on the other hand, don't much like dealing with technicalities. In a sense it boils down to different approaches to passion. The expert tries to be dispassionate and wants the concerned citizen to be dispassionate, too. The citizen, on the other hand, is passionate and expects the expert to be compassionate.

What are the implications for journalists of this hazard-versus-outrage distinction? To start with, the media are not really very interested in hazard, unless it's huge. A 1 in 10,000 risk, for example, is serious enough to matter greatly to public health experts, but it's not a very good news story. A villainous company or government official would make it newsworthy; a victim (dying and accusing) would make it newsworthy; a controversy would make it newsworthy. In other words, outrage is what makes risks newsworthy.

There are many reasons for reporters typically paying more attention to outrage than to hazard. It is, of course, an easier story to cover, especially if the reporter has relatively little technical training. It's more interesting to readers and viewers (and editors). And the sources of outrage information are far likelier to be available, cooperative, and quotable than technical sources.

This focus on outrage is legitimate. Outrage isn't just a distraction from hazard; it is a real issue in its own right. A community that is exposed to a risk it didn't agree to, doesn't benefit from, and wasn't told about has a right to be outraged—even if the risk is small. A news story that reports an outrage of this sort is a real public service. Outrage, in short, deserves the coverage it gets.

But hazard sometimes deserves more coverage than it gets. It would be a public service as well for journalists to pay more attention to hazard (not less attention to outrage). High-hazard low-outrage risks need the public's attention. And high-outrage low-hazard risks need to be put into context, so that readers and viewers begin to understand that the risks that make people angry or frightened may or may not be the risks that endanger their health and environment.

The main thrust of this book is to clarify the hazard side of high-outrage environmental risks. These risks are heavily covered because they are controversial, that is, because they are significant outrages. The briefs that follow should make it easier to judge and report their hazard.

REFERENCES

Doll, R., and R. Peto. 1981. *The Causes of Cancer.* New York: Oxford University Press.

Higginson, J., and C. Muir. 1979. Estimated carcinogenesis: Misconceptions and limitations to cancer control. *Journal of the National Cancer Institute* 63:1291–1298.

U.S. Environmental Protection Agency. 1987. *Unfinished Business: A Comparative Assessment of Environmental Problems.* Washington, D.C.: Environmental Protection Agency.

Wynder, E., and G. Gori. 1997. Contributions of the environment to cancer incidence: An epidemiologic exercise. *Journal of National Cancer Institute* 58:825–832.

TRACKING DOWN A COMPANY'S ENVIRONMENTAL RECORD

Reporters are frequently assigned stories about companies or institutions that have been involved in an environmental controversy. How do you find out the environmental track record of a company? How do you find out whether a chemical spill caused by a company is unusual or whether the firm has a long history of pollution problems?

▪ NEWSPAPERS ▪

One of the first things you should do is check with your newspaper's librarian to dig out all of the clips about the company that have appeared in your own paper over the past five or ten years. By reviewing these clips you may see a pattern (e.g., the company has been cited for numerous air pollution problems but appears to have had a good record concerning water pollution). If your own library has no clips, check with other papers in town that may have done stories about the company and review their clips.

▪ COMMUNITY ACTIVISTS ▪

From these clips you may find out the names of community activists who have complained about the company in the past. Call these people to learn their perspective. If there are environmental organizations in your community, such as the Sierra Club or Audubon Society, give their officers a call to see what they know about a company's environmental record.

This chapter was written by James Detjen, Director, Knight Center for Environmental Journalism, Michigan State University, East Lansing.

■ NEIGHBORS ■

Talk to neighbors of the plant. You can walk through the neighborhood knocking on doors. Or you can check city directories to find out the names, addresses, and phone numbers of people living near the plant. And don't forget to talk to officials in police and fire departments. They have tremendous street knowledge about companies and institutions in their neighborhood.

■ LABOR UNIONS ■

Track down the local offices of labor unions that have workers employed at the company. Sometimes union officials are unwilling to talk publicly about a company's environmental record because of fear that jobs will be lost. Others may be very helpful because they are concerned about workers who are being exposed to unsafe levels of toxic chemicals. Unions may be able to track down the names and phone numbers of workers for you. Companies with poor occupational health records often have poor environmental records as well.

■ CHECKING ENVIRONMENTAL AGENCY FILES ■

Most state and federal environmental laws require that permits be issued to companies intending to discharge pollutants to the air and water or to send toxic waste to disposal facilities. Review the agency files on these companies, looking at permits, inspection reports, enforcement actions, environmental impact statements, and correspondence. Different records may be kept in different offices of these agencies. If you have the time, check the files in environmental agencies in neighboring states as well. Be firm and ask to see the complete files yourself, not just a few documents that a public relations officer pulls for you.

If officials refuse to let you see these files, be firm and say you have a right to see them. File an open records request with state and local agencies and a Freedom of Information Act request with federal agencies if you have to.

■ USING THE FREEDOM OF INFORMATION ACT ■

One of the most powerful tools available to journalists is the Freedom of Information Act (FOIA). This law enables you to look at records that officials in federal agencies may not want you to see. Before sending a letter, find out the name of the FOIA officer and address the request to that person.

Any agency's FOIA officer can be found by calling the agency or looking up the agency's FOIA regulation in the *Code of Federal Regulations* (CFR), which is in any law library and many public libraries.

When requesting records, be as specific as possible. You can obtain more information on the FOIA by contacting The Reporters Committee for Freedom of the Press, 1815 N. Fort Myer Drive, Suite 900, Arlington, VA 22209; located at 222/rcfp.org on the Internet.

A sample letter might took something like this:

Freedom of Information Officer
U.S. Environmental Protection Agency
Your regional office

Dear Mr. Cleanwater:

This request is being made under the federal Freedom of Information Act, 5 U.S.C. 552. Please send me copies of, or make available to me for review, the following records: all permits, inspection records, enforcement actions, and correspondence between your agency and the XYZ corporation concerning their Backwater factory, from the years 1970 to the present. As you know, the FOIA provides that if portions of a document are exempt from release, the remainder must be segregated and disclosed. I reserve the right to appeal your decision to withhold any materials.

Please notify me in advance if the total fees for this request exceed $ [fill in the amount you are willing to pay]. Please call me at my office [provide phone number] if you have any questions pertaining to this request.

Thank you for your assistance. I look forward to receiving your reply within ten working days, as required by law.

Very sincerely,
Your name

If you don't hear from the agency within a reasonable amount of time, call and ask them why there has been a delay. You have the right to file an appeal and ultimately to sue them for the records if you think they are being illegally witheld.

▪ CHECKING OTHER RECORDS ▪

Check court records to see if people living near the plant or government agencies have sued the company for environmental problems. Check records kept by your county health department, your local sewer district, and any other government agency that might have records on the company's environmental problems. If it is a publicly held corporation, ask the federal Securities and Exchange Commission (SEC) to look at the company's 10-K reports, which list any actions, such as enforcement actions, by environmental agencies that could adversely affect the company's profits. And don't forget to talk to the company or institution. Once they know how much information you have gathered, they will be less likely to try to snow you. Try to talk to those company officials with direct knowledge of pollution incidents.

▪ DO YOUR OWN TESTING ▪

If no records about a pollution problem exist but people think that a company is illegally discharging pollution into a stream, consider taking your own samples and conducting laboratory tests on these samples. These tests can be expensive, but often they are the only way you can get answers. Sometimes a local college will run these tests for you for free or at a very low cost.

▪ AVOIDING PITFALLS ▪

- Make sure you have checked with the company or institution about each pollution incident you are covering. Be fair to the company or institution. Let them respond to any negative statements that environmental activists or environmental agency officials may have made.

- Don't try to "prove" connections that don't exist. If ten neighbors of a plant say their relatives have died of cancer because of the air pollution a company emits, be very cautious. Such cancer connections are almost impossible to prove. People die of cancer for many reasons, such as smoking tobacco and eating improperly.
- Make sure your reporting is technically accurate. Double check all of your facts, calculations, and quotations.

FINDING AN EXPERT

▪ HOW DO YOU FIND AN EXPERT? ▪

Experts are not always easy to find. You will develop your own lists of individuals whom you trust and with whom you feel comfortable.

A major state university that has active graduate programs is a good source of experts. Graduate programs tend to emphasize specialization, while undergraduate programs are more apt to emphasize generalization. Consult university catalogs that describe graduate courses and faculty.

Most professional organizations have statewide and local offices, and they often will provide the right expert. If the situation is one of health risk, try contacting organizations that raise money for the disease at risk, for example, the American Cancer Society for cancer or the March of Dimes for birth defects. Contact Media Resource Service at (800) 223-1730 or online at www.mediaresource.org. Media Resource Service was formerly a program of the Scientists' Institute for Public Information (SIPI). At no charge, they provide help to journalists in locating expert sources of information on science and technology to interview for news and feature stories. They maintain a database of 30,000 (primarily American) scientists, engineers, physicians, and policy-makers who have agreed to provide information on short notice to print and broadcast journalists.

In certain situations, state and local governments can be helpful, as can industry associations. Obviously, everyone has a bias of some sort. Governments may have their own biases. Try to get a range of opinions, especially on controversial topics where objectivity is rare. Since experts tend to know one another, ask an expert in one area to refer you to an unbiased expert in another area, but make sure that the first expert does not have a vested interest in the second area.

This chapter was written by Bernard D. Goldstein, M.D., Dean of the School of Public Health, University of Pittsburgh.

▪ IS THE EXPERT REALLY AN EXPERT? ▪

How do you find out if a person has the credentials to make an expert statement? Gentle probing can elicit information about educational background and current affiliation. However, there are potential pitfalls; for example, someone addressed as doctor could be a doctor of optometry or a Ph.D. in an unrelated field.

An affiliation claimed by, or attributed to, a person also should not be taken at face value. Ask these questions:

- What do you do at the university?
- Do you work there full-time?
- What precisely is your field?
- Have you been involved in a situation like this before?

Avoid asking experts about something outside of their immediate area. There is the human tendency not to be willing to admit ignorance. This age of technology often requires that a person's knowledge be highly specialized. Thus, an engineer who is an expert in hydraulics may know little or nothing about hazardous waste control technology. A physician does not necessarily know about the risks of environmental pollutants or workplace chemicals.

▪ IS THE EXPERT PROVIDING FACTUAL INFORMATION OR OPINION? ▪

It is perfectly legitimate for an expert to provide an opinion based on knowledge. However, it is important to determine if the expert is stating fact or opinion.

A "fact" can be defined as something that is known with certainty and is verifiable. An "opinion" is an evaluation or judgment based on special knowledge. It is a conclusion not substantiated by positive proof or knowledge. Most experts know the distinction but could assume you are asking for their judgment or opinion.

Ask the expert if the information they are giving you is indeed fact. Also, be careful not to interpret an opinion and report it as a fact. Ask the expert for names of individuals with opposing points of view and seek additional information from them.

▪ IS THE EXPERT UNBIASED? ▪

There are two major sources of bias on the part of experts. One source is an obvious conflict of interest, such as owning stock in an affected industry or a riverside home if flood control is the issue. The second source is more subtle and occurs when an expert's scientific reputation is involved in an outcome, leading to a willingness to jump to conclusions or to make unjustified pronouncements. Further investigation and the use of more than one expert are the best means of overcoming bias.

THE LARGER CONTEXT

JOURNALISTS' VIEWS OF THE ENVIRONMENT

ISSUES AND CHALLENGES

Most Americans worry about the environment (Gallup/CNN/*USA Today* poll April 1999). At the same time, many do not fully understand environmental issues. In a 1999 nationwide survey of 1,500 adults eighteen years of age or older conducted by the National Environmental Education and Training Foundation (NEETF), respondents could correctly answer an average of only three out of ten simple knowledge questions about the environment (NEETF 1999).

Over time, environmental issues and the risks they present have become more complex; therefore, presenting information on these issues in a form that can be easily understood and acted upon is critical. Studies show that the news media play a vital role in conveying information to the public about the environment (Byrd et al. 1997). People turn to their televisions, radios, and newspapers for the information they need on environmental issues and the risks they present.

While playing a critical role in helping the public understand environmental issues, journalists often feel ill-prepared to cover the environment. According to a 1993 survey of environmental journalists, very few journalists who cover environmental issues believe they have the knowledge needed to cover their beat adequately. Seven in ten reporters said they lack the training and background to cover technical environmental issues (Foundation for American Communications [FAC] Survey 1993). Covering environmental stories requires an understanding of both the "science" involved as well as the many complex environmental laws that govern these issues.

A slightly altered and expanded version of this article by Bernadette West, Jane Lewis, and Michael Greenberg originally appeared in *Risk: Health, Safety and Environment* 12, nos. 3/4 (2001): 299–310. *Risk*, the official journal of the Risk Assessment and Policy Association, is published by Franklin Pierce Law Center and can be accessed via its website at http://www.fplc.edu/risk/profRisk.htm.

To ensure that the third edition of *The Reporter's Environmental Handbook* addresses issues of concern to journalists in their communities, we surveyed a sample of environmental journalists to identify environmental issues important to them. This research was supported by a grant from the Hazardous Substance Management Research Center (HSMRC) at the New Jersey Institute of Technology (NJIT). We asked the journalists about the challenges they face in covering these issues in their community and their perceptions of the priorities placed on the environment by both the public and their newsrooms. The survey findings are reported here.

▪ METHOD ▪

In October 1999, a survey was mailed to members of the Society of Environmental Journalists (SEJ). Membership includes journalists who work in radio, television, print media, government, and academic settings (N = 877). It should be noted that membership itself in the SEJ is not equal across all four regions of the United States. There are more members from the South and West (28.9 and 29.6 percent, respectively) compared with members from the Northeast and Midwest (21.8 and 18.9 percent, respectively). An overall response rate of 32 percent was obtained after sending out a follow-up mailing to nonrespondents. While a higher response rate was desirable, reporters warned us to expect a much lower rate of between 10 and 15 percent.

The survey included an open-ended question asking journalists to list three environmental health issues of importance in their communities and a series of fixed-response questions. Journalists were asked to gauge (e.g., very well, somewhat, not very well, or not at all) the public's level of understanding of environmental health issues. The survey also asked journalists to rate, on a 10-point scale, the priority attached by their newsrooms and the public to environmental health issues and to rate how "hot" these issues are in newsrooms today compared with five years ago. Finally, using a 5-point Likert scale, journalists were asked about the extent to which factors such as scarcity of information, lack of editorial support, community misunderstanding, and pressure from industry and environmental groups present challenges in covering environmental health issues today.

Analysis of responses to the open-ended question concerning "the most important environmental health issues" involved development of an initial list of all responses. Each journalist identified up to 3 issues. The 280 respondents identified a total of 633 issues. This list of 633 responses included much duplication. For example, a single issue such as water pollution was listed by many journalists. In an attempt to further limit the list to issues of general concern, we eliminated from the analysis duplications and issues that were identified by only one journalist. The eliminations resulted in 165 subtopic areas. The remaining issues that were identified by only one journalist were grouped into an "other" category and set aside for further analysis at a later date.

Review of this list by project team members showed that many journalists identified specific, discrete issues rather than broad, general ones. Next, all project team members individually reviewed the initial list and then, as a group, discussed the issues in an attempt to develop broad, general categories that would cover the lengthier list of very specific issues. Project team members grouped the 165 issues into thirty-nine broad categories designed to capture all of the more specific issues. For example, issues involving environmental factors impacting reproductive health, synthetic chemicals, and estrogen mimics were regrouped under the broader category of estrogen disruptors. Issues such as automobiles, SUVs and air pollution, diesel emissions, deregulation of utilities, and tire fires were grouped together under the broader category of lower atmospheric air pollution. Low-level radiation concerns, ionizing versus nonionizing radiation, electromagnetic fields, and cell phone towers were regrouped under radiation. Biodiversity, species extinction, wetlands, logging, destruction of habitat, overfishing, and endangered species were regrouped under habitat protection and biodiversity. Mercury contamination, leaching of plastics, and leaking aboveground tanks were combined under water pollution. Asthma in children, exposure to lead in the home, and secondhand tobacco smoke were regrouped under children's health. After further discussion among project staff, the list of thirty-nine categories was further condensed into a more manageable number of twenty-three broader categories that were used as the basis for seventeen new briefs in this edition of the *Handbook*.

In addition to our analysis of the open-ended question regarding most important environmental issues, data from the fixed-response questions were analyzed using the Statistical Package for the Social Sciences (SPSS). As noted, journalists were asked to rate issues using 5- and 10-point scales. For purposes of analysis, responses to the seriousness of challenges presented by various factors were grouped, with 1–3 coded as "not serious" and 4–5 as "serious." Ratings of the level of priority attached to environmental issues by newsrooms and the public were later grouped, with 1–5 coded as "low priority" and 6–10 as "high priority." Similarly, ratings of how "hot" environmental health issues were today and five years ago were also grouped, with 1–5 coded as "not hot" and 6–10 as "hot."

▪ FINDINGS ▪

There were slightly more male respondents than female respondents (55 percent compared with 45 percent, respectively). The breakdown of respondents by region of the country is presented in Table 1. Respondents were classified according to the four census geographic areas: northeastern states, southern states, midwestern states, and western states. The largest percentage—30 percent of our respondents—were from the West, while only 19 percent of respondents were from the Midwest. When we compared respondents with nonrespondents in our sample, we found that between 31 and 34 percent of potential respondents from each region responded to the survey, keeping in mind that regions were not proportionately represented in our sample of all SEJ members.

▪ JOURNALISTS' VIEWS OF IMPORTANT ENVIRONMENTAL ISSUES

Water concerns topped the list of environmental health issues. They were identified by more than a third of respondents (37 percent). Issues included in this broad category included water contamination by various pollutants; sources of pollution, including industries such as mining and agriculture; and issues of water quantity and water rights. Atmospheric air pollution concerns were the second most frequently listed environmental health issues. Review of these concerns showed they fell into three broad categories: lower atmospheric air pollution, upper atmospheric air pollution, and indoor air pollution. Twenty-seven percent of journalists identified issues grouped under the category of lower atmospheric air pollution. Concerns here included issues such as air pollution and automobiles, in general, and SUVs, in particular; diesel pollution and particulates; and the impact of tire fires on surrounding communities. Eighteen percent of respondents identified

TABLE 1. DEMOGRAPHICS OF RESPONDENTS

Geographic Region	Number of Potential Responders	Number of Actual Responders	Response Rate Per Region	Regional Representation in Total Sample (N = 280)
Northeast	192	61	32%	21.8%
South	258	81	31%	28.9%
Midwest	157	53	34%	18.9%
West	268	83	31%	29.6%
Unknown	2		0.7%	
Total	875	280 (32%)		*

*Because of rounding, percentages may not add up to 100 percent.

issues grouped under upper atmospheric air pollution, such as global warming, ozone, and cyclical solar activity. In addition, 2 percent of respondents identified issues grouped under indoor air pollution concerns, such as radon, chemicals in the home environment, secondhand smoking concerns, and "sick building syndromes." The complete list of broad categories identified most often by respondents can be found in Table 2.

Several broad categories of issues stand out regardless of what region respondents were from. Included here are issues grouped under upper air pollution, issues involving endocrine disrupters, and issues grouped under waste management. Other issues were raised more frequently in certain regions of the country and less often in other regions. For example, journalists from the West were twice as likely to identify water issues and concerns about pesticide and herbicide use compared with journalists from the Midwest. Three times as many journalists from the Northeast compared with those from the Midwest identified lower air pollution issues. Respondents from the West were four times as likely as respondents from the Northeast to list habitat protection as an issue (48 percent compared with 10 percent).

Journalists from the Midwest were more likely to raise animal livestock issues compared with journalists from the northeastern and western states. Journalists from both the South and Midwest were almost twice as likely to identify issues related to urban/suburban sprawl compared with journalists from the Northeast and West. Of the fifty-nine journalists who identified issues related to genetic modification, only 12 percent were from the Midwest. Journalists from the

TABLE 2. TWENTY-THREE ENVIRONMENTAL CATEGORIES RANKED IN ORDER OF THE PERCENTAGE OF RESPONDENTS WHO IDENTIFIED ISSUES INCLUDED WITHIN THE CATEGORY AS "IMPORTANT"

Categories	Northeast	Midwest	South	West	%/# of all Respondents
1. Water Issues	20%	17%	30%	34%	37% (103)
2. Air Pollution—Lower Atmosphere	32	12	31	25	27 (75)
3. Genetic Modification of Plants and Animals	26	12	31	31	21 (59)
4. Air Pollution—Upper Atmosphere	20	20	32	28	18 (50)
5. Endocrine Disrupters	24	22	26	28	16 (46)
6. Pesticides/Herbicides	27	16	22	36	16 (46)
7. Waste Management—Hazardous and Nonhazardous	27	23	27	23	11 (31)
8. Urban/Suburban Sprawl	18	32	32	18	10 (28)
9. Marine/Ocean/Coastal Issues	29	21	17	33	9 (25)
10. Habitat Protection/ Biodiversity	10	19	24	48	8 (21)
11. Animal Livestock Issues (Farm)	10	40	35	15	7 (20)
12. Food/Nutrition Issues	25	19	31	25	6 (16)
13. Future of Environmental Policy/ Regulation/Politics	15	31	23	31	5 (13)
14. Risk Issues	15	0	62	23	5 (13)
15. Cancer and Other Clusters	46	23	15	15	5 (13)
16. Radiation	8	17	8	67	4 (12)
17. Population Growth	17	17	33	33	4 (12)
18. Cross Border/Global Env. Health Issues	9	18	18	55	4 (11)
19. Children's Health Issues/Asthma/Lead/ Tobacco Smoke	30	40	10	20	3 (10)
20. Weapons of Mass Destruction/Biological Hazards	13	13	38	38	2 (8)
21. Dioxin	13	13	50	25	2 (8)

TABLE 2. (CONTINUED)

Categories	Northeast	Midwest	South	West	%/# of all Respondents
22. Brownfields	43	29	29	0	2 (7)
23. Air Pollution—Indoor	33	33	0	33	2 (6)
Total Issues Identified					633

other three regions were two times more likely to list genetic modification issues.

Radiation issues and cross-border concerns were raised primarily by journalists from the West. No journalists from the South identified indoor air pollution as an issue. Concerns regarding the nature of risk and how it is reported were expressed most often by journalists from the South, while no Midwest journalists identified risk concerns. Half of all respondents who identified dioxin as an issue were from the South.

One can speculate about the reasons for these regional variations. For example, the greater concern with dioxin in the South may be linked to the Times Beach, Missouri, incident involving dioxin. In 1983, TCDD-contaminated waste oil was sprayed on local roads in Times Beach to keep the dust down. This forced some residents to leave their tainted community permanently. The greater emphasis on radiation issues in the West may reflect concerns over burial of spent radioactive materials. With regard to habitat protection, the emphasis placed by journalists from the West may be related to the success of environmental groups in bringing the issues to the forefront.

▪ JOURNALISTS' VIEWS OF THE PUBLIC AND THE NEWSROOM

As shown in Table 3, almost all respondents described the public as wanting more information on environmental issues. However, while viewing the public as interested in environmental issues, journalists in our survey thought the public does not understand these issues. Only 7 percent of our respondents thought that the public understands environmental health issues "very well," and another 39 percent believed the public understands them "reasonably well."

While 77 percent of our respondents believed that environmental issues are "high priority" stories for the public, they are less inclined to

TABLE 3. FINDINGS FROM STUDIES OF THE PUBLIC, JOURNALISTS, AND NEWSROOMS WITH REGARD TO ENVIRONMENTAL ISSUES

Importance of environmental news	
For the public . . .	
■ % of the public who said they were very or somewhat interested in environmental news stories[1]	86%
■ % of our journalists who felt public wants more information on environmental health issues	97%
■ % of our journalists who felt environmental health issues are a high priority for the public	77%
For newsrooms . . .	
■ % of our journalists who felt environmental health issues are a high priority for newsrooms	62%
■ % of news directors who thought the general public are "very interested" in environmental stories[2]	17%
■ % of our journalists who said lack of support from editorial staff represented a "serious challenge" in presenting environmental health info to the community	33%
Knowledge of environmental issues	
Of the public . . .	
■ % of the public who rate themselves as having either "a lot" or "a fair amount" of knowledge about environmental issues and problems[3]	69%
■ % of our journalists who felt the public understands environmental health issues "very well" or "reasonably well"	46%
■ Average # correct answers (out of 10) for the public on a test of knowledge on basic environmental issues[4]	3.2
Of journalists . . .	
■ Journalists who report lacking the training needed to cover environmental issues[5]	72%

1. Radio and Television News Directors Foundation (RTNDF), 1998.
2. Ibid.
3. National Environmental Education and Training Foundation (NEETF), 1999. Up from 64 percent in 1995.
4. Ibid. Random guessing would have produced 2.5 correct answers. Respondents with college degrees averaged 3.1 correct.
5. Foundation for American Communication Survey, 1993.

describe their newsrooms as having the same opinion. Only 62 percent of journalists said these issues were high priority issues for their newsrooms. There was some variation by region in terms of the extent to which newsrooms were described as placing a high priority on environmental health issues. Journalists from western and southern states were more likely to rate environmental issues as "high priority" issues in their newsrooms—74 and 60 percent, respectively, compared with 56 percent of journalists from the Northeast and 50 percent of journalists from the Midwest ($p < .05$).

■ JOURNALISTS' VIEWS OF THE CHALLENGES THEY FACE

As shown in Table 4, community misunderstanding represents the greatest challenge journalists face with regard to covering environmental issues. Half of our respondents identified it as a "serious" challenge. A third of our respondents identified lack of support by their editorial staffs as a "serious challenge" in covering environmental news stories. Overall, more journalists (37 percent) believed that pressure from industry represented a "serious" challenge in covering environmental health issues compared with 20 percent who described pressure from environmental groups as a "serious" challenge.

Perceptions of these challenges varied somewhat by region. Journalists from the Northeast were more likely to view community misunderstanding as serious and reporters from the South least likely (58 and 42 percent, respectively). Journalists from the West and South were twice as likely to rate pressure from industry as "serious" compared with those from the Midwest. Journalists from western states were

TABLE 4. PERCENTAGE OF JOURNALISTS REPORTING "SERIOUS" CHALLENGES FROM VARIOUS FACTORS BY REGION

	Northeast	South	Midwest	West	Total
Community Misunderstanding	58%	42%	47%	51%	50%
Pressure from Industry	38	40	21	41	37
Scarcity of Information	37	37	30	36	35
Lack of Editorial Staff Support	24	38	33	34	33
Identifying Experts	32	31	26	27	28
Pressure from Environmental Groups	18	24	7	27	20

almost four times as likely to rate pressure from environmental groups as a "serious" challenge compared with journalists from the Midwest.

▪ DISCUSSION ▪

There are many similarities in our findings from our journalists and their work covering environmental issues and those of other studies that have examined environmental issues in relation to both the public and newsrooms. There are similarities in terms of what journalists identified as the important environmental issues and issues identified by NEETF as critical for the future by the scientific community. The NEETF list includes polluted water, air pollution, freshwater shortages, cutting of large forests, population increases, loss of animal and plant species, and climate change (NEETF 1999). Given the important role of the media in conveying environmental information to the public, it is encouraging to note that journalists and scientists in the field considered the same environmental issues to be important.

The perceptions of our journalists regarding the public's high level of interest in environmental issues are in line with recent studies that show most Americans are very interested in the environment. A 1998 study by the Radio and Television News Director Foundation (RTNDF) found that 86 percent of the public said they were either "very" or "somewhat" interested in environmental news stories (FAC Survey 1993).

While recognizing the importance of environmental issues for the public, respondents believed that the issues are not always a high priority for newsrooms. A third of our journalists said environmental health issues were "low priority" issues for their newsrooms—despite the fact that in 31 percent of these "low priority" newsrooms, the public was described as placing a "high priority" on environmental health issues. In other words, journalists suggest that the media's focus in some communities may not be in sync with the priorities of the public. A similar disconnect between the priorities of the public and the media has been observed elsewhere. In the same 1998 RTNDF survey, eight out of ten members of the public said they were "very interested" in environmental stories; only 17 percent of news directors thought the general public was "very interested" in these stories.

It is important to learn more about why the environment is considered a lower priority in some newsrooms. From the findings, it is not possible to determine the basis for the lower priority observed by journalists in certain newsrooms. It is not clear if it reflects a general tendency in newsrooms to devalue environmental health issues or if it is only a possible reduction in their importance relative to other events occurring when the survey was conducted in 1999. The disjuncture between what the public sees as a priority and what newsrooms view as a priority may be linked to the complexity of environmental health issues. These complexities make environmental reporting difficult for reporters covering the general beat. Almost three-fourths (72 percent) of journalists surveyed by the Foundation for American Communication reported they lacked the training needed to cover complex environmental issues (FAC Survey 1993). Perhaps as a consequence, these issues have been less enthusiastically embraced by newsrooms that find it more cost-effective for reporters to cover stories about crime, sports, and celebrities, which lack the complexity of environmental stories.

Regardless of the basis for the lack of interest on the part of newsrooms, it appears that today we face a challenge. The public wants and needs more information on environmental health issues, but the complexity of these issues means that journalists cannot provide useful information to the public without adequate background information themselves. The third edition of *The Reporter's Environmental Handbook* has been designed to meet some of these challenges by providing succinct background information, "pitfalls to avoid" in reporting that might confuse the public, important points for researching each issue, and sources for additional information, including important Internet sites.

REFERENCES

Byrd, Theresa, et al. 1997. Variation in environmental risk perceptions and information sources among three communities in El Paso. *Risk: Health, Safety and Environment* 8:355.

Foundation for American Communications (FAC). 1993. *Survey* (annual), California.

Gallup/CNN/*USA Today* poll. 1999. (April).

National Environmental Education and Training Foundation (NEETF)/ Roper Starch Worldwide. 1999. *Eighth Annual National Report Card on Environmental Attitudes, Knowledge, and Behaviors.* Washington, D.C.: National Environmental Education and Training Foundation.

WHO SETS THE ENVIRONMENTAL AGENDA?

Who sets the environmental agenda in the United States? Who determines what environmental issues the American people are thinking about? The answer that immediately comes to mind is the federal government, which since 1965 has taken control of environmental policy-making in the United States. President Lyndon B. Johnson was one of those politicians who realized that being against pollution could be a popular as well as a relatively safe issue. Johnson told Congress in 1965:

> In the last few decades entire new categories of waste have come to plague and menace the American scene. These are the technological wastes—the by-products of growth, agriculture and science. . . .
>
> Almost all these wastes and pollution are the results of activities carried on for the benefit of man. A prime national goal must be an environment that is pleasing to the senses and healthy to live in. (Burton 1966, 207–208)

▪ GOVERNMENT OFFICIALS SET POLICY ▪

From the 1960s on, government officials and agencies saw themselves as the primary decision-makers concerning environmental issues, and they produced a tremendous number of environmental press releases, which were regularly used by the news media (Sachsman 1973, 7). Early on, it dawned on politicians that the environment was not a pass-

This chapter was written by David B. Sachsman, the holder of the West Chair of Excellence in Communication and Public Affairs at the University of Tennessee at Chattanooga, and is based on a paper presented at the International Congress on Hazardous Waste: Impact on Human and Ecological Health in Atlanta on June 7, 1995.

ing trend and that they would be expected to produce legislation to match their rhetoric. As Walter J. Hickel (1971, 65) explained: "When I took office in 1969 as Secretary of the Interior, pollution was no longer a joke; this fact was made clear by the nature of my confirmation hearings. The subject was aggravating millions of Americans; frustration and hostility were growing. The nation was desperately looking for leadership, and I decided that we should take the lead."

President Richard M. Nixon signed into law much of what is thought of as the backbone of modern environmental legislation, no matter what he really thought of the importance of the environment. For most of the next two decades, it was generally expedient for many politicians to support environmental issues rather than to develop the reputation of being overly responsive to special business interests. Only occasionally did politicians vocalize their lack of support for the environment, as did Reagan administration secretary of the interior James G. Watt and Environmental Protection Agency (EPA) administrator Anne Burford, both of whom were eventually forced to resign. Not until the Republican congressional takeover brought on by the 1994 election did large numbers of politicians actively work against the environment, though most of them continued to speak as if rewriting legislation was what was really best for environmental protection.

▪ ENVIRONMENTAL ACTIVISTS USE PRESS RELEASES ▪

The first wave of environmental activism came with the creation of the national parks and forests more than a hundred years ago, according to Philip Shabecoff in *A Fierce Green Fire* (1993). This environmental movement was about the conservation of nature, not the environmental health risks due to pollution. Some say it was Rachel Carson's *Silent Spring* in 1962 that turned the attention of activists toward the global danger of pollution.

The established environmental activist groups sent out their own fair share of environmental press releases in the 1960s aimed at awakening the American people to an environmental agenda. If they could marshal public support, their efforts to lobby government might carry greater weight. In addition, new activist groups were being born on local, regional, and national levels concerning every environmental issue imaginable. Among the things these groups had in common with the established movement were direct communication with government and the use of press releases to reach the public through the mass media. This was Shabecoff's second wave of environmentalism, a middle-class white environmental movement that was in full flower on the first Earth Day in 1970. The third wave of environmentalism in the Shabecoff lexicon was created in the 1980s by local environmental groups that involved diverse social classes, women, African Americans, and Native Americans and included supporters of the environmental justice movement against the environmental degradation of inner-city and rural human poverty (Perrin 1993).

▪ INDUSTRY AND INDUSTRY-RELATED GROUPS TELL GOOD-NEWS STORY OF INDUSTRIAL PROGRESS ▪

What was the effect of American business on the environmental agenda? Through most of the industrial age—from the nineteenth century to the 1960s—pollution and the use of natural resources were commonly accepted trade-offs for manufactured goods. In the period following World War II, American industry thought it necessary to explain what it was doing to the environment using press releases aimed at the business pages. The picture that was created during this era was one of corporate concern for the environment. In a sense, the environment itself was a business story at this time, the public relations–supplied good-news story of the progress of American industry.

This view of the environment changed in the 1960s. The mass media were receiving environmental press releases from government officials and citizen-action pressure groups as well as from industry, and the picture presented to the American people was one of conflict. Richard W. Darrow, president of the Hill and Knowlton public relations company, in 1971 called this conflict among public relations sources "the great ecological communications war." Darrow was concerned not just that the environment was on the public agenda but that corporate America could be crippled in the process:

> The hour is later, Communications Time than it is Mountain Standard Time, for you and me and our colleagues at the control points of industry. We will do those things that earn us attention and gain us understanding, or we will live out the remainder of our professional lives in the creeping, frustrating,

> stultifying, stifling grasp of unrealistic legislative restraints and crippling administrative restriction. A public that ought to understand us—and thank us for what we are and what we do—will instead clamor for our scalps. (Darrow 1971, 18)

▪ INDUSTRY, GOVERNMENT, AND ACTIVISTS FIGHT WAR OF CONFLICTING PRESS RELEASES ▪

For the next three decades, industry and industry-related groups fought for the attention of journalists and the public against the perceived threats of government and environmental activist groups. By the 1990s, there were many different industry positions, ranging from those who hoped to dismantle existing environmental regulations, through the "wise-use movement," to corporate efforts toward sustainable development. As the decade progressed, many companies supported Republican congressional efforts to dismantle existing environmental laws, the wise-use representatives and environmental activists were in conflict, and the Clinton administration's Council on Sustainable Development included many corporate leaders as well as several members of the cabinet. All wished to place their agenda before the American people, and by this time their press releases featured beautifully designed, glossy brochures.

Also involved in attracting the attention of the American people were other institutions, such as universities and institutes, as well as scientific programs. These institutions and programs had something to say about the environment and something to gain from publicity (such as government funding and even fame). From the 1970s on, universities, institutes, and scientific programs were centers of environmental research and study, and they initiated many press releases and contacts.

▪ THE RISE OF PUBLIC ENVIRONMENTAL AWARENESS ▪

Though many credit the publication of Carson's *Silent Spring* in 1962 for the rise of American environmental awareness, her message was adopted only by environmental activists at that time. While President Johnson spoke out on the environment in the mid-1960s, most of America's environmental legislation, including the EPA, began under President Nixon. The key year was 1969.

In 1969, the environment burst onto the networks, onto the front pages, and into public discussions. The specific story was a spill from a Union Oil rig in the Santa Barbara Channel (Shabecoff 1993, 111). Why was it that this particular story put the environment on the American public agenda? The answer may lie in the decision by the networks to tell the story in terms of the death of birds caught in the muck and the heartbreak of young people who had gone down to the beaches to try to save them. Night after night an oil spill was turned into a story of disaster and sorrow by the dramatic visual images of young people in tears trying to save dying, oil-soaked birds.

Some say it was the accumulation of negative environmental events in the late 1960s that led to the rise of environmental awareness on the American agenda and cite, along with the Santa Barbara oil spill, numerous notorious episodes involving phosphates, PCBs, mercury, smog, and even a river on fire (the Cuyahoga River in Cleveland on fire due to flammable chemicals) (Shabecoff 1993, 111). While the accumulation of negative incidents deserves a place on the list of factors influencing the environmental agenda, it was the dramatic visual impact of the way the television networks decided to play the Santa Barbara oil spill story that shocked Americans into public discussion in 1969. In 1995, when Teya Ryan, then the executive producer of CNN's Environment Unit, was asked how she approached environmental news, she said she looked for the human element. The traditional news value called "human interest" (MacDougall 1977, 56) clearly was at work in the 1969 decision by the networks to concentrate on pictures of crying young people with dying birds in their arms. And local journalists across the nation were just as affected by the story as was the general public. Watching the networks night after night, local broadcasters and newspaper reporters turned to their own local environmental problems, sorted through their own stacks of conflicting environmental press releases, and went out looking for their own local sidebars, their own local human interest environmental stories (Sachsman 1973, 2).

In 1969, *Time* and *Saturday Review* started regular sections on the environment, *Life* increased its coverage, *Look* gave over virtually a whole issue to the crisis, and *National Geographic* carried a 9,000-word article on the topic. This was also the year that the *New York Times* followed the lead of others and created an environment beat, a development that would soon take place in a number of major newspapers across the nation (Sachsman 1973, 2–3).

▪ ENVIRONMENTAL REPORTING BECOMES SPECIALIZED BEAT ▪

In the 1970s, the influence of specialized environmental reporters proved to be another factor in setting the environmental agenda. A study conducted in the San Francisco Bay Area found that regular environmental reporters were the only Bay Area journalists given the time to do local environmental enterprise stories. They also received the most environmental press releases and were, in fact, more influenced by public relations than were their colleagues (Sachsman 1973, 241).

The common notion that the best way to cover the environment was to use specialized reporters prevailed in the 1980s and was supported to some extent by the creation and growth of the Society of Environmental Journalists (SEJ) in the 1990s. But while many editors thought that specialized reporting improved environmental coverage and that SEJ members generally knew their field, the total number of environmental reporters remained comparatively small from the 1970s to the turn of the century. One major reason was cost. Another was the distinction that would arise in the 1970s and 1980s between science writers and environmental reporters.

In the 1970s, environmental reporting was often seen as part of the broader topic of science writing. This remained the way it was generally taught in journalism schools into the 1990s. But environmental reporting had many roots (such as outdoor and nature writing) besides science writing and included many elements (such as politics and economics) other than science. So by the 1990s, the reporters who joined the SEJ appeared somewhat different from the journalists who attended the major scientific meetings.

▪ PRESS RELEASES INFLUENCE COVERAGE ▪

The study of Bay Area environmental coverage conducted in the early 1970s showed the tremendous number and variety of environmental press releases and the very significant influence of these releases on environmental coverage. Over two months, eleven Bay Area journalists received 1,347 environmental items. These reporters saved (268) and used (192) large numbers of releases. A content analysis of environmental coverage in a related period found that public relations efforts influenced at least a fourth and perhaps as many as half of the stories whose sources could be identified. This high degree of influence was apparently related to the fact that the environment was a complex area of news that was difficult to cover. The study supported the analysis that a comparatively high percentage of the coverage of new, complex areas of the news, such as science, health, education, social welfare, and the environment, was influenced by public relations (Sachsman 1973, 50, 275, 276, 277).

▪ GOVERNMENT SOURCES DOMINATE ▪

The content analysis and the study of press releases found that government officials were the sources of information most often identified within environmental stories as well as the largest providers of press releases. In the content analysis, sources from other institutions, industry, and pressure groups followed in order, with industry-related groups a distant last. The number of releases journalists received included 566 from the government, 315 from the combination of industry (175) and related groups (140), 234 from other institutions, and 229 from pressure groups (Sachsman 1973, 113, 88).

The dominance of government officials and agencies as environmental news sources continued through the rest of the century, as did the influence of a wide variety of conflicting sources. One study of four newspapers' coverage of the *Exxon Valdez* oil spill across six months found 254 sources in 1,086 articles. Of these, 102 (40.2 percent) came from government, 46 (20.5 percent) from the oil industry, 21 (8.3 percent) from scientists, 20 (7.8 percent) from environmentalists, 16 (6.2 percent) from fishermen and women, and the rest from individuals (6.2 percent), affected businesses (4.3 percent), animal rescuers (3.5 percent), oil experts (2.3 percent), legal experts (1.9 percent), and media observers (0.8 percent) (Smith 1993, 397).

▪ TRADITIONAL NEWS VALUES CONTROL COVERAGE ▪

The findings of a five-year study at Rutgers University and the University of Medicine and Dentistry of New Jersey in the 1980s supported the concept that the media's traditional news values themselves influenced the public environmental agenda and that practical, everyday newsroom factors influencing news judgment likewise influenced the public agenda. Victor Cohn, in *Reporting on Risk* (1990), coined the term "Rutgers group" to describe the researchers whose work was supported by the Hazardous Substance Management Research Center (HSMRC) in New Jersey:

> Dr. Michael R. Greenberg, professor of urban planning and public health; Dr. Peter M. Sandman, professor of environmental journalism and director, Environmental Communication Research Program, Rutgers University; and Dr. David B. Sachsman, dean, School of Communications, California State University at Fullerton. For convenience I have referred to them in several instances as "the Rutgers group" or "the Rutgers professors," since Sachsman is a former New Jerseyite. They are authors of two highly recommended manuals. (61)

The Rutgers group was charged with the task of teaching journalists about environmental risk. The idea was that environmental news stories that did not discuss risk might be improved if risk information were included. From a scientific and health standpoint, it made sense to think of environmental issues in terms of the degree of risk involved, and more and more it seemed that within these circles the most appropriate terms to use were environmental risk or even environmental health risk. The Rutgers group was trying to improve an area of journalism it called environmental risk reporting, and was itself involved in a field that some called risk communication or environmental risk communication.

In the 1990s, environmental reporters belonged to the SEJ and talked about environmental coverage, not environmental risk reporting. Even those who were directly concerned with environmental health risk issues, such as the environmental justice movement, did not regularly seem to use the term "risk." At the same time, two academic fields had developed: environmental communication and risk communication. Risk was part of the field of environmental communication, and the environment was an issue within risk communication. "Risk" remained a scientific and medical term, and risk assessment continued to be an important scientific approach, but the public did not generally appear to discuss issues in terms of their scientific degrees of risk.

In its work, the Rutgers group had learned that while it was possible to teach reporters and editors about risk and risk assessment, these journalists normally would not adopt risk as a basic news value in their coverage of environmental or health issues. The Rutgers group's studies showed that journalists viewed risk as one aspect of the traditional news value of consequence or importance (which itself was just one of the profession's standards). If something was really risky, it was important and worth coverage. If the degree of risk was not quite so high or scientists disagreed about the danger, journalists did not know what to do with the risk (Sandman et al. 1987). Meanwhile, if a prominent person like Robert Redford was involved in an environmental story (such as the 1994 SEJ convention), the story received national attention.

▪ DRAMA AND GEOGRAPHY INFLUENCE NETWORK NEWS ▪

Environmental coverage was determined by the traditional journalistic news values of proximity, timeliness, prominence, and human interest, as well as consequence, the Rutgers group learned, standards that had little to do with the values of science. In addition to the traditional determinants of news, network television environmental coverage also involved the availability of dramatic visual images, the researchers found, and practical newsroom considerations such as cost and convenience, which the Rutgers group called geographical factors (Greenberg et al. 1989).

▪ WHO SETS THE ENVIRONMENTAL AGENDA? ▪

Public awareness of the environment appears to be influenced by many different factors: government, activists, business, universities, scientific institutions, conflicting press releases, big environmental events, traditional news values, dramatic visual images, and the media's cost and convenience in providing coverage. Some of these factors influence the public directly; all of these factors influence media coverage, which in turn influences public knowledge and discussion:

> The actual influence of the press . . . will vary with the selective interest and experience of readers. In esoteric areas of science and technology where readers have little direct information or preexisting knowledge to guide an independent evaluation (e.g., the effect of fluorocarbons on the ozone in the atmosphere), the press, as the major source of information, in effect defines the reality of the situation for them. During the period of maximum press coverage of the ozone controversy, for

> example, 73.5 percent of the general public had heard about this highly technical issue, previously remote from their experience, for the first time in the press. (Nelkin 1987, 77)

Some environmental events are so big that they seem to make the public agenda immediately, even before the television cameras arrive. Bhopal and Chernobyl involved so many deaths and were such catastrophes that they became the subjects of discussion as soon as the public found out about them (information about Chernobyl was not immediately released by the Soviets). But the attention paid by the general public to the Santa Barbara oil spill, Three Mile Island, and the *Exxon Valdez*, on the other hand, apparently was influenced by many factors, from government officials to conflicting press releases, traditional news values, dramatic images, and even the relatively short distance between Santa Barbara and Three Mile Island and the media centers of Los Angeles and New York, respectively.

These events became disasters in the public mind partly because of the amount of damage done to the environment but also because numerous people called them disasters and the mass media decided to treat them as such. Other events in other locations did not make the public agenda either because the press did not know about them or because they were not defined by government or by the mass media in crisis terms. While many people remember the 10.1-million-gallon oil spill of the *Exxon Valdez* off Alaska in 1989, who outside of Texas remembers the 10.7-million-gallon spill that resulted from the 1979 collision of the *Burmah Agate* with another ship in Galveston Bay?

Government is the official source for most environmental stories. It is government that officially declares a crisis. Government legislates and regulates the environment, and government sources supply the most press releases and other public information about the environment. Government wants to be the principal agenda-setter concerning the environment, and in many cases it is. Under these circumstances, what is interesting is how much power all the other actors have to influence the public agenda.

When the mass media decides to treat an environmental event as a crisis, then the act of putting it on the front page or on the airwaves sets the public agenda in those terms (Sachsman 1993, 3). An open conflict among those involved in an environmental problem is likely to result in increased press and public attention, especially when there are accusations of impropriety. For example, Robin Gregory (1991, 5) states, "the appearance of incompetence or callousness on the part of risk managers is likely to foster a split between perpetrators and victims of an accident (e.g., witness public anger at the delayed response of the Exxon company to the March 1989 Alaska oil spill)."

The question of who sets the public agenda may be even more complex when it comes to those chronic environmental issues where no event exists to form a news peg on which to hang a story. In those mass media that employ specialized environmental reporters, chronic environmental problems occasionally receive in-depth feature treatment, but the majority of American news media give their environmental assignments to local-beat and general-assignment reporters who generally know as little about chronic environmental problems as they do about scientific risk assessment. The very substantial number of local environmental stories that are produced by these beginning reporters demonstrates that the environment has become a central issue in local reporting, just as it has become one of the key components of K–12 science education. But are these local journalists truly agenda-setters, as are the specialized reporters, or is it their news sources (conflicting and otherwise) who really set the public agenda through their influence of the press?

The public relations efforts of government officials, environmental activists, business leaders, and university scientists would have enormous influence over the public agenda if they did not tend to balance each other out. The open conflicts among these news sources tend to give the power back to the journalist, whose responsibility it is to make a meaningful story out of contradictory public communications. Furthermore, the reliance by both reporters and editors on their traditional news values, drama, and geography also tends to keep the agenda-setting power in the hands of the mass media.

■ SUMMARY ■

Government and the mass media are the two principal agenda-setters regarding the environment. Each has a story to tell the American public. When they agree in their viewpoints, there is substantial cooperation between them. When they disagree, they become adversaries, each vying for the public's attention. The other actors on the environmental stage try to affect the public agenda by lobbying government or by convincing the press. The influence of public relations on journalism is substantial, but it is not overwhelming because the mass media are insulated by journalism's traditional standards and because reporters often get to pick and choose among the contradictory statements of various sources.

REFERENCES

Burton, P. 1966. *Corporate Public Relations*. New York: Reinhold.

Cohn, V. 1990. *Reporting on Risk*. Washington, D.C.: The Media Institute.

Darrow, R. W. 1971. *Communication in an Environmental Age*. New York: Hill and Knowlton.

Greenberg, M. R., D. B. Sachsman, P. M. Sandman, and K. L. Salomone. 1989. Risk, drama, and geography in coverage of environmental risk by network TV. *Journalism Quarterly* 66:267–276.

Gregory, R. 1991. Risk perceptions as substance and symbol. In *Risky Business: Communications Issues of Science, Risk, and Public Policy*, ed. L. Wilkins and P. Patterson. New York: Greenwood Press.

Hickel, W. J. 1971. The making of a conservationist. *Saturday Review*, October 2, 65.

MacDougall, C. 1977. *Interpretative Reporting*. 7th ed. New York: MacMillan.

Nelkin, D. 1987. *Selling Science*. New York: W. H. Freeman.

Perrin, N. 1993. Think globally, act locally. Review of *A Fierce Green Fire*, by P. Shabecoff. *New York Times Book Review*, January 24, 8.

Ryan, T. 1995. Speech to the Conference on Communication and Our Environment. Chattanooga, March 31.

Sachsman, D. B. 1993. The mass media and environmental risk communication: Then and now. In *Proceedings of the Conference on Communication and Our Environment*, ed. James G. Cantrill and M. Jimmie Killingsworth. Marquette: Northern Michigan University Printing Services.

Sachsman, D. B. 1973. Public relations influence on environmental coverage (in the San Francisco Bay Area). Ph.D. diss., Stanford University.

Sandman, P. M., D. B. Sachsman, M. R. Greenberg, and M. Gochfeld. 1987. *Environmental Risk and the Press: An Exploratory Assessment*. New Brunswick, N.J.: Transaction.

Shabecoff, P. 1993. *A Fierce Green Fire: The American Environmental Movement*. New York: Hill and Wang, 1993.

Smith, C. 1993. News sources and power elites in news coverage of the *Exxon Valdez* oil spill. *Journalism Quarterly* 70, no. 2:397.

THOUGHTS ON THE FUTURE OF ENVIRONMENTAL POLICY AND REGULATION

While many reporters today take a deregulated environment as a given, it is important to remember that the modern environmental movement of the late 1960s began as a regulated system. Under a regulated environment, governmental laws were established that limited pollution and exposure and imposed penalties enforcing these laws. This regulatory approach was responsible for the enormous strides made in protecting the environment over the last thirty years. Our water and air have become demonstrably cleaner as a result of landmark legislation such as the Clean Air Act and the Clean Water Act.

In the 1980s, however, the Reagan administration took the United States in a new direction—away from intervention and regulation and toward acceptance of the role of the marketplace, competition, and deregulation. This new thinking was applied not only to prices and quality but also in determining what is acceptable to consider within the environmental arena. Because of this sea change, the emphasis in environmental policy has shifted away from efforts to determine whether pollution is acceptable toward efforts to set acceptable limits for pollution. The political spectrum in which environmental debates take place has become much more narrow.

As has happened more than once in the past, shifts in policy swing back and forth. The shift in environmental policy toward deregulation in the 1980s is likely to shift at some point in the future again toward a more regulated environment. Shifts usually occur when society is confronted with a new crisis that once again demands government intervention. Because pollution knows no borders, the next swing back

This brief is based on a conversation with former governor of New Jersey James Florio, who is now on the faculty of the Edward J. Bloustein School of Planning and Public Policy, Rutgers University, New Brunswick, New Jersey.

toward regulation will likely occur on the global environmental front. An international governance system will be needed for some measure of control over the environmental process.

In the current paradigm, deregulation and competition are defined as the prevailing mechanisms to be used in solving environmental problems. At one time, regulation and taxation were acceptable parts of the paradigm used to effect change. Over time, however, these policy strategies have been taken off the table and are no longer even contemplated as options. For example, no one argues for increasing gas taxes in order to achieve greater fuel efficiency and cleaner air. No one suggests establishing new regulations to improve air quality. The public is exposed to only one set of ideas and values in the media, and this becomes the framework that people use to evaluate options and propose solutions to problems. This mindset impacts on environmental matters, especially when we are confronted by problems that require possibly more regulation.

A competitive model relies on market forces to produce better environmental quality and lower pollution. The model works like this: If the actions of company X cause financial problems for them, then it is assumed they will change their course of action. If they produce a byproduct that they discharge into a nearby river and it is found to cause illness or death, the financial problems this generates will eventually cause them to change their practices. Under the market approach, policy will eventually change for the better. Meanwhile some—often many—people are sickened or die in the process. The question one needs to ask is whether corrective action is better than preventive action. Is this "body count" approach the best way to protect the environment—rather than imposing regulations that prevent pollution of the water, soil, and air before it starts?

The logic of the argument supporting the competitive model is that market forces internalize penalties from bad policies. Rational decision-making tells companies they are better off doing something about pollution because they can't afford the damages associated with it, the public relations price tag, or the impact it will have on their ability to raise capital.

Some argue, however, that it is counterintuitive to rely on market forces to produce better environmental quality and lower pollution. After all, the Superfund concept was put in place because companies randomly dumped hazardous substances prior to strong laws, and we are all now living with this legacy. "Right-to-know" laws require companies to make risk data on the materials they use and produce available to the community. The rationale behind the laws is that companies will feel pressure from communities if they are required to report risks—and act responsibly as a result. While there is some value in this thinking (the "right to sue" in addition to the "right to know" really focuses people's attention), the idea of expecting goodwill ultimately to result in good environmental policy is naive.

In looking toward the future of environmental policy, cost-benefit analysis and risk assessment will be important concepts for journalists to grasp. If $100 is spent to comply with an environmental regulation that ends up cleaning 95 percent of the problem, how do we deal with the remaining 5 percent for which cleanup will cost another $50? According to cost-benefit analysis, the marginal return for that 5 percent is not great. Therefore, the remaining cleanup may not get done, and, since pollution is not static, what is 5 percent this year can easily become 10 percent next year and 20 percent the following year.

Risk assessment is another important issue for journalists to understand. Supporters of risk assessment believe it is capable of always producing the right outcome. In fact, risk assessment is an extremely subjective process rather than a scientific tool applied in a strict, unchanging model. The model depends on built-in assumptions regarding how to quantify costs and benefits, but as a rule, costs are much easier to quantify than benefits. Depending on the values one chooses to assign to benefits in the equation, it is possible to dictate the outcome of a risk assessment. Risk assessment can also be used to delay change. There are some who argue against doing anything until a risk assessment is completed and costs and benefits have been evaluated. This can become an ongoing procedural delaying tactic. Without any conclusions, maintaining the status quo is often the only choice.

Cost-benefit analysis and risk assessment are not easy concepts to understand. While the public is capable of grasping these concepts if they are explained well, this kind of explanation is not easily conveyed in a thirty-second piece on the 6:00 evening news. This represents a challenge for journalists.

BRIEFS

AIR POLLUTION (INDOOR)

▪ BACKGROUND ▪

It is commonly accepted that outdoor air can be unhealthy. People with respiratory conditions are accustomed to following news and weather reports that monitor levels of ozone (smog), pollen, molds, and spores before they go outdoors. Most people do not realize, however, that indoor air can be even more polluted than outdoor air. Indoor air levels of some pollutants can be more than a hundred times higher than outdoor levels. Given that people spend up to 90 percent of their time indoors, it is important to investigate and evaluate the health significance of these exposures.

Indoor air pollution is the accumulation of a substance or substances within the air of a home, workplace, school, or public building to such a degree that the health of persons within that structure are negatively affected. The U.S. Environmental Protection Agency (EPA) consistently ranks indoor air pollution among the top five environmental health risks. The EPA's 1989 "Report to Congress on Indoor Air Quality" estimated the costs of indoor air pollution in the United States to be in the tens of billions of dollars per year.

The health effects associated with poor indoor air quality vary widely and depend upon the contaminants, their concentrations, and the individual susceptibilities of the people exposed. The health effects may be immediate or occur years after exposure; they may be distinct and severe or mild and transient. In many cases, where complaints are vague or mimic cold symptoms, it may be difficult to determine if the symptoms are indeed related to indoor air quality. The problem of poor indoor air quality is further compounded by the fact that those who are most vulnerable to its effects—infants, the sick, and the elderly—tend to spend most of their time indoors.

This brief is based on an earlier version included in the second edition of *The Reporter's Environmental Handbook*. Additional information and comments were provided by Paul Lioy, Deputy Director of the Environmental and Occupational Health Sciences Institute (EOHSI), Piscataway, New Jersey.

Sources of indoor air pollution include building materials and furnishings, combustion sources, household cleaning products, pesticides, personal care products, hobby products, radon, central heating and ventilation systems, and outdoor air pollution. The relative importance of these sources can vary significantly among buildings. The types and levels of indoor air contaminants depend upon many factors, including the age and condition of the structure, maintenance of heating and ventilation systems, housekeeping practices, pesticide use, smoking practices, time of year, geographic location, and types of activities carried out within the building.

■ IDENTIFYING THE ISSUES ■

In terms of cancer risk, the most significant indoor air pollutants are radon and environmental tobacco smoke ("secondhand smoke").

■ RADON

Radon is an odorless, colorless, tasteless, radioactive gas that occurs naturally around the globe. Radon enters buildings through dirt floors, through cracks in foundation floors and walls, and through floor drains, sumps, and other underground openings. It is estimated that one out of every fifteen homes in the United States has radon levels above the EPA's action level of 4 picocuries per liter (pCi/l). The National Research Council (NRC) estimates that radon is responsible for 15,400 to 21,800 lung cancer deaths each year. Smoking in combination with radon exposure greatly increases the risk of developing lung cancer. NRC data suggest that the number of lung cancer deaths due to radon may be as low as 3,000 per year among nonsmokers and as high as 33,000 per year among smokers.

■ ENVIRONMENTAL TOBACCO SMOKE

Environmental tobacco smoke (ETS) is a mixture of more than 4,000 chemicals, including 200 compounds known to be toxic and more than forty known carcinogens. The EPA estimates that exposure to ETS may be responsible for 3,000 lung cancer deaths per year. The American Heart Association reports that ETS is responsible for 37,000–40,000 heart disease deaths per year. In addition, the EPA estimates that

150,000–300,000 cases of lower respiratory tract infections occur annually in children less than eighteen months of age due to exposure to ETS. Exposure to ETS in children is also associated with middle ear infections and reduced lung function. The number and severity of asthma attacks in children are also aggravated by exposure to ETS. The EPA estimates that ETS may cause thousands of children to develop asthma each year. (See the brief on "Children's Health [Asthma].") Exposure to ETS is also associated with eye, nose, and throat irritation and chest pain.

■ ASBESTOS

Indoor air pollutants associated with building materials include asbestos, formaldehyde, lead, and other volatile organic compounds (VOCs). Asbestos is the most notorious source of indoor air pollution related to building materials. Asbestos is a fibrous natural mineral that, before 1973, was commonly used in building construction for fireproofing and insulation. When inhaled, asbestos fibers can cause asbestosis (asbestos-related scarring of the lung), lung cancer, and mesothelioma. Mesothelioma is a cancer of the mucous membrane lining of the chest that can also affect the linings of the heart and abdomen. Mesothelioma is generally preceded by asbestosis and is almost always fatal. Asbestosis and asbestos-related cancers have a latency period of twenty to thirty years or more. Therefore, the incidence of asbestosis, mesothelioma, and other asbestos-related cancers today is the result of asbestos exposures that took place decades ago—exposures that are rare today.

■ FORMALDEHYDE

Another indoor air contaminant related to building materials is formaldehyde. The most significant indoor sources of formaldehyde emissions are pressed wood products made with urea-formaldehyde adhesives. Other possible indoor sources of formaldehyde include carpets, upholstery, permanent-press clothing and draperies, paints, and coating products. Formaldehyde exposure is associated with watery eyes; coughing; eye, nose, and throat irritation; skin rashes; nausea; headaches; dizziness; and, at high levels, difficulty in breathing. High concentrations of formaldehyde can trigger asthma attacks in people with asthma. Some people develop a sensitivity to formaldehyde, where subsequent exposure to even low concentrations causes symptoms to develop. Formaldehyde is classified as a "probable human carcinogen" by the EPA and by the International Agency for Research on Cancer (IARC).

▪ LEAD

Most people are aware that lead-based paint in older homes presents a health threat to young children who may eat paint chips. Lead can also be an important indoor air pollutant. Sources of indoor airborne lead include resuspended dust from flaking lead-based paint and dust tracked or blown in from outdoors. Other sources include lead emitted during soldering and stained-glass making. Recently, lead used as a stiffener in household candlewicks has been identified as a significant source of lead in indoor air. Lead exposure can adversely affect the brain, central nervous system, blood cells, and kidneys. Lead is stored in the bones, where it accumulates with continued exposure. Young children exposed to lead and children whose mothers were exposed to lead can suffer delays in mental and physical development, lower IQs, shortened attention spans, and behavioral problems. (See the brief on "Children's Health [Lead].") Nonairborne lead can dominate the total exposure of children and adults. Settled lead dust and subsequent hand-to-mouth or object-to-mouth ingestion can be a significant source of exposure. Older homes with lead-containing soldered water pipes (or even older lead piping) can cause elevated lead exposure via drinking water or its use in cooking.

▪ OTHER SOURCES

Other sources of indoor air pollution include space heaters, gas stoves, wood stoves, fireplaces, and poorly ventilated or poorly maintained furnaces. The airborne contaminants from these sources include carbon monoxide, nitrogen dioxide, sulfur dioxide, particulates, and VOCs. Carbon monoxide is a colorless, odorless, and tasteless gas that interferes with oxygen uptake by the body. At low concentrations, carbon monoxide causes headaches, dizziness, weakness, nausea, confusion, disorientation, and fatigue. The symptoms of carbon monoxide poisoning may mimic the flu. At high concentrations, carbon monoxide results in unconsciousness and death. Nitrogen dioxide and sulfur dioxide act as strong irritants of the eye, nose, throat, and respiratory tract. Airborne particulates can lodge in the lungs, causing irritation and lung tissue damage. Other indoor air pollutants, including radon, can attach to inhaled particulates and be carried deep into the lungs.

VOCs are released from burning fuel (gasoline, oil, wood, coal, natural gas, etc.) as well as from a variety of household products, including cleaners, personal care products, solvents, paints, glues, carpeting, wallpaper, and other building materials. In addition, benzene and other VOCs can escape from storage containers kept in attached garages and seep into homes. Exposure to high concentrations of VOCs can cause eye and respiratory tract irritation, headaches, dizziness, rashes, vomiting, and memory impairment. Many VOCs found in household products are known to cause cancer in animals and are known or suspected to cause cancer in humans. Formaldehyde (see above) is one example of a VOC. In recent years, scientists have begun to study chemical reactions that occur in household indoor air. These reactions involve VOCs from consumer products (e.g., limonene in air fresheners) and ozone from indoor and outdoor sources. The products of these reactions include other VOCs and particulates that can be as much of a concern or even greater concern for exposure than the reactants.

Housekeeping practices can be a large determinant of indoor air quality. On the one hand, poor housekeeping can result in elevated airborne levels of "biological contaminants," including bacteria, molds, mildew, animal dander, and dust mites. On the other hand, misuse or overuse of household cleaning agents and pesticides can result in harmful levels of VOCs and other compounds in the indoor air.

Biological contaminants are associated with a wide range of symptoms and diseases. Some biological contaminants—animal dander, dust mites, dust from cockroaches, and rat and mouse urine—trigger allergic reactions. Inhalation of microorganisms and their toxins can cause fever, chills, and lung inflammation. Legionnaires' disease is an example of a pneumonia caused by an airborne bacterium. The bacterium that causes Legionnaires' disease has been found in cooling systems, whirlpool baths, humidifiers, food market vegetable misters, and tap water. "Humidifier Fever" is a flulike illness associated with exposure to bacteria, fungi, and amoebae found in humidifiers, air conditioners, and aquariums. Microbial and fungal contaminants need a source of nutrients and moisture in order to grow. Control of moisture (especially roof, window, and plumbing leaks or extensive moisture condensation in building ventilation systems) is a key to keeping biologic contaminants under control.

Indoor and outdoor pesticide use also contributes to indoor air quality problems. Overexposure to household and commercial pesticides can cause headaches, dizziness, muscle twitching, weakness, tingling sensations, and nausea. Long-term exposure to pesticides is associated with liver and central nervous system damage and increased risk of cancer. Pesticide products also include ingredients listed as "inert." These ingredients are typically VOCs.

Indoor air pollution has become a serious concern following the terrorist attacks of September 11, 2001. The collapse of the World Trade Center Towers covered the streets of lower Manhattan with debris that has also filtered into ventilation systems, carpets, and walls in buildings otherwise seemingly untouched. Hundreds of building cleanup workers came into the area to clean adjacent office buildings surrounding the World Trade Center and have subsequently reported health symptoms. People living downtown have complained that dust in the air inside their buildings is making them sick. Some residents have filed complaints regarding possible asbestos contamination in their apartments. In May 2002, the EPA announced that it would clean and test 31,000 apartments south of Canal Street.

▪ ADDRESSING THE ISSUES ▪

Three basic strategies are used to remedy indoor air quality problems: source control or removal, improved ventilation, and air cleaning.

▪ SOURCE REMOVAL AND CONTROL

Source removal and control includes routine maintenance of heating, ventilation, and air-conditioning (HVAC) systems and combustion sources; encapsulation or removal of intact asbestos insulation, sealing or removal of lead-based paint; replacement of water-damaged building materials; the banning or restriction of smoking; frequent cleaning to remove household dust; the use of household chemicals and pesticides in well-ventilated areas and during periods when the building is not occupied; and switching to nonpolluting household products and nonchemical pest control. (It should be noted that asbestos and lead-paint removal should only be conducted by trained professionals who specialize in abatement.) To control household dust, high-efficiency vacuum cleaners equipped with high-energy particulate absorption (HEPA) filters should be used. Maintaining indoor relative humidity between 35 and 55 percent and indoor temperature between 20 and 23 degrees Celsius (68 and 73 degrees Fahrenheit) can inhibit or prevent the growth of some molds and bacteria. This, however, will have a high cost in terms of energy consumption. Source removal, when practical, is the most effective means of improving indoor air quality. To avoid microbial growth and air contamination, it is very important to prevent and promptly correct water leaks in the building or extensive condensation in ventilation systems.

■ IMPROVED VENTILATION

Improved ventilation is often a cost-effective means of removing indoor air pollutants. Many home HVAC systems circulate indoor air as opposed to drawing in fresh air from outdoors. In these cases, simple measures such as opening windows and doors and operating window or attic fans can increase the amounts of fresh air drawn indoors. For large buildings, HVAC systems should be designed and operated to meet ventilation standards contained in local building codes, including an adequate supply of fresh, clean outdoor air. Local exhaust ventilation can be used to remove air contaminants in areas where they routinely accumulate, such as copy and printing areas, kitchens, and rest rooms. Proper maintenance and operation of the building ventilation system are important since poorly maintained or improperly operated systems can themselves be the source of an indoor air quality problem.

■ AIR CLEANERS

Air cleaners may be useful in addressing some indoor air pollution problems. Air cleaners range from simple furnace filters to tabletop appliances to whole-house systems and are predominately used for particle removal. The effectiveness of an air cleaner depends upon the strength of the pollutant source, the efficiency of the air cleaner's particle collector, and the air cleaner's air-circulation rate. As with HVAC systems, routine maintenance of air cleaners, including changing filters, is required to maintain their effectiveness. The effectiveness of an air cleaner can be greatly enhanced by simultaneous efforts to control or remove the source.

To address the issue of indoor air quality in the general workplace, the Occupational Safety and Health Administration (OSHA) published a proposed rule on April 4, 1994 (59 FR 15968-16039). The proposed rule applied to nonindustrial indoor work environments, including schools and training centers, offices, commercial establishments, health care facilities, cafeterias, and factory break rooms. The proposed rule set requirements for workplace ventilation and required designated smoking areas with separate exhaust systems. The proposal generated the largest public response in OSHA's history, with more than 100,000 comments received during the open comment period. OSHA eventually withdrew the proposal on December 17, 2001. Citing widespread positive actions taken to curtail smoking in public areas and workplaces since the rule's proposal, the agency found that withdrawal of the proposal would allow it to direct its resources to other projects.

▪ IMPORTANT POINTS FOR RESEARCHING A STORY ▪

- The important task for the reporter in an indoor air quality controversy is to find out which pollutant(s) is thought to have caused the problem and then to determine if scientists think the pollutant(s) is likely to cause that problem and what outside exposures or factors are associated with that problem.
- Consider the potential impacts of outdoor pollution when investigating indoor air quality problems and vice versa. For example, outdoor contaminants such as sulfuric acid from smokestack emissions may seep into buildings and cause symptoms indoors. Likewise, neighbors of an industrial facility or Superfund site may blame these "sources" for a myriad of health problems that may be in fact related to problems with their own indoor air quality (e.g., smoking).
- To address an indoor air quality problem, homeowners or building managers may choose to install indoor air cleaners. In the case of ozone-generating air cleaners, the air cleaner itself may cause or exacerbate an indoor air quality problem. Ozone, the main component of outdoor photochemical smog, is highly irritating to the upper respiratory tract; can aggravate chronic respiratory conditions, including asthma; and can cause lung damage. (See the brief on "Air Pollution [Outdoor].") Studies show that, at concentrations below public health standards, ozone emitted from indoor air cleaners is not effective in removing air contaminants. Further, in the process of reacting with chemicals indoors, ozone can produce other harmful chemicals. Again, removal of the contaminant source (rather than cleanup by filtration or absorption) is generally the preferable approach.

- The phrases "sick building syndrome" and "building-related illness" refer to two separate phenomena. "Sick building syndrome" describes cases where occupants of a building suffer from a variety of acute symptoms and complaints that appear to be related to time spent in the building. Symptoms associated with sick building syndrome may include headaches, nausea, drowsiness, and eye, nose, and throat irritation. In cases of sick building syndrome, the symptoms typically disappear soon after leaving the building. "Building-related illness" refers to situations where individual cases of diagnosable illness caused by specific indoor air contaminants are identified among building occupants. Symptoms of building-related illness vary but may include cough, chest tightness, fever, chills, and muscle aches. The symptoms of building-related illness persist after leaving the building, and recovery time may be prolonged.

▪ AVOIDING PITFALLS ▪

- General complaints of poor indoor air quality are notoriously difficult to diagnose. An investigation into indoor air quality complaints should include information gathered from building occupants, an assessment of the HVAC system, and identification of possible contaminants, sources, and exposure pathways. Air sampling is often one of the first things building occupants request. However, air sampling can only provide a "snapshot" of indoor air quality in a specific location within the building at a specific time. Air sampling results can often be misleading and often fail to show any contaminant concentrations above recognized exposure standards or guidelines. One notable exception to this is radon. The EPA recommends measurement of radon levels in living areas for comparison against a specific "action level" of 4 pCi/l. However, for general indoor air quality complaints, unless specific sources and contaminants are suspected, it is impossible to design an appropriate air sampling strategy. In fact, it is generally simpler to solve an indoor air quality problem through source elimination or improved ventilation than it is to diagnose the problem and identify the offending pollutants via air sampling.
- Typical symptoms associated with poor indoor air quality—headaches, nausea, drowsiness, fatigue, and skin rashes—may also

result from other causes ranging from illness unrelated to the building or seasonal allergies to personal or job-related stress and other psychosocial factors.

- Use caution when indoor air sampling data are compared to "standards." With the exception of the EPA's action level for radon, there are currently no standards for air contaminants in homes, offices, or public buildings. OSHA's Permissible Exposure Limits (PELs) and the American Conference of Governmental Industrial Hygienists' (ACGIH) Threshold Limit Values (TLVs) have been developed to address high levels of exposure in specific industrial settings under specific conditions of exposure for defined periods of time. It is unlikely that any contaminant involved in an indoor air quality complaint in an office building would exceed a PEL or TLV, and demonstrating that contaminant levels in nonindustrial settings are below these limits does not ensure that the air is "clean" or "safe."

▪ INFORMATION RESOURCES ▪

▪ GOVERNMENT/ACADEMIA

Local, county, and state departments of health and environment are generally the first agencies to investigate complaints of indoor air pollution. Other resources include:

- Centers for Disease Control and Prevention (www.cdc.gov)
  Office of Communications
  1600 Clifton Rd., MS D25, Atlanta, GA 30333
  (404) 639-3286 or (800) 311-3435; fax: (404) 639-7394
  E-mail: in.the.news@cdc.gov
- Indoor Air Quality Information Clearinghouse
  (http://www.epa.gov/iaq/)
  P.O. Box 37133, Washington, DC 20013-7133
  (800) 438-4318 or (703) 356-4020
  E-mail: iaqinfo@aol.com
- Montana State University–Healthy Indoor Air for America's Home (www.montana.edu/wwwcxair)
  Montana State University Extension Service
  109 Taylor Hall, Bozeman, MT 59717

(406) 994-3451; fax: (406) 994-5417
E-mail: mvogel@montana.edu

- National Safety Council–Environmental Health Center (www.nsc.org/ehc.htm)
  1025 Connecticut Ave. NW, Suite 1200, Washington, DC 20036
  (202) 293-2270; fax: (202) 293-0032
  E-mail: ehc@nsc.org
- New York Committee for Occupational Safety and Health (www.nycosh.org)
  Contains links for World Trade Center safety and health information
- U.S. Consumer Product Safety Commission (www.cpsc.gov)
  Office of Information and Public Affairs
  4330 East-West Highway, Bethesda, MD 20814-4408
  (301) 504-0580 or (800) 638-2772; fax (301) 504-0862
- U.S. Environmental Protection Agency–Indoor Environments Division (www.epa.gov/iaq)
  Ariel Rios Bldg., Mailcode 66093
  1200 Pennsylvania Ave. NW, Washington, DC 20460
  (202) 564-9370; fax: (202) 565-2039

▪ INDUSTRY

- Association of Home Appliance Manufacturers (www.aham.org)
  Suite 402, 1111 19th St. NW, Washington, DC 20036
  (202) 872-5955; fax (202) 872-9354
- Building Owners and Management Association International (www.boma.org)
  1201 New York Ave. NW, Suite 300, Washington, DC 20005
  (202) 408-2662; fax: (202) 371-0181

▪ NONPROFIT/CONSUMER ORGANIZATIONS

- American Lung Association—Indoor Air Quality (www.lungusa.org/air/air_indoor_index.html)
  1740 Broadway, New York, NY 10019
  national: (212) 315-8700; press_contact@lungusa.org
  local: (800) 586-4872

AIR POLLUTION (OUTDOOR)

▪ BACKGROUND ▪

Since the adoption of the Clean Air Act in 1970, air quality in most areas of the United States has improved for all criteria pollutants. Nevertheless, more than 100 million Americans breathe air that does not meet national minimum standards for air quality. The health-related costs of outdoor air pollution in the United States are estimated at $40 billion to $50 billion per year.

Outdoor air pollution affects human health, the environment, and property. The health effects from air pollutants range from eye, nose, and throat irritation to difficulty in breathing and premature death. Environmental effects of outdoor air pollution include reduced visibility due to smog, damage to forests, and the acidification of lakes and rivers by acid rain. Air pollution dirties buildings and other structures, erodes stone structures and monuments, and damages crops.

The National Ambient Air Quality Standards (NAAQS) established under the 1970 Clean Air Act cover six air pollutants of particular concern in the United States: carbon monoxide, lead, nitrogen dioxide, ozone, particulate matter, and sulfur dioxide. These air pollutants are collectively referred to as the criteria pollutants. The NAAQS set limits on the amount of each criteria pollutant that can be present in outdoor air and are intended to provide all Americans with the same minimum standards for clean air. "Primary" ambient air quality standards are designed to protect human health, and "secondary" standards are designed to protect the environment, including crops, natural vegetation, and structures. Compliance with the ambient air quality standards is the responsibility of the individual states, which are required to develop state implementation plans (SIPs).

This brief is based on material included in the second edition of *The Reporter's Environmental Handbook*. Additional information and comments were provided by Bernard D. Goldstein, M.D., Dean of the School of Public Health, University of Pittsburgh, and Paul Lioy, Deputy Director of the Environmental and Occupational Health Sciences Institute (EOHSI), Piscataway, New Jersey.

The EPA measures compliance with the Clean Air Act through the National Ambient Air Quality Monitoring Program. Geographic regions in compliance with the ambient air quality standards are called attainment areas. Regions where air quality measurements routinely exceed the standards are designated as nonattainment areas for the offending pollutant(s).

In addition to the criteria pollutants, the Clean Air Act regulates emissions of 188 hazardous air pollutants (HAPs, or air toxics). Air toxics include pollutants that are known or suspected of causing cancer, birth defects, or other serious health or environmental effects.

▪ IDENTIFYING THE ISSUES ▪

The most notable improvements in criteria pollutants include a reduction in the average airborne concentration of lead by more than 94 percent. Concentrations of carbon monoxide and sulfur dioxide are less than half of their 1980 levels. Despite these overall improvements at the national level, some locations have poorer air quality now than they did twenty years ago.

▪ FINE PARTICULATE MATTER

As of July 2000, a total of 114 areas—containing more than 100 million Americans—were designated as nonattainment areas for one or more criteria air pollutants. Of these, two-thirds were nonattainment for PM10, particulate matter measuring 10 micrometers or less in diameter. Particulate matter includes solid particles and liquid droplets emitted by a wide range of sources, including motor vehicles, construction operations, power plants, industry, residential fireplaces, wood stoves, volcanic eruptions, and windblown dust. Particulate matter is also formed by condensation of, or chemical reactions between, pollutant gases in the atmosphere. Particulate matter itself can consist of toxic compounds or can carry toxic or radioactive materials that become attached to the particles. When inhaled, fine particulate matter (generally < 1–10 micrometers) settles and accumulates in the respiratory tract. The smaller the particle, the deeper it can penetrate into the lungs. Particulate matter aggravates existing respiratory problems, including asthma, and is associated with decreased lung function and premature death. Particulate matter also soils and erodes structures and is a major cause of reduced visibility. A study of half a million people conducted over a sixteen-year period of time and reported in the *Journal of the American Medical Association* in 2002 found that long-term exposure to combustion-related fine particulate matter—soot emitted by cars, trucks, coal-fired power plants, and factories—significantly raises the risk of dying from lung cancer and is about as dangerous as living with a smoker. While this translates into just two additional lung cancer fatalities per 100,000 people, it suggests a cause for many otherwise unexplained lung cancer deaths.

■ OZONE

In 2000, ground-level ozone contributed to the nonattainment status of thirty-one areas. While ozone is beneficial in the upper atmosphere (see the brief on "Ozone Depletion"), ground-level ozone is a primary component of photochemical smog and threatens public health and the environment. Exposure to ozone damages lung tissue and reduces lung function, causing symptoms such as cough, chest pain, and congestion in otherwise healthy adults and children. Those at greatest risk from ground-level ozone are the elderly, infants, pregnant women, people with asthma, individuals who work or exercise outdoors, and victims of chronic lung and heart disease. Work done by the Environmental Occupational and Health Sciences Institute (EOHSI) of New Jersey has shown that there is up to a 25 percent increase in asthmatic visits to the emergency room on summer days with high ozone levels.

Ozone is not directly emitted by industry into the air but is formed by chemical reactions between volatile organic compounds (VOCs) and nitrogen oxides (NO_x) (known collectively as ozone precursors) in the presence of heat and sunlight. VOCs are compounds capable of changing quickly to a gas. Ground-level ozone concentrations, therefore, typically peak during the summer and at warmer, brighter times of the day, often at significant distances from industrial areas. In fact, ground-level ozone pollution is a particular problem in rural areas and the national parks, where ozone levels have steadily increased since 1990.

■ SULFUR DIOXIDE

National average levels of sulfur dioxide (SO_2) fell by 50 percent between 1980 and 1999. However, SO_2 pollution remains a problem in many urban locations and contributed to the status of a quarter of the nonattainment areas in 2000. The major source of SO_2 emissions is combustion of sulfur-containing fuel by coal-fired power plants. SO_2 acts as a lung irritant. High concentrations can impair breathing and aggravate existing respiratory conditions and cardiovascular disease. Populations most sensitive to SO_2 include children; the elderly; individuals with asthma, bronchitis, or emphysema; and those who work or exercise outdoors.

■ ACID RAIN

In addition to its adverse effects on health, SO_2, along with NO_x, is a precursor to fine particle formation, including particles responsible for acid rain. Acid rain is formed when SO_2 and NO_x react chemically with air and water in the presence of sunlight to produce mineral acids. These chemical reactions take place in the atmosphere and may be transported great distances before being washed out of the atmosphere in precipitation or falling out of the atmosphere in dust or gases.

Health effects linked to acid air pollution include breathing problems in children and people with asthma and lung damage in otherwise healthy people. Acid rain changes the acidity of lakes and streams, killing fish and making water undrinkable. Acid rain damages trees, affects forest and crop growth, and causes erosion of stone structures and monuments.

■ CARBON MONOXIDE

In 2000, 15 percent of nonattainment areas were in chronic violation of the ambient air quality standard for carbon monoxide. Carbon monoxide is produced by the incomplete burning of carbon-based fuels. Overall, mobile sources are responsible for approximately 80 percent of carbon monoxide emissions in the United States. However, this figure may be markedly higher in areas with high population and traffic density. Other major sources of carbon monoxide emissions include wood-burning stoves, incinerators, and industry. When inhaled, carbon monoxide enters the bloodstream, where it interferes with oxygen delivery to internal organs and tissues. At low concentrations, carbon monoxide causes headaches, dizziness, weakness, nausea, confusion, disorientation, and fatigue. At high concentrations, carbon monoxide exposure results in unconsciousness and death. Individuals with cardiovascular disease are most susceptible to the effects of exposure to carbon monoxide.

▪ LEAD

Average airborne levels of lead have fallen by more than 94 percent since the adoption of the Clean Air Act. Much of this improvement is a direct result of the removal of lead additives from gasoline. In 2001, the EPA amended SARA 313 rules (which require companies to submit a Toxic Chemical Release Inventory Form—Form R—for specified chemicals) in two areas to include PBT chemicals (persistent, bioaccumulative, and toxic chemical substances and chemical categories), one of which is lead. The EPA says anyone burning oil or other fuels in large quantities can produce lead. This is based on measurements taken at large utilities companies. Since no one measures lead, it is most likely not present. The EPA, however, says companies must use these factors anyway. Therefore, lead may show up in SARA 313 reports.

The major sources of lead emissions today are smelters and battery manufacturers. In July 2000, a total of six areas were designated nonattainment for lead. Lead exposure can adversely affect the brain, central nervous system, blood cells, and kidneys. Lead is stored in the bones, where it accumulates with continued exposure. Young children exposed to lead and children whose mothers were exposed to lead can suffer delays in mental and physical development, lower IQs, shortened attention spans, and behavioral problems. (See the brief on "Children's Health [Lead].")

▪ NITROGEN DIOXIDE

Nitrogen dioxide (NO_2) was the only criteria pollutant for which all areas were in attainment in the year 2000. Overall, national average levels of NO_2 have fallen by 25 percent since 1980. However, nationwide emissions of NO_x, which include nitrogen monoxide (NO), NO_2, and other oxidation states of nitrogen, increased by several percent during this period. NO_x emissions are of concern because of direct health effects (irritation and changes in lung function in sensitive individuals and children) and because of their direct role in the formation of acid rain, ground-level ozone, and fine particulate matter.

▪ AIR TOXICS

Unlike the criteria pollutants, the EPA does not have a nationwide monitoring system for air toxics. Air toxics are typically discussed in terms of emission rates as opposed to airborne concentrations. According to the EPA's National Toxics Inventory, nationwide emissions of air toxics dropped 23 percent between 1990 and 1996, although data for individual air toxics vary widely. Air toxics are emitted from a wide range of sources, including refineries and power plants, cars, trucks, construction equipment, dry cleaners, and indoor sources. A study by the EPA's Cumulative Exposure Project found that, based upon emissions data for 1990, modeled concentrations of air toxics exceeded established benchmarks for health effects in all census tracts in the contiguous United States. The study estimated that an average of fourteen air toxics per census tract exceeded benchmarks for cancer or other chronic health effects.

▪ ADDRESSING THE ISSUES ▪

The 1990 amendments to the Clean Air Act made major changes to the law, including establishing a permit program for large sources, called the Title V program. Sources with the potential to release more than 100 tons per year of any criteria pollutant are considered "major" sources and must apply for a Title V permit. Within nonattainment areas, some source categories with lower emission rates are considered "major" and also require Title V permits.

The 1990 amendments gave stronger enforcement powers to the EPA. The amendments established interstate commissions to address regional air quality and introduced market-based approaches to reduce emissions. They also provided economic incentives for businesses to reduce their emissions. The market-based approaches for reducing air pollution emissions in nonattainment areas include emissions offsets and pollutant trading. An offset is a reduction in the emission of a criteria pollutant at one stack or source that is used to counterbalance a smaller increase in the emission of that pollutant at another source or stack. Emission offsets for criteria pollutants may be traded or bought and sold between sources within the same nonattainment area.

Risk Management Programs (RMPs) were also established under the 1990 amendments. The RMP is a community right-to-know regulation designed to inform citizens and local emergency management organizations about chemical hazards in the community. They contain worst-case and more likely chemical release and fire scenarios, with estimates of injuries and deaths to nearby populations. Each facility's RMP includes a five-year history of releases, its emergency response program, and its release prevention activities. These emergency response programs have become even more important to communities worrying about preparedness following terrorist events on September 11, 2001.

The 1990 amendments to the Clean Air Act also required the EPA to identify and rank nonattainment areas according to the severity of the pollution and to establish deadlines for cleanup. Cleanup methods include using the act's permit system to reduce emissions from large sources (e.g., power plants, refineries, industry) and instituting new controls for mobile sources and smaller sources, including construction sites, agricultural burning, and home heating systems.

Since the adoption of the Clean Air Act, there have been significant reductions in automobile emissions. According to the EPA, automobiles in 1993 were producing 60 to 80 percent less pollution than cars in the 1960s. The removal of lead from gasoline has had a significant positive impact on national air quality. Other improvements in automobile emissions include the use of catalytic converters, oxygenated fuels, and reformulated gasoline to reduce emissions of carbon monoxide and VOCs. However, many of these improvements are counteracted by significant increases in automobile use.

To further address emissions from mobile sources, the 1990 amendments required the development of cleaner fuels and cleaner cars, the establishment of vehicle inspection and maintenance programs, and the development of transportation policies to discourage automobile use in ozone nonattainment areas. A number of these initiatives have met with significant resistance from consumers and small businesses.

The Clean Air Act also allows the EPA to revise air quality standards as needed to protect human health and the environment. In 1997, the EPA revised the NAAQS for ozone and particulate matter. The ground-level ozone standard was changed from a one-hour standard to a stricter eight-hour standard to provide better protection of human health, particularly among those who work or play outdoors for long periods of time. A new standard for fine particulate matter less than 2.5 microns in diameter (PM2.5) and a less stringent standard for particulate matter less than 10 microns in diameter (PM10) were also adopted to better reflect the public health significance of different particle sizes. (Fine particulate matter is of greater concern to public health, as it is small enough to travel deep into the lungs.) A lawsuit brought by industry groups resulted in the court of appeals remanding the revised standards back to the EPA for further consideration. The revised standards were in limbo for four years until the Supreme Court ruled in 2002 that the EPA acted within its power when it enacted the standards and that the agency is not required under the Clean Air Act to consider financial costs when setting air quality standards. At this writing, the EPA must develop an implementation plan for the new standards, while opponents vow additional legal challenges in the lower courts. The EPA maintains that the new standards will result in significant public health benefits, including 15,000 fewer premature deaths annually and 250,000 fewer cases of severe respiratory problems among children each year.

The EPA has also revised its approach for setting standards for air toxics. Originally, the agency used a strictly risk-based, chemical-by-chemical approach for developing standards for air toxics. However, this process proved difficult and time consuming—only seven standards were adopted from 1970 to 1990. The 1990 amendments to the Clean Air Act established a new approach for regulating air toxics based upon source categories and available air pollution control technology. This new approach identifies "maximum achievable control technology" (MACT) (also known as National Emission Standards for Hazardous Air Pollutants [NESHAPS]) which are used to set industry-specific emission standards for air toxics. To date, the EPA has issued MACT standards covering eighty-two source categories. When fully implemented, these standards will reduce emissions of annual air toxics by approximately 1.5 million tons. Efforts to reduce emissions of air toxics also include stricter car emissions standards. The EPA estimates that these efforts will result in a 75 percent reduction in air toxics emissions from automobiles by 2020.

▪ IMPORTANT POINTS FOR RESEARCHING A STORY ▪

- Americans strongly resist any effort to regulate their lifestyles. Because people love the freedom of their own cars, they prefer to attribute pollution to stationary industrial sources rather than admit to a role in the problem. As a result, efforts to enact and enforce car-pool laws, for example, have largely failed. The most successful efforts to reduce automotive air pollution have instead required changes in car design and fuels.

- The highest ozone levels typically occur in the summertime, although the timing and length of the ozone season vary across the United States. Ozone levels generally peak in the mid to late morning and linger until after sundown. Broadcast ozone alerts should advise the public to limit outdoor exercise to the early morning hours. Those at most risk—the elderly, people with asthma, and individuals with chronic lung or heart disease—should be advised to remain indoors during peak ozone hours.
- The Emergency Planning and Community Right-to-Know Act (also known as EPCRA or SARA Title III) is designed to help states and communities develop a better understanding of potential chemical hazards and chemical emissions from industrial facilities. Among other reporting requirements, facilities must report annual air emissions of listed toxic compounds.
- At present, new source reviews apply to old plants that were exempt from meeting new pollution standards. Under the current rule, when these industries—including utilities—upgrade their operations, they must upgrade pollution control equipment. Representatives of the utility industries want to relax this rule. They see it as analogous to a car owner who buys new tires one week and consequently is required to buy a new engine. When the owner buys a new fan belt the next week, if engine standards have improved during that week, he or she would be required to buy a new engine again. Those who support maintaining the rule argue that companies are supposed to reduce their total emissions as time goes by, not increase them.

▪ AVOIDING PITFALLS ▪

- Ozone has two roles in the atmosphere that are sometimes confused. In the upper atmosphere, ozone absorbs ultraviolet radiation and is essential to life. In the lower atmosphere, ozone is the major component of smog. Many people confuse these two issues. It is important to note that these two phenomena are unrelated.
- Poor air quality is not always a function of living in an urban or

industrialized area. Industry in one county can contribute to downwind air quality problems in other counties, other states, or even other countries. The transport of acid precipitation from the Ohio River Valley into New England and Canada is a well-known example. These issues tend to become quickly and highly politicized, pitting one region's economy against another's health and environmental quality.

- When covering a story on acid rain, it is important to remember that pH (the measure of acidity) follows a logarithmic scale—that is, a change of one point represents a tenfold change in acidity—and that the lower the figure, the greater the acidity. For example, if a lake shows an acidity of pH 5, it is ten times more acidic than a reading of pH 6.
- Recent history has demonstrated that the use of fuel additives or reformulated fuels can result in the replacement of one problem with another. The most notorious example of this is the use of the chemical compound Methyl *tert*-Butyl Ether (MTBE) in oxygenated and reformulated gasoline to reduce emissions of carbon monoxide and VOCs. MTBE has resulted in extensive groundwater pollution and in reports of headaches, nausea, dizziness, and respiratory problems among drivers and passengers. (For further discussion of MTBE and groundwater pollution, see the brief on "Groundwater Pollution.")
- Less than 5 percent of the current fleet of automobiles in use are old, out-of-tune cars. However, these vehicles are responsible for most uncontrolled automobile pollution.

▪ INFORMATION RESOURCES ▪

▪ GOVERNMENT/ACADEMIA

- Centers for Disease Control and Prevention, National Center for Environmental Health (www.cdc.gov/nceh/ncehhome.htm)
  4770 Buford Highway NE, MS F-29, Atlanta, GA 30341-3724
- Centers for Disease Control and Prevention, Office of Communications
  1600 Clifton Rd., MS D25, Atlanta, GA 30333
  (404) 639-3286; fax: (404) 639-7394
  E-mail: in.the.news@cdc.gov

- U.S. Environmental Protection Agency (www.epa.gov/oar)
  Office of Air and Radiation
  Ariel Rios Bldg., 1200 Pennsylvania Ave. NW, Washington, DC 20460
  (202) 564-7400; fax: (202) 501-0986

INDUSTRY

- Air and Waste Management Association (www.awma.org)
  One Gateway Center, Third Floor, 420 Fort Duquesne Blvd., Pittsburgh, PA 15222
  (412) 232-3444; fax (412) 232-3450
  E-mail: info@awma.org
- American Trucking Associations (www.trucking.org)
  2200 Mill Rd., Alexandria, VA 22314-4677
  (703) 838-1700
  430 First St. SE, Washington, DC 20003
  (202) 544-6245

NONPROFIT/CONSUMER ORGANIZATIONS

- American Lung Association (www.lungusa.org)
  1740 Broadway, New York, NY 10019
  national: (212) 315-8700; press_contact@lungusa.org
  local: (800) 586-4872
- Environmental Defense (www.scorecard.org) or (www.environmentaldefense.org)
  257 Park Ave. South, New York, NY 10010
  (212) 505-2100; fax: (212) 505-2375

ANIMAL WASTE MANAGEMENT

▪ BACKGROUND ▪

Animals play an important role in our world. The manure from livestock farms contains usable nutrients such as nitrogen, phosphorous, and potassium. However, as livestock farms grow in size, the disposal of wastes becomes a bigger responsibility. Nitrogen, phosphorous, and potassium, as well as pathogens, ammonia, and sediment that also are present in manure, may contribute to diminished water or environmental quality.

Food and fiber products derived from animals contribute significantly to our diet. In addition, animals contribute to the environmentally sound use of natural resources and the economic vitality of the United States. Livestock in the United States annually consume nearly 750 million metric tons of harvested and grazed forage, food-processing by-products, and feed grains. Animals also play a role in the United States as medical models; they provide numerous products of medicinal value (hormones, heart valves, enzymes, and blood-clotting factors). They also provide companionship and entertainment, and in the case of draft animals, they work. Animal production contributed over $500 billion to the U.S. economy in 1990, and the export of animal products contributes positively to the nation's balance of trade. The use of animals plays an important role in our lives but also raises concerns. As livestock farms increase in size, the disposal of animal waste in an environmentally benign manner becomes more difficult.

In the past, when most farmers produced all their own feed and owned smaller herds of livestock, it was easier to dispose of manure by spreading it on the land as a fertilizer. Today, however, large operators such as cattle and hog feedlots, poultry operations, and dairy farms produce tremendous amounts of animal waste. This is particularly a problem when most feed is purchased from outside sources and

This brief was written by Michael Westendorf, Associate Extension Specialist in the Animal Sciences, Cook College, Rutgers University, New Brunswick, New Jersey.

acreages are small, because waste must be disposed of outside of the owned acreage. This can influence entire regions of the country. For example, in parts of the Southeast, feed grains are imported to feed the expanding swine and poultry industries. Although the swine and poultry will leave as meat for consumption, the manure will stay.

▪ IDENTIFYING THE ISSUES ▪

A lactating dairy cow can help to illustrate both the problems and potentials in managing animal wastes. In one day, a lactating cow producing 31.75 kilograms (70 pounds) of milk and consuming 20.41 kilograms (45 pounds) of dry feed will produce 72.57 kilograms (160 pounds) of raw manure (feces plus urine). This manure will be composed of 8.165 kilograms (18 pounds) of dry solids, 6.804 kilograms (15 pounds) of volatile solids, 350 grams (0.79 pound) of nitrogen, 68 grams (0.15 pound) of phosphorous, and 163.3 grams (0.36 pound) of potassium in addition to small quantities of minor nutrients. A 100-cow herd producing milk for a year would excrete approximately 2,268,000 kilograms (5 million pounds) of raw manure containing 226,800 kilograms (500,000 pounds) of total solids, 208,700 kilograms (460,000 pounds) of volatile solids, 11,070 kilograms (24,400 pounds) of nitrogen, 2,075 kilograms (4,575 pounds) of phosphorous, and 4,150 kilograms (9,150 pounds) of potassium. This only includes manure from lactating cows. Dry cows, calves, and replacements produce additional manure. Animal bedding and milking parlor washout generate further wastes and nutrients. Since these figures will vary considerably based on age and life stage of the animals, species, and so forth, it is important to tailor manure management programs to individual farm conditions.

The nutrients essential for animal production provide value for plant growth as fertilizers when present in the soil but may be considered contaminants when present in groundwater or surface water. Principal among these nutrients are nitrogen and phosphorous. Nitrogen is a major component of protein; livestock animals need protein for maintenance, growth, reproduction, lactation, and work. Phosphorous is needed for maintenance, growth, and other physiologic functions. Nitrogen, phosphorous, and potassium are all required for plant growth. The manure from a 100-cow dairy herd is estimated to be worth $11,437 as fertilizer because of the nitrogen, phosphorous, and potassium it contains. In addition, manure supplies organic matter to the soil. However, when land is overmanured and the ability of crops to take up nutrients is exceeded, these nutrients will build up in the soil and pose a possible hazard in groundwater or surface water. Nitrogen can leach as nitrate (NO_3) unless crops are present to take it up. NO_3 can also undergo the process of denitrification in the soil and be lost into the atmosphere as gaseous nitrogen monoxide (NO) or nitrous oxide (N_2O). Phosphorous can contribute to long-term phosphorous loading of the soil. If applied at the wrong times of the year and/or when soil erosion occurs, it will run off. It can also leach if soil becomes saturated and contaminate groundwater or surface water. This can result in nutrient enrichment and algae growth, a process known as eutrophication. Eutrophication and algae growth have been associated with outbreaks of the bacteria *Pfiesteria piscicida* in the Chesapeake Bay and other locations.

A challenge in large animal facilities or feedlots is how to dispose of manure on a regular basis. Traditional methods used on some smaller farms include hauling manure to the fields daily for spreading on cropland. Other farms stockpile manure for later spreading. The land required for spreading manure goes up as animal numbers increase. A small farmer could spread the manure from 50 cows on less than 40.5 hectares (100 acres). However, a farmer with 10,000 cows would need many times that acreage, and finding this acreage could be a challenge. For facilities having large numbers of animals and manure often high in moisture content, it is impossible either to stockpile it or spread it every day. Large animal operations now use long-term storage facilities for holding manure with space for up to six months' storage. Manure, usually liquid, is then spread on available cropland. For farms with a large number of animals, this requires hundreds, if not thousands, of hectares. These structures can contain millions of gallons of waste and pose increased risks for leakage or overflow.

There have been several well-profiled accidents involving waste leakage problems. For example, in September 1999 Hurricane Floyd dumped heavy rains on the coastal floodplain regions of North Carolina where many large swine farms are located and where hog manure waste is stored in liquid form in large lagoons. These open-air lagoons were flooded, resulting in the contamination of groundwater, surface water, and drinking water. In addition, thousands of hogs either drowned during the storm or perished in the aftermath. The accident raised concerns over the placement of hog lagoons in portions of the coastal plain. New regulations in North Carolina since the flood have served to restrict where and how hog facilities may be built.

Other concerns with animal manure are odor and related airborne particulate matter as well as pathogens that may infect both humans and animals. The chief odor-producing gasses in manure are ammonia, hydrogen sulfide, carbon dioxide, and methane. Dust, particulate matter, and airborne insects such as flies that reproduce in manure pose risks. Some animal diseases that may be transferred in manure are Johne's disease, bovine viral diarrhea, salmonella, E. coli, and cryptosporidiosis. Salmonella, E. coli, and cryptosporidiosis can also be human health risks.

▪ ADDRESSING THE ISSUES ▪

Animal facilities, manure storage methods, animal feeding practices, level of production, climate, presence of streams or wetlands near animals, available land for spreading, topography of land, soil types, and cropping systems all influence manure management.

A farmer's use of Best Management Practices (BMPs) will help to reduce hazards and make the best use of the beneficial qualities of animal manures. BMPs are those practices, commonly accepted both through research and practical experience, that take all of these factors into consideration to develop appropriate measures for managing animal waste. In many states, farms are now required to have an approved management plan for manure disposal. These plans include comprehensive information about the number of animals on a farm, the manure produced, and an approved plan for disposing of manure on either owned or rented acreage or off-farm, for example, compost. In some states, farms with even a few animals are required to have such a plan. State governments often oversee these plans, called Comprehensive Nutrient Management Plans (CNMPs). Assistance in developing CNMPs can come from either the U.S. Department of Agriculture Natural Resources Conservation Service (USDA-NRCS), land-grant colleges of agriculture, the state, or professional consulting services.

Because of the risks involved in long-term waste storage, the facilities must be designed according to very stringent specifications and require approval of the state department of environmental protection, as well as the USDA-NRCS. These long-term storage facilities require a greater level of management than does the farmer who spreads daily or who stockpiles and spreads manure only infrequently. Mistakes made in the design process can have dire consequences at some future date.

Another storage method used by larger facilities for managing manure is composting. Composting facilities are less expensive than in-ground storage facilities and, if properly designed, pose less environmental risk from runoff than the risks associated with leaks from in-ground storage facilities.

A key aspect of the Clean Water Act is to minimize public health risks and environmental impacts of runoff from animal feeding operations (AFOs). When not managed properly, runoff from animal waste can pose risks to public health and water quality by depositing ammonia, nutrients, pathogens, and sediment in the environment. For most of the past twenty-five years, most segments of agriculture have been exempt from the act. However, concentrated animal feeding operations (CAFOs) are not exempt. To be regulated as a CAFO, an animal farm must contain at least a threshold number of animals. For example, a dairy farm is designated as a CAFO if it contains the equivalent of 700 mature dairy cattle.

Farms designated as CAFOs must go through a permit process that may require eliminating the discharge of animal wastes into U.S. waters. This process may also require construction of retention structures for animal wastes (including specifications on construction, maintenance, and operation), periodic reporting of water quality monitoring results, proper land application of wastes, BMPs, and pollution prevention plans. CAFO permit holders are given legal protection in the case of overflows resulting from catastrophic events (including tornadoes, hurricanes, twenty-five-year/twenty-four-hour storms, and chronic rainfall—a series of wet weather conditions that prevent waste removal from properly maintained waste retention structures). CAFO permits are generally issued by state agencies. Smaller farms are generally not considered CAFOs.

The CAFO permit process focuses on cleaning up point sources of pollution (pollution from a particular pipe or leak). The Total Maximum Daily Load (TMDL) focuses on efforts to reduce nonpoint sources within individual watersheds. A TMDL is the maximum pollutant loading a body of water (e.g., stream or lake) can accept and still meet water quality standards. It considers all pollutant sources and takes into account seasonal variations, with a margin for error. The state or U.S. Environmental Protection Agency (EPA) determines a maximum loading rate, estimates all potential sources of the pollutant, and then develops an action plan for meeting the level. Some livestock producers view TMDLs with alarm because there is concern TMDLs will circumvent the CAFO permitting process. They believe the inclusion of nonpoint sources is beyond the scope of the Clean Water Act; however, recent court action has forced the EPA to implement the TMDL program.

CAFO regulations are currently under review as EPA considers changes in the regulatory process to provide improved environmental protection with minimal disruption to farming operations. For example, under proposed CAFO regulations, all but the smallest livestock owners will be affected.

In recent years, Congress has made funding available to farmers for assistance in designing and building manure management systems through the Environmental Quality Incentives Program (EQIP). The USDA-NRCS administers EQIP; however, these funds may or may not be available to animal facilities designated as a CAFO, depending on the state.

▪ IMPORTANT POINTS FOR RESEARCHING A STORY ▪

- All animal farms, irrespective of size, can be a water quality threat when not managed properly. A small farm with fewer animal numbers may be at just as great a risk as a larger farm if manure is handled or stored inappropriately.
- Conversely, larger farms, when well managed, should not pose any risks to the environment. Most farms are managed in an environmentally beneficial manner. A farmer's use of BMPS will help to reduce hazards and make the best use of the beneficial qualities of animal manures.
- Manure can be a valuable source of nitrogen, phosphorus, and other crop nutrients when it is applied to land in proper amounts. When managed properly, animal manure can provide nutrients that promote crop growth and environmental sustainability. However, increasing animal numbers on small acreages may result in insufficient cropland to use all of the manure. If this results in inappropriate storage or spreading, there is an increased likelihood that accidents will happen.
- While concern has focused on the impact of animal waste on aquatic ecosystems, there is also human health concerns associated with animal waste. Manure contains pathogens to which humans

are vulnerable, including salmonella and cryptosporidium, and can pollute groundwater with nitrates potentially fatal to infants.

- Nutrient pollution can come from a number of sources, but in areas of intensive livestock production, animal waste is a leading suspect in blooms of toxic microbes in bodies of water. These blooms are linked to excessive nutrients in the water (eutrophication). The microbes produce compounds that may be toxic to animals and people.
- It has long been recognized that nitrogen is highly soluble and susceptible to leaching and run off, but only recently has it been fully understood that when soils are saturated with phosphorous, excess phosphorous can also run off. Application rates of manure have traditionally been determined by calculating the amount of nitrogen going onto the land. Because the phosphorus content of manure is proportionally much higher than nitrogen (in relation to crop nutrient needs), this practice can lead to the application of excess phosphorous. In the future, most farms will have to base spreading rates on phosphorous content and not on nitrogen.
- The risk of water pollution from dry manure is greatest after it is spread on cropland. The risk of waste spills and chronic pollution from liquid waste storage and application systems is greatest when liquid waste is being transported, stored, or applied on land or as a result of equipment or structural failure or human error.
- There are software programs available to estimate the production of waste materials within an animal feeding operation and then determine the size of needed storage/treatment facilities. These can also be used for determining land requirements for spreading.
- Animal waste consists of not only manure and urine but also of used bedding, waste feed, and other residual organic matter. While all of these materials are potential sources of crop nutrients, they also can be a source of pollution.
- The storage and disposal of animal mortalities can also lead to environmental pollution.

▪ AVOIDING PITFALLS ▪

- Remember that the regulatory atmosphere is constantly changing, with various federal, state, and local controls that may affect the management of animal waste. Many states have "right to farm" or nuisance ordinances to protect the rights of farmers and/or their neighbors.

- Remember that in some areas there can be multiple sources of water pollution including storm water runoff, septic contamination, construction runoff, runoff or contamination from new housing developments, recreational pollution (e.g., marinas, golf courses), and contamination by wildlife. All of these could be in addition to any agricultural pollution.
- Remember that one size may not fit all with respect to animal waste management. The issues related to animal waste management in populous states such as New Jersey may be different from those in less populous states. In addition, coastal or wetland areas may have more stringent regulations for animal waste management than might other locations.

▪ INFORMATION RESOURCES ▪

▪ GOVERNMENT/ACADEMIA

- Midwest Plan Service (MWPS) (www.mwpshq.org).
  22 Davidson Hall, Iowa State University, Ames, IA 50011-3080
  (800) 562-3618
- National Council for Science and the Environment (www.cnie.org)
  1707 H St. SW, Suite 200, Washington, DC 20006
  (202) 530-5810
- Natural Resource, Agriculture, and Engineering Service (NRAES) (www.nraes.org).
  Cooperative Extension, 152 Riley-Robb Hall, Ithaca, NY 14853-5701
  (607) 255-7654
- U.S. Department of Agriculture (www.nrcs.usda.gov).
  Natural Resources Conservation Service, 14th and Independence Ave., Room 6032-S, Washington, DC 20250
  (202) 720-1845
- U.S. Environmental Protection Agency (www.epa.gov/oeca/ag).
  The National Agriculture Compliance Assistance Center, 901 North 5th St., Kansas City, KS 66101
  (888) 663-2155.

▪ NONPROFIT/CONSUMER ORGANIZATIONS

- American Farm Bureau Federation (AFBF) (www.fb.org)
  600 Maryland Ave. SW, Suite 800, Washington, DC 20024
  (202) 484-3600
- Council for Agricultural Science and Technology (CAST)
  (www.cast-science.org)
  4420 West Lincoln Way, Ames, IA 50014-3447
  (515) 292-2125
- Food Animal Integrated Research (FAIR)
  Coordinating symposia for animal research goals and priorities (1995 and 2002)
  Federation of Animal Science Societies
  1111 N. Dunlap Ave., Savoy, IL 61874
  (217) 356-3182
- Northeast Organic Farming Association (www.nofa.org)
  State affiliates in Connecticut, Massachusetts, New Hampshire, New Jersey, New York, Rhode Island, and Vermont

BIODIVERSITY

▪ BACKGROUND ▪

Biological diversity, or biodiversity, refers to the number and variety of plant, animals, and other organisms on earth. Biodiversity includes species diversity, which describes the variety of animals, plants, and microorganisms; genetic diversity, which describes the many differences that occur within individual species; and ecological or ecosystem diversity, which describes the variety of ecosystems and habitats in which organisms thrive. To date, scientists have identified nearly 2 million species of animals, plants, and microorganisms. Estimates of the total number of species living on the planet range from 5 million to 100 million.

Scientists maintain it is important to protect the earth's biodiversity for the resources we draw from it—food, energy, medicines, fiber, horticultural plants, and other raw materials—and for the resources we have yet to discover. Much attention has been given in recent decades to the wealth of medicines that may exist within the vegetation of tropical rain forests, for example. Human beings rely on complex ecological systems and food webs to provide the food we eat. We also rely on the earth's rich vegetation to provide us with the oxygen we breathe and to recycle and purify the water we drink. Many believe it is important to protect biodiversity for its own sake, as well as for aesthetic or religious reasons or out of respect for the complex evolutionary processes that developed it over billions of years.

▪ IDENTIFYING THE ISSUES ▪

In its history, the earth has experienced five mass extinctions. A meteor collision with earth 65 million years ago is believed to have resulted in

Information for this brief was provided by Joanna Burger, Division of Life Sciences and Environmental and Occupational Health Sciences Institute (EOHSI), Piscataway, New Jersey.

the extinction of many species of plants and animals, including the dinosaurs. Scientists estimate that the planet is currently losing species to extinction at a rate of 17,000 to 100,000 per year. Some sources estimate that up to 20 percent of the world's species will become extinct within the next twenty years. The plant and insect species being lost to extinction include many that have never been classified or studied. The significance of their loss may never be known. Some scientists suggest that the current mass extinction will have serious implications for human survival.

There are many threats to biodiversity today. These include habitat loss, overfishing and overharvesting, and biological invasion (the introduction of nonnative species).

▪ HABITAT LOSS

A habitat is the specific environment in which a species thrives. A habitat is defined by its location, climate, vegetation, and physical environment. Development, deforestation, and pollution all contribute to habitat loss. The loss of tropical forests is of greatest concern because of the rapid rate at which they are being consumed and the high degree of biological diversity they contain—most of the world's species live in tropical forests. An estimated 13 million hectares (32,123 million acres) of tropical forests are lost to agriculture and development each year. Significant amounts of habitat loss also continue to occur in wetlands, estuaries, river basins, savannas, grasslands, and northern forests.

In addition to the direct loss of habitat due to agricultural conversion, urban development, and pollution, scientists also predict that rapid changes to habitats will occur as the global climate changes. (See the brief on "Global Climate Change.") Species that are unable to adapt to rapid changes in their habitat or to migrate to other suitable habitats may be lost to extinction. The loss of an individual species unable to adapt will likely have consequences for many other species in the region, from populations of direct prey and predators of that species to populations of plants and animals at either end of the food chain.

▪ OVERFISHING AND OVERHARVESTING

Overfishing and overharvesting of species for food, sport, or other purposes have endangered and eliminated many species throughout human history. Many species of fish have suffered great declines. Well-known examples of overharvesting include the overhunting of African elephants for their tusks and rhinos for their horns; the overfishing and "by-catch" (i.e., accidental catch) of whales, dolphins, and porpoises in drift nets cast by those engaged in commercial fishing; and the overharvesting of caviar resulting in the endangerment of beluga in the Caspian Sea. Overharvesting issues also include clear-cutting of trees and deforestation.

■ BIOLOGICAL INVASION

Another threat to biodiversity is biological invasion, or "bio-invasion," the introduction of nonnative species into an area. Nonnative species have been intentionally and unintentionally introduced to countries across the globe as travel and trade have expanded. Nonnative species threaten biodiversity by introducing disease and competition for resources into native ecosystems. Competition from nonnative species can lead to the extinction of native species. Populations of nonnative species can grow to pest levels, threatening crops and natural vegetation.

Examples of biological invasion by nonnative species include gypsy moths, foot and mouth disease, West Nile virus, and Africanized honeybees (a.k.a. "killer bees"). The zebra mussel was inadvertently introduced into the U.S. Great Lakes from Eastern Europe in the mid-1980s. It has since spread throughout the Great Lakes and into the Mississippi, Ohio, and Hudson Rivers. Zebra mussels are small in size, can attach to almost any hard surface, and multiply at a rate of millions of offspring per year. They have become a major nuisance in the Great Lakes region, where they compete with native species for plankton, clog water intake structures for public and industrial water supplies, and disrupt recreational boating by clogging motors and colonizing watercraft and docks.

The advent of biotechnology has introduced a new set of concerns for genetic diversity. First, scientists are concerned that genetic diversity will be lost as farmers across the globe switch to one or a few genetically engineered versions of each food crop. At one time, farmers, particularly those in developing nations, selectively cultivated crops that thrived in their specific region. This led to the development of many different varieties of the major food crops. The concern with biotechnology is that a globally homogenous crop would leave the world's food supply vulnerable to the catastrophic spread of a plant disease or pest. In the past, the spread of plant diseases and pests has often been halted by locally resistant varieties. Another concern with biotechnology is the potential for outcropping of genetically engineered traits. The concern is that genetically modified crops may transfer their engineered traits to nearby fields of the same crop and to wild varieties of the crop through cross-pollination. Wild varieties that gain the engineered traits would then have a competitive advantage and, through natural selection, the unaffected wild varieties would eventually disappear. At the same time, biotechnology also provides a new argument for species preservation. That is, it creates the potential for discovering and using hitherto unknown beneficial uses of genetic traits in organisms. (See the brief on "Genetically Modified Crops.")

■ ADDRESSING THE ISSUES ■

The issue of biological diversity was a key issue at the United Nations Earth Summit in Rio de Janeiro in 1992. The focus of the Earth Summit was developing a worldwide strategy for "sustainable development"—allowing continued economic growth and progress while conserving and maintaining resources for future generations. The Convention on Biological Diversity was one of the key agreements reached at the summit. The convention has been signed by more than 180 countries and, at this writing, ratified by 168 governments. To date, the United States has not ratified the convention.

The goals of the Convention on Biological Diversity are to conserve biological diversity, maintain sustainable use of biological resources, and achieve "fair and equitable" sharing of the benefits from the commercial use of genetic resources. To protect the rights of developing nations, the convention established national sovereignty over genetic resources. (As stated earlier, most of the world's biodiversity is found in tropical forests and, hence, in developing nations.) In the past, the genetic diversity of developing nations has been "mined" by foreign companies and "bioprospectors" who developed native resources into commercial products, such as crops and drugs. Biotechnology has increased this practice by allowing the accelerated inclusion of specific genetic traits from native sources into commercial products. Along with modern bioprospecting, biotechnology firms have begun to secure patents and intellectual property rights on native resources, with little or no benefit given to the source country. This practice has been termed biopiracy. One example of biopiracy is the legal battle over a patent awarded to a small U.S. seed company for the Enola bean, a strain of yellow bean that has been grown in Mexico for centuries.

To manage the risks posed by nonnative species and the products of biotechnology, the Conference of Parties to the Convention on Biological Diversity developed the Cartagena Protocol on Biosafety. (Because the United States has not ratified the Convention on Biological Diversity, it is not a party to the convention and did not have an official voice in the development of the biosafety protocol.) The biosafety protocol was developed to address concerns regarding biotechnology, international trade, and possible risks to human health and the environment. The protocol includes notification requirements prior to the initial export of a genetically modified organism. The protocol also provides for information and technology exchange, risk assessment, and public education regarding the products of biotechnology. The biosafety protocol will become legally binding once it has been signed and ratified by fifty governments. To date, the United States has not signed the biosafety protocol.

Although the U.S. government has not fully participated in the above U.N. efforts to protect biodiversity, it is involved in a number of international programs through the United Nations Environment Program. Also, in association with Mexico and Canada, the United States has entered the North American Agreement on Environmental Cooperation. Under the agreement, the North American Commission for Environmental Cooperation (CEC) addresses regional environmental concerns and supports the environmental provisions of the North American Free Trade Agreement (NAFTA). The CEC supports and funds numerous projects and initiatives to protect biodiversity.

At the national level, the United States has undertaken a number of efforts to protect biodiversity. For example, the Endangered Species Act (ESA) was passed in 1973 and amended in 1996. The act protects plants and animals that are listed by the federal government as "endangered" or "threatened." It makes it unlawful for anyone to "take" a listed animal and includes significantly modifying its habitat. This applies to private parties and private land, prohibiting landowners from harming an endangered animal or its habitat on their property. The ESA is enforced by the U.S. Fish and Wildlife Service (FWS) and the National Marine Fisheries Services (NMFS).

The United States has also formed the National Invasive Species Council, which coordinates federal activities to protect against and manage invasive species. The council includes the U.S. Departments of the Interior, Agriculture, Commerce, State, Treasury, Transportation, Defense, and Health and Human Services; the U.S. Environmental Protection Agency (EPA); and the U.S. Agency for International Development.

Nongovernmental organizations as well as some industries are also addressing biodiversity issues. For example, some companies are conducting biodiversity assessments of their major facilities, with a goal of developing and implementing site-specific biodiversity management plans.

■ IMPORTANT POINTS FOR RESEARCHING A STORY ■

- Protection of biodiversity and of individual species and their habitat is always juxtaposed against economic development. The issue is not always as straightforward as it seems. There are many economic benefits that are derived from biodiversity. Some benefits of biodiversity may lie in the potential for future medicines, energy sources, or raw materials. Other benefits of biodiversity may be more immediate, such as ecotourism. Ecotourism is an increasingly popular form of tourism in which tourists look for wild, scenic areas such as rain forests or mountains for a trip that is both active and educational. Destinations are usually in the developing world. It has also become popular among people interested in both environmental conservation and sustainable development. In fact, the encouragement of ecotourism is one strategy that has been used to protect regions that otherwise would have been lost to agricultural conversion or other development. In many cases, the economic growth associated with ecotourism is far greater than the gains from development. However, ecotourism, like all exploitation of resources, can be overdone. And tourism brings its own social and environmental concerns, including waste, traffic, pollution, and crime.

■ AVOIDING PITFALLS ■

- It is important to distinguish efforts to protect biodiversity from efforts to protect individual species and their habitat. Protection of biodiversity requires protection of entire ecosystems, which include many habitats and species, and requires a much broader effort. Protection of biodiversity, therefore, begins with protection of individual species but does not end there.

- Very commonly, the economic impacts of biodiversity (or species) protection on development are exaggerated. Reporters should press those who predict such impacts to specify the assumptions on which the expected impacts are based and ask for evidence. In some cases, the "evidence" is simply prior similar predictions.

▪ INFORMATION RESOURCES ▪

GOVERNMENT/ACADEMIA

- Convention on International Trade in Endangered Species of Wild Fauna and Flora (CITES) (www.cites.org)
  International Environment House
  Chemin des Anémones, CH-1219 Châtelaine, Geneva, Switzerland
  +412-2-917-8139/40; fax: +412-2-797-3417
  E-mail: cites@unep.ch
- National Biological Information Infrastructure (NBII) (www.nbii.gov)
  NBII National Program Office
  USGS Biological Informatics Office
  302 National Center, Reston, VA 20192
  (703) 648-6244; fax: (703) 648-4224
- NatureServe (www.abi.org)
  1101 Wilson Blvd., 15th Floor, Arlington, VA 22209
  (703) 908-1800; fax (703) 908-1917
- United Nations Cartagena Protocol on Biosafety (www.biodiv.org/biosafety/)
  World Trade Centre, 393 St. Jacques St., Office 300
  Montreal, Quebec, Canada H2Y 1N9
  +1-514-288-2220; fax: +1-514-288-6588
  E-mail: secretariat@biodiv.org

NONPROFIT/CONSUMER ORGANIZATIONS

- Conservation International (www.conservation.org)
  1919 M St. NW, Suite 600, Washington, DC 20036
  (800) 406-2306 or (202) 912-1000

- Environmental Defense (www.environmentaldefense.org)
  257 Park Ave. South, New York, NY 10010
  (212) 505-2100; fax: (212) 505-2375
- Natural Resources Defense Council (www.nrdc.org/media)
  40 West 20th St., New York, NY 10011
  (212) 727-2700; fax: (212) 727-1773
- The Nature Conservancy (www.nature.org)
  4245 North Fairfax Drive, Suite 100, Arlington, VA 22203-1606
  (800) 628-6860
- World Rainforest Movement (www.wrm.org.uy)
  Ricardo Carrere
  Maldonado 1858, Montevideo 11200, Uruguay
  +598-2-413-2989; fax: +598-2-418-0762
  E-mail: wrm@wrm.org.uy
- World Wildlife Fund (www.worldwildlife.org)
  P.O. Box 97180, 1250 24th St. NW, Washington, DC 20037
  (202) 293-4800; media can contact staff experts at (202) 778-9541; fax: (202) 293-9211

BROWNFIELDS

▪ BACKGROUND ▪

Once thriving centers of economic activity and community pride, many American industrial centers have been all but abandoned to decay. For years, brownfields—former industrial and commercial sites—have been passed over in favor of new development in suburban and rural areas—greenfields. As Americans reexamine our past land-use practices, we are turning back to brownfields and looking for economically and environmentally feasible means to redevelop and revitalize these sites and their neighborhoods.

Brownfields are abandoned or neglected industrial or commercial sites whose redevelopment is hindered by concerns about environmental contamination. The U.S. General Accounting Office estimates that there are at least 450,000 brownfield sites "affecting virtually every community in the nation." The 1999 U.S. Conference of Mayors, representing 168 cities nationwide, estimated that restoration and reuse of brownfields would create more than 675,000 jobs and generate between $955 million and $2.7 billion annual tax dollars.

▪ IDENTIFYING THE ISSUES ▪

One of the many obstacles to the redevelopment of brownfields is the presence or perceived presence of environmental contamination. This can represent a problem for several reasons. First, the costs of environmental cleanup can be prohibitive, possibly exceeding the current market value of the property. Second, developers and financiers are often unwilling to invest in brownfields for fear of becoming finan-

This brief is based on information provided by Frances Hoffman, former Vice President for Planning and Research, Institute for Responsible Management, New Brunswick, New Jersey.

cially responsible for future cleanup of existing environmental problems, should the U.S. Environmental Protection Agency (EPA) or the state investigate the site under the Comprehensive Environmental Response, Compensation and Liability Act (CERCLA, or Superfund) or state cleanup program. Section 107 of CERCLA broadens liability for environmental cleanup costs to past and present site owners and even to banks that take possession of a site through foreclosure. Financial liability under Section 107 of CERCLA applies to past and present site owners and operators, even if they did not contribute to the contamination.

Equating brownfields with Superfund sites is a common misconception. Although some brownfield sites may have been considered in the past for inclusion on the National Priorities List of Superfund sites, most have never been formally investigated by the EPA or state environmental agencies. In fact, brownfields are typically much less contaminated than Superfund sites.

The processes and goals of brownfield and Superfund projects also have significant differences. Superfund projects focus on remediation and follow a strict set of procedures set forth in law and regulations. In contrast, the focus of a brownfield project is redevelopment and reuse, with cleanup designed to support a specific future use.

The issue of cleanup standards often arises in brownfield projects. The question, as always, is "how clean is clean?" Under Superfund, remediation is driven by a generic standard of acceptable health risk—that of a one in one million additional lifetime cancer risk. The one in one million risk standard is designed to ensure minimal health risk should a site be used for future housing development. In practice, this conservative standard has been adopted by many state agencies and environmental groups and has set the standard for declaring a site "clean." The focus of brownfield cleanup and redevelopment supports the intended site-specific development while maintaining protection for human health and the environment. The cleanup goals for future use as an industrial park, office space, or retail space generally require different controls than do the cleanup goals for residential or recreational development. The selection of cleanup standards that are lower than the one in one million benchmark for cancer risk can be a point of contention for environmental and community groups. The debate then becomes a case of "protective" versus "pristine."

▪ ADDRESSING THE ISSUES ▪

To address the obstacles associated with developing contaminated brownfields, the EPA set forth the Brownfields Action Agenda in January 1995. The program has since expanded to include the EPA's Brownfields Economic Redevelopment Initiative and the federal Brownfields National Partnership. These programs are designed to help facilitate the efforts of federal, state, and local governments; communities; and developers to clean up and reuse brownfields.

The Brownfields National Partnership provides assistance to the brownfield redevelopment efforts of more than thirty federal agencies and departments. The partnership has provided technical and financial assistance to twenty-eight Brownfields Showcase Communities since 1998. The Brownfields Showcase Communities highlight projects where government agencies work in collaboration throughout the brownfields process and serve as models for future projects. The EPA's Brownfields Economic Redevelopment Initiative has awarded more than 360 brownfields assessment demonstration pilot grants. The pilot grants are funded up to $200,000 each for a period of two years for site assessment and site identification. The pilot grants are not used to cover cleanup costs.

As cleanup costs are sometimes counted in the millions of dollars, securing additional funds for remediation is a major focus at the outset of brownfield projects. Much of the funding currently comes from the private sector and traditional sources. For example, some banks include cleanup costs in project financing. Additional funding for cleanup is often secured in the form of grants and technical assistance from state and regional agencies. The EPA also offers a Brownfields Cleanup Revolving Loan Fund (BCRLF). BCRLF grants are currently available in amounts up to $1 million.

EPA and state agencies are also easing the process of obtaining private funding and insurance for brownfield redevelopment. EPA regional offices provide site-specific information on possible environmental risks and liabilities in the form of "comfort letters" to developers, owners, purchasers, municipalities, lenders, and other interested parties. Comfort letters address any previous federal investigation of the site, the current status of federal Superfund interest in the site, and whether the state has assumed authority over environmental response at the site. While these letters do not release a site from future environmental liability under Superfund, they can provide developers, financiers, and insurers with important information and a certain level of comfort. At the state level, letters of "no further action," "promise not to sue," and "certificate of completion" provide similar assurances.

The focus of brownfield projects on end use often requires community support and involvement from the outset. Neighbors are stakeholders in the redevelopment of a brownfield site and can contribute significantly to the project's success or failure. Community involvement and risk communication can be particularly important when site-specific cleanup goals are at issue. A community is much more likely to accept site-specific cleanup standards when all parties have been operating in an atmosphere of trust. Community involvement has, to date, been an important part of federally funded brownfield projects. In contrast, privately funded and state-sponsored brownfield projects have sometimes been criticized for their failure to include neighbors in the redevelopment process.

Community workforce development is a formal component of the EPA's Brownfields Economic Redevelopment Initiative. The EPA works with community educators and colleges to provide environmental education, recruitment of students from disadvantaged communities, worker training in the environmental field, and job opportunities associated with local brownfield sites. The EPA has awarded more than thirty Job Training Development Demonstration Pilots since 1998.

■ IMPORTANT POINTS FOR RESEARCHING A STORY ■

- Media coverage can either rally community support for a brownfield project or turn the tide of public opinion against it. A review of newspaper coverage of brownfields found that, during the early years of brownfield redevelopment, most articles were overwhelmingly positive and presented unbalanced coverage of the risks and benefits in favor of benefits. As brownfield programs expand, the challenge is to provide balanced coverage while avoiding the temptation to sensationalize the risks associated with contaminated sites or, conversely, to overemphasize benefits and neglect risks.
- Brownfield sites are not limited to urban areas. More than half of all brownfield pilot grants have been awarded in small municipalities and rural areas. The impact of a brownfield in these areas may be even more significant than in a large urban center. A

brownfield may be the result of the failure of an area's single industry, with the community's economic past and future tied heavily to the fate of the site. Such areas may also face greater pressure for greenfields development, due to the simple availability of large areas of land.

- Most states have voluntary cleanup programs that include the redevelopment of brownfields. These programs are similar to the federal program in approach and usually offer some release from future environmental liability at the state level. However, unless they are covered by a Memorandum of Agreement (MOA) with the EPA, these programs do not release site owners or developers from potential future liability under CERCLA.

▪ AVOIDING PITFALLS ▪

- Focusing solely on the issue of cleanup of the brownfield site may miss the point. More important than the cleanup of the site itself may be how that cleanup and redevelopment can improve neighborhood quality and stimulate revitalization.
- Brownfield redevelopment works well to improve communities when there are no accompanying issues of crime and blight. When neighborhood crime is a problem, brownfield redevelopment alone cannot spark revitalization. The redevelopment plan must also address crime prevention.
- Don't automatically equate a brownfields site with a Superfund site. Brownfields are typically much less contaminated than Superfund sites, and only some brownfields have been considered in the past for inclusion on the National Priorities List of Superfund sites. Most have never been formally investigated by the EPA or state environmental agencies.

▪ INFORMATION RESOURCES ▪

▪ GOVERNMENT/ACADEMIA

Start with state departments of environmental protection. They often provide case managers to facilitate regulatory oversight and permitting of brownfield projects. The Northeast Midwest Institute website (see below) maintains a current list of state agencies overseeing brownfield projects.

- U.S. Environmental Protection Agency, Office of Solid Waste and Emergency Response (OSWER) (www.epa.gov/swerosps/bf)
  401 M St. SW, Washington, DC 20460
  Outreach and Special Projects Staff
  (202) 260-4039; fax: (202) 260-6606
- U.S. Environmental Protection Agency, Technology Innovation Office (www.clu-in.org)
  U.S. EPA (5102G)
  Ariel Rios Bldg., 1200 Pennsylvania Ave. NW, Washington, DC 20460
  (703) 603-9910; fax: (703) 603-9135

▪ NONPROFIT/CONSUMER ORGANIZATIONS

- Brownfields Non-Profits Network (www.brownfieldsnet.org)
  c/o Phoenix Land Recycling Company
  105 North Front St., Suite 106, Harrisburg, PA 17101-1436
  (717) 230-9700; fax: (717) 230-8808
- Institute for Responsible Management (www.instrm.org)
  317 George St., Suite 202, New Brunswick, NJ 08901-2152
  (732) 296-1960; fax (732) 296-1972
  E-mail: mail@instrm.org
- International City/County Management Association (ICMA) (www.icma.org)
  777 North Capitol St. NE, Suite 500, Washington, DC 20002
  (202) 289-4262; fax: (202) 962-3500
- National Center for Neighborhood and Brownfields Redevelopment (http://policy.rutgers.edu/brownfields)
  Edward J. Bloustein School of Planning and Public Policy
  33 Livingston Ave., Suite 100
  Rutgers University, New Brunswick, NJ 08901-1958
  (732) 932-4104, ext. 673; fax: (732) 932-0934
- Northeast Midwest Institute (www.nemw.org)
  218 D St. SE, Washington, DC 20003
  (202) 544-5200; fax: (202) 544-0043

CANCER AND OTHER DISEASE CLUSTER CLAIMS

▪ BACKGROUND ▪

Apparent clusters of cancer, birth defects, or other health conditions are tragic events that capture the public's heart and imagination and therefore are routinely covered by the media. Most journalists are frustrated in their efforts to build a story around these events because cluster investigations take a long time to conduct and the results are almost always inconclusive.

A disease "cluster" is the occurrence of a greater number of cases within a group of people than normally would be expected. The cluster usually occurs within a specific area, which can be as small as a single block or as large as a county. When a larger than expected number of cases of the same disease occur at approximately the same time as well as in the same place, it is called a time-space cluster.

When people hear the term "cluster," cancer most frequently comes to mind. However, other chronic and infectious diseases can appear in clusters. Common examples include outbreaks of influenza, measles, and food poisoning. Recent examples of noncancer disease clusters include clusters of variant Creutzfeldt Jakob disease linked to "mad cow disease" in Britain and a suspected autism cluster in New Jersey. While identifying and validating true clusters is a difficult and expensive process, a number of important health hazards have been brought to light through the observation of apparent clusters. Examples include the observation of Legionnaires' disease (which is caused by a bacterium), the carcinogenicity of vinyl chloride, and sterility induced by the pesticide dibromochloropropane.

This brief is based on an earlier version included in the second edition of *The Reporter's Environmental Handbook*. Additional information and comments were provided by Daniel Wartenberg, Environmental Health Division, Environmental and Occupational Health Sciences Institute (EOHSI), University of Medicine and Dentistry of New Jersey/Robert Wood Johnson Medical School, Piscataway, New Jersey.

▪ IDENTIFYING THE ISSUES ▪

Cluster investigations typically begin with a phone call to a local health department or other health agency from a concerned individual or citizen's group. About 1,500 requests for cancer cluster investigations are made annually to state agencies in the United States. More than three-quarters of these requests end with the initial phone conversation and/or a letter from the health agency to the caller. In these instances, one or more factors may speak against the probability of an actual cluster. A true disease cluster meets all of the following conditions: (1) the cases share the same unusual diagnosis—the same rare disease or type of cancer; (2) the number of cases is greater than expected in comparison with similar populations; and (3) the cases share a common exposure to a plausible causative agent. While this seems simple and straightforward, disease clusters are notoriously difficult to investigate and confirm.

In determining whether to conduct a scientific investigation of a cluster claim, the health agency must first determine whether excess in disease has actually occurred. Other considerations include:

- How serious is the cluster, if it exists?
- How verifiable is the cluster—that is, even if it exists, is the disease or condition common enough and the population large enough that it can be found?
- How big is the budget for cluster investigations, and what other demands are being made on that budget?
- How much political pressure is the community putting on the agency?

▪ ADDRESSING THE ISSUES ▪

Suspicion of a cancer cluster, for example, typically begins when someone who is affected by the disease begins to notice that other people in his or her neighborhood or workplace also have cancer. This may lead to the perception that there is an unusually high cancer rate within their community. However, it is important to note that cancer is not a single illness. There are more than 200 different types of cancers, each with its own set of risk factors. Further, cancer is a common illness. The American Cancer Society reports that one in every four deaths in the United States is due to cancer. It is, therefore, not unusual to find several people with cancer living within the same neighborhood or sharing the same workplace.

The first step in investigating a cluster claim is to confirm that the cases share the same diagnosis—the same type of cancer or the same rare disease—or are at least attributable to a common exposure. The confirmation process is labor intensive, involving examination of records of mortality (death certificates) and incidence (found in state disease registries), talking to people with the disease, and checking with attending physicians and coroners to verify the diagnoses. During this process, investigators may exclude some cases due to misdiagnosis or inaccurate reporting or, conversely, may find additional cases that were not included in the initial cluster claim.

Once the cases have been defined and identified, investigators then determine if the number of cases is larger than expected and if the difference is "statistically significant"—that is, the excess in disease is unlikely to have occurred by chance. In simplest terms, this is done by comparing the number of cases with the number that would be expected for a similar population in the state or nation. There are a number of factors that need to be carefully considered in these calculations. It is important to properly define the study population in terms of location—neighborhood, town, school, job function, or common water source, for example—so that all possible cases are included in the calculation. The study population must also be defined in terms of demographics—gender, age, race, socioeconomic status. These characteristics are used to define not only the study population but also to define the reference population to which their disease rate will be compared.

Cancer and other disease rates vary by age, race, ethnicity, occupation, and behaviors such as smoking. In many areas, neighborhoods are comprised of people with very similar racial and socioeconomic backgrounds who have similar lifestyles, all of which could put them at higher risk of getting a specific disease or type of cancer. For example, higher than expected rates of melanoma (skin cancer) in Florida are associated with the age of the population—melanoma rates are higher among older adults—and a lifestyle that includes sunbathing with little or no sunblock, for sun exposure is a known risk factor for melanoma.

Statistical significance is often difficult to prove in cluster investigations. Cluster investigations are declared to be inconclusive when more disease cases are found than would be expected to occur by chance but the excess is not found to be statistically significant. A lack of statistical significance does not necessarily mean that a cluster is not real. It may simply indicate that the total number of cases was not large enough to perform meaningful statistical analyses—statistical analyses generally require sample sizes in the tens to hundreds in order to achieve statistical significance.

Many cluster investigations are halted upon finding a lack of statistical significance. If, however, an excess in disease has been found that has potential public health significance and if sufficient funds and personnel are available, officials may attempt to find a cause for the cluster. This stage of the investigation involves the search for all possible causes of the disease within the cluster population. One component of this research may be a community survey to identify common risk factors. Many cluster investigations stop at this point, because investigators are unable to isolate a common exposure that is plausible as a risk factor for the disease.

It is difficult to identify possible causes for disease clusters and even more difficult to prove causation. One reason is the problem of latency—when a cancer is due to a specific exposure, there may be a latency period of ten to forty years between the exposure and the onset of the cancer. The problem is in pinpointing the individual past exposures that may be associated with recent diagnoses of cancer. Another involves situations where a hazardous waste site is considered as a possible cause. Investigators must identify a specific contaminant or set of contaminants as the possible disease agent, as well as confirm a definitive exposure pathway from the site to the cluster population. Such sites typically involve hundreds of contaminants at varying concentrations and multiple potential exposure pathways, including air, surface water, and potable groundwater supply.

In the rare event that a cluster investigation finds an excess of disease and a likely source, researchers may survey a comparison population or control group—persons similar in age, race, and gender to the affected population who do not share exposure to the suspected cause of the disease. This is called a cohort study, and it requires extensive resources. Less than 3 percent of requests for cluster investigations lead to such in-depth field studies.

As stated at the outset of this brief, most requests for cluster investigation end following the initial call to a local or state health agency. The cluster claims that do get investigated are typically those where the people have either the political or media connections to bring public attention to their plight, the affluence to spend the time lobbying for the investigation, and the persistence to keep up their fight and keep it in the public eye. There is no guarantee, therefore, that the clusters being investigated are the only ones in existence or that they represent the biggest public health threats.

■ IMPORTANT POINTS FOR RESEARCHING A STORY ■

- Consider possible exposures (e.g., occupation) and lifestyle factors (e.g., smoking, diet, or poor nutrition) that could be responsible for the reported cluster.
- There is an important distinction to be made between incidence and prevalence. The incidence of a disease refers to the number of new cases of the disease diagnosed during the present year. Prevalence refers to the total number of cases of the disease that currently exist in an area, regardless of when they were first diagnosed. Those who have died from the disease in question are not included in the calculation of incidence or prevalence. Deaths due to the disease constitute the mortality rate. It is important to determine if the cases under investigation are, for example, cancer deaths. If the cases are not deaths, it should then be determined when they were diagnosed.
- Occasionally, officials have not heard about supposed disease clusters. Journalists should share information they have gathered with health officials and researchers.
- When officials are aware of a suspected cluster but have not investigated, determine why an investigation has not been conducted. Often, the bottom line is a lack of funding, since cluster investigations are labor intensive. New stories may prompt the government to find appropriate funding for the research. Sensational stories, however, may only serve to cause public panic.
- Try to identify the population at risk. Determine whether the problem is localized in one neighborhood or whether it might be affecting the entire community or county.
- It is sometimes assumed that a common exposure will cause the same type of cancer. This is often not the case, since some known human carcinogens—dioxin is a good example—cause cancer at multiple sites; in this case, then, the best indicator would be total cancer frequencies.
- In situations where the population at risk is too small to achieve

statistical significance, public health agencies should not ignore these cases. Disease prevention practices and strategies still need to be put in place. It is important that journalists include in their stories ways for the public to minimize exposure and/or reduce the risk of disease.

▪ AVOIDING PITFALLS ▪

- Community residents report most clusters, so it is not unusual for stories to be based only on this anecdotal evidence. Health surveys conducted by citizens are not worthless, but neither are they a replacement for scientific study by trained investigators. If a story is based upon data gathered by citizens, the limitations of such surveys and the need for government studies should be emphasized. Use disclaimers where necessary.
- Journalists should use caution in selecting expert opinion. Always verify the credentials for "experts." An advanced academic degree does not necessarily make someone an expert in a particular cluster investigation or in epidemiology (the study of diseases in populations).
- Keep in mind that cluster investigations rarely reach definitive conclusions about cause. Failure to reach such conclusions does not mean that local officials are incompetent or are covering up to protect polluters. Nor does the failure to reach definitive conclusions mean that the problem is not real and that citizens are hysterical. Usually it simply means that the problem is too small to measure conclusively—even though it may be big enough to take seriously. Cluster investigations are difficult, expensive, and *usually* inconclusive.
- Cluster investigations are declared to be inconclusive when more disease cases are found than would be expected to occur by chance but the excess is not statistically significant. A lack of statistical significance does not necessarily mean that a cluster is not real or that the potential risk is unimportant—statistical analyses generally require sample sizes in the hundreds to achieve statistical significance. In such cases, it is appropriate to report the number of cancers observed, the number expected, and that the results were not statistically significant perhaps because of the small size of the population under study. Conversely, a finding of statistical

significance does not necessarily mean that the excess disease will be traceable to some local environmental exposure. In a large enough population, simple random variation in the distribution of a disease can result in regionally high or low rates that are statistically significant.

- Consider whether there was exposure and whether there are alternative explanations for the suspected cluster. These factors should not only go into the story, but they should also go into the decision as to how "big" to play the story. This is especially true when writing stories about neighborhoods affected by hazardous waste sites.
- Government agency unresponsiveness should not be confused with the actual health risk. Both deserve coverage, but a good risk story avoids treating one as a symptom of the other.

▪ INFORMATION RESOURCES ▪

Local, county, and state health departments should know what clusters are currently being investigated. Physicians who practice in the community, hospital administrators, and academic researchers are also possible sources of information—but beware. They may also have strong opinions about possible causes.

▪ GOVERNMENT/ACADEMIA

- Centers for Disease Control and Prevention (www.cdc.gov)
  Office of Communications
  1600 Clifton Rd., MS D25, Atlanta, GA 30333
  (404) 639-3286 or (800) 311-3435; fax: (404) 639-7394
  E-mail: in.the.news@cdc.gov
- National Cancer Institute (www.nci.nih.gov)
  Office of Cancer Communications
  Building 31, Room 10A24, Bethesda, MD 20892
  (301) 496-6641

▪ NONPROFIT/CONSUMER ORGANIZATION

- The Brain Tumor Society (www.tbts.org)
  124 Watertown St., Suite 3-H, Watertown, MA 02472

(800) 770-TBTS (8287) or (617) 924-9997; fax (617) 924-9998
E-mail: info@tbts.org

- Center for Health, Environment and Justice (www.chej.org)
  P.O. Box 6806, Falls Church, VA 22040
  (703) 237-2249; fax: (703) 237-8389
  E-mail: chej@chej.org
- Children's Environmental Health Network (www.cehn.org)
  110 Maryland Ave. NE, Suite 511, Washington, DC 20002
  (202) 543-4033; fax: (202) 543-8797
  E-mail: cehn@cehn.org
- Toxic Environment Affects Children's Health (TEACH)
  (www.tr-teach.org)
  Toms River, NJ
  E-mail: contact@tr-teach.org

CHEMICAL EMERGENCIES

▪ BACKGROUND ▪

A warehouse catches fire, possibly releasing toxic chemicals into the air. A tank truck carrying chemicals fails to negotiate a turn on a road and flips on its side; the contents leak out into a nearby stream. A freight train derails, and a chemical begins to leak. These are the makings of a chemical emergency. Covering such an emergency can be difficult for many reasons: the scene is often tense and hectic, emergency personnel at the scene may not yet know the risk, and emergency response teams often use unfamiliar technical jargon.

Chemical emergencies such as the accident at Bhopal and other large-scale chemical release fire and explosion emergencies are significant hazards. Some of these emergencies pose an acute risk to a small number of people at the site where they occur and/or to people close by. However, except for those living in the vicinity, chemical emergencies pose a smaller threat to public health than do asbestos, radon, and other indoor air pollutants, smoking, alcohol, and drug abuse. In fact, most fatalities connected with chemical emergencies are not chemical related but rather the result of related accidents (e.g., trucks crashing and people falling off scaffolding at emergency sites).

The identity of the facility or transportation company is usually evident. A description of what material is involved may or may not be available. Company transportation representatives can provide this information, but they may be reluctant to do so. Right-to-know legislation now requires that all hazardous materials be inventoried and recorded in an easy-to-find fashion. The state or county health department, as well as the local fire and police departments, should now have access to information on the material involved in the emergency. In addition, several other state disclosure acts, licensing permits, and even zoning requirements may provide the needed information.

This brief was written by James Ross, Supervising Program Development Specialist, Office of Site Safety and Health, Division of Publicly Funded Site Remediation, New Jersey Department of Environmental Protection and Energy, Trenton, New Jersey.

Information on the chemicals involved in an emergency can be obtained in several ways. For chemical emergencies occurring at a facility, Toxics Release Inventories (TRIs) are the best key. However, they only include "covered chemicals." For transportation accidents, the best sources are the U.S. Department of Transportation (DOT) placards displayed on the vehicle or the manifest held by the driver. These numbers identify the chemical being transported. For example, trucks carrying gasoline will have a red placard with the DOT number and hazard class (e.g., DOT 1203—gasoline, hazard class number 3, flammable liquid).

Determining the effects of the material is more complicated. Finding out whether a material is toxic, explosive, or corrosive is usually easy because there are simple tests for these designations. For emergencies, short-term acute effects are the important parameter. Long-term health and environmental effects, such as groundwater pollution, cancer, and birth defects, depend on the situation. Days after the accident, experts may disagree about the effects even after all the information is collected. If there is disagreement, reporters have to start asking detailed questions to pin down the disagreement. Some of the best answers can come from industrial hygienists, safety specialists, toxicologists, and environmental specialists.

■ IDENTIFYING THE ISSUES ■

The type of accident can give important clues to the kinds of effects to expect. In transportation accidents, the spill usually, though not always, stays close to the accident site. The toxic material may be highly concentrated but is usually confined to a small area. The potential for environmental damage is severe, but the risk to public health is relatively low. Often there is an acute risk for those present and a chronic risk for those nearby. In the case of a factory fire involving chemicals, the toxic material is spread over a much larger area in a lower concentration, increasing the public health risk. Fumes from both chemical fires and spills may require evacuation of downwind residents. Information on downwind protective actions can be obtained from the DOT *Emergency Response Guidebook* (2000). This document (often called the orange book) is distributed for placement in almost every emergency vehicle in the United States today.

Responders to a chemical emergency—and that includes journalists who want to get close to it—often must wear protective clothing and use self-contained breathing apparatus (SCBA) or an air-purified respirator with chemical filters. Equipment and training are to be provided by the employer. In most instances, a respirator, protective suit, gloves, boots, and hood cost under $300.

Decontamination of protective equipment and supplies takes place when the emergency is declared to be over. Tyvek plastic-coated protective suits are washed down, scrubbed with a harsh soap, and covered with bleach before being given to the waste removal contractor for disposal. They are never to be mixed with regular garbage since they are considered to be hazardous waste. Showers can be set up in the field, and large waste contractors even have modular units containing showers that are trucked to emergency sites. Wastewater from the decontamination process is also removed by the contractor, but if injured personnel have to be treated at a hospital, the hospital must perform the decontamination. Today, more and more hazardous material response agencies have the capability to decontaminate accident victims at the scene, before transport to the medical facility. Once at the hospital, the chemical substance is usually so diluted that it is safe to treat the contaminated water in the hospital's sewage system. Schools and other facilities with showers are sometimes used following chemical emergencies for mass decontamination of large populations.

▪ ADDRESSING THE ISSUES ▪

There are three steps to any remedial action plan: containment, disposal, and follow-up environmental surveillance. Containment and disposal are often handled by private cleanup vendors licensed by the states and the U.S. Environmental Protection Agency (EPA).

▪ CONTAINMENT

For land spills, contractors employ a method of diking, using earth, sand, or tarps made of plastic or other impervious material to cover sewer manholes and drains to prevent runoff. They may also use absorbent materials such as Dri-Rite, which resembles kitty litter, and absorbent pads or rolls of material that soak up certain organic matter, such as gasoline and alcohols. During excavation, contaminated soil is put in reclaiming containers, such as drums.

Contractors employ floating booms for water spills, made of material that absorbs chemicals but not water. Oil-spill contractors are now using removable booms that attract the oil floating on the surface of the water. Booms are squeezed out using a wringer, and the oil is reclaimed. Contractors never rely on just one containment source. There is always a series of dikes or a row of booms.

When the materials to be cleaned up are corrosives or acids, it may be better to dilute and neutralize the substance with lime, water, or other buffering agents, rendering it less hazardous. However, the substance is always removed after it is safely diluted and neutralized.

Not all chemical fires are contained by efforts to extinguish them. Some are allowed to burn because the hazardous chemical or by-product may be rendered safer by burning off. For example, emergency response personnel routinely allow pesticides to burn off unless the fire can be extinguished rapidly. Scientists claim that it is less risky to release burning pesticides into the atmosphere than to have contaminated water run off. If a leaking tanker or sealed storage tank contains a flammable liquid or gas and there is a threat of explosion, the most urgent task for firefighters is to quench the heat and prevent a deadly boiling liquid expanding vapor explosion (BLEVE). To do this, fire personnel evacuate to safer positions and use automated fire sprays to bathe the tank in cooling water until the threat has passed. This is typically recommended when dealing with corrosive materials such as dimethyl-sulfate and nitrogen tetroxide and poisons such as arsine (arsenic gas).

■ DISPOSAL

With land-bound spills, material trapped by dikes is vacuumed out into special trucks and deposited into containment tankers. Disposers must get temporary storage disposal licenses from the EPA to move the tankers and reclaiming drums that carry the excavated material to approved rendering facilities that break down and neutralize contaminated matter or to chemical burial sites. Under the Resource Conservation and Recovery Act (RCRA), the chemical waste must be manifested so that state and federal officials know the history of that waste from point of production to final disposal, sometimes referred to as "cradle to grave."

■ ENVIRONMENTAL SURVEILLANCE

Monitoring wells may be placed to assure there was no penetration or intrusion into the groundwater. Officials can require an analysis of potable water supplies; air monitoring; ground, soil, and vegetation sampling; and, if necessary, medical and epidemiological surveillance of responders and the affected populace. This latter step is done less frequently—usually in more catastrophic situations.

▪ IMPORTANT POINTS FOR RESEARCHING A STORY ▪

- Determine what quantity and form of material has been released into the environment and whether it is going into the surface water, groundwater, soil, or air. This will determine the route of human exposure.
- Find out if the material is persistent in the environment and the material's other properties. For example, even though a volatile material may be confined to a small container, it may evaporate easily and spread over a large area.
- Be sure to ask what quantities are considered dangerous, especially to specific vulnerable groups such as children, the elderly, and pregnant women.
- Find out why the material is considered to be dangerous, whether effects are acute or chronic, and whether it reacts with air, water, or other chemicals found nearby. Determine what happens when these materials react and whether they are more dangerous or less dangerous after a reaction. For instance, a spill of methyl chloroform will evaporate harmlessly if flushed with water into the nearest stream but may turn into a persistent contaminant of local well water if allowed to seep into the groundwater supply. Likewise, a spilled mercuric salt will not percolate deeply into most soils and can be confined in place if scooped up, but if flushed into surface water it may make fish unacceptable for human consumption.
- Learn the symptoms of exposure and determine if they can be differentiated from other symptoms (e.g., a cold, the flu, or difficulty breathing).

▪ AVOIDING PITFALLS ▪

- Be certain you are dealing with a chemical accident and not an act of terrorism or a release of a weapon of mass destruction (WMD). The latter are intentional releases and intended to do the greatest harm to the largest population. Most chemical emergencies today usually involve the accidental discharge of the substance from a container or system that was constructed to prevent or at least minimize its release.

- WMD emergencies involve materials that are intended to utilize the wind and other environmental currents to move or disperse the material over a large area, usually undetected, and to hit large populations.
- Chemical emergencies are tough situations to cover because they are difficult technical stories occurring in the midst of crises. While covering crises is basic to a reporter's job, covering technical issues in the midst of crisis requires special skills and knowledge.
- A common source of misinformation stems from asking the wrong person for technical information. People working to clean up an accident may not necessarily be qualified to discuss the health risks it poses. At the same time, people at the site of an emergency may be too busy dealing with the emergency to give thorough answers, even if they have the technical background to provide them.
- Keeping the reporter from getting close may not be a cover-up. The risks involved often necessitate this. Also, reporters at chemical emergencies sometimes assume that emergency responders know everything and therefore that what they will not say is a cover-up of very alarming information. Consider the possibility that they simply may not know the answer to a question (yet).
- Reporters at the site of a chemical spill or factory fire run the risk of being forced to leave the scene by police because they, too, are at risk. Every newspaper should consider investing in protective equipment and have suppliers in to train reporters in its use.
- The chemical emergency is often better reported than the health risk. Exposure information may not be known accurately for several days. Follow-up stories on health risks are extremely critical if a community is to be kept informed.
- Not all questions are best answered at the scene. Many times the cause and effect of the accident cannot be determined until after the dust has settled.
- On significant stories, reporters should stay with the story not just in terms of who was to blame and who was indicted or fined. Lessons for other facilities can be highlighted in follow-up. When company X had a fire, authorities may have determined that a leak in Y was the problem. Has company Z—located five miles

down the road—done anything about Y, or are they waiting for a fire, too?

- In some situations, not doing anything (e.g., letting a fire burn) is sometimes the right response.
- If it is a big story, then the story is more than the emergency itself. It also includes technical information on health risk (or ecosystem risk), how an area is being decontaminated, where the disposal site is located, follow-up surveillance, assessment of responsibility, and lessons to be learned. It is hard to imagine an emergency that deserves extensive coverage when it happens and merits no follow-up coverage at all. Yet disposal, surveillance, and what went wrong are often parts of the story that get less media attention than they deserve.

▪ FIRST CONTACTS ▪

Emergency responders are good news sources. They may include state and local police, environmental agency emergency teams, and health departments, as well as fire departments, first aid squads, and emergency management officials. Police and fire departments are the best sources for logistical information. They will know what is being done to contain the emergency, how traffic is being affected, whether there are injuries, and if there is need for an evacuation. For information on health effects, talk to health department and environmental agency officials, since in most cases, other on-site responders have little training in this field.

In the event of a large emergency (e.g., a factory fire involving chemicals), a command post often called the Emergency Operations Center (EOC) may be set up. This command post is where sources gather and where decisions are made. There you may find company representatives and experts from industry and academia called in by responders. In the event of minor emergencies, a command post probably will not be established. Reporters should look for an on-scene coordinator, the person responsible for seeing that each group does its job and has the support it needs. Federal law requires that every state and county have this form of emergency management. Small accidents, such as a minor transportation spill, may not have coordinators, and reporters should direct their attention to the local fire or police chief or perhaps a health officer or state/county emergency management coordinator. Expect that on-site experts may be busy managing the emergency and that reporters may have trouble finding out the information. In the event of a transportation spill, find out what materials were spilled by asking officials about the manifest. The manifest can be followed like a trail of bread crumbs to the original source of the material. It documents every movement and change in material from origin to final resting place. For complete information on placarding, see the Title 49 CFR (Code of Federal Regulations), specifically Title 100-177. Section 172.500 is the section that explains placarding. The state police and often the environmental agencies may have information on the shipment and storage of the hazardous material.

■ INFORMATION RESOURCES ■

■ GOVERNMENT/ACADEMIA

- Federal Emergency Management Agency (FEMA) (www.fema.gov)
  500 C St. SW, Washington, DC 20472
  (202) 566-1600
  emergency information and media affairs: (202) 646-4600
  fax: (202) 646-4086
  E-mail: pao@fema.gov
- U.S. Coast Guard, Oil Spills National Response Center (NRC)
  (www.nrc.uscg.mil)
  (800) 424-8802

■ INDUSTRY/PROFESSIONAL ASSOCIATIONS

- Association of American Railroads, Bureau of Explosives
  (www.aar.org)
  Emergency Handling of Hazardous Materials in Surface Transportation
  50 F St. NW, Washington, DC 20001-1564
  (202) 639-2100; fax: (202) 639-2558
  E-mail: information@aar.org
- CHEMTREC (www.chemtrec.org)
  1300 Wilson Blvd., Arlington, VA 22209

(800) 262-8200; (800) 424-9300 (24-hour emergency response communication); fax: (703) 741-6037
E-mail: chemtrec@americanchemistry.com

- INFOTRAC (24-hour emergency response communications service)
  (800) 535-5053
- 3E Company (24-hour emergency response communications service)
  (800) 451-8346

See also:

- *Covering an Environmental Accident.* A half-hour videotape analysis of how reporters and emergency response teams communicate during (and after) an accident. It is available through Human Ecology/CEC, Rutgers University, 31 Pine St., New Brunswick, NJ 08901 (732) 932-8795 (http://www.cook.rutgers.edu).
- Transportation Department. 2000. *The Emergency Response Guidebook.* It can be obtained in commercial bookstores as well as through the government (http://bookstore.gpo.gov).
- Lewis, Richard J., Sr., ed. 1999. *Sax's Dangerous Properties of Industrial Materials.* 10th ed. New York: John Wiley and Sons.
- Merck. 2001. *The Merck Index.* 13th ed. Rahway, N.J.: Merck.
- NIOSH. 1997. *Pocket Guide to Chemical Hazards (NPG).* It can be ordered or downloaded at www.cdc.gov/niosh/npg/npg.html.

CHEMICAL WEAPONS (DISARMAMENT)

▪ BACKGROUND ▪

Chemicals have been used in warfare since people first discovered poisons and dipped the tips of arrows and spears to inflict their enemies. Historians report that chemical warfare, in the form of arsenic gas, was used during the Peloponnesian War (431–404 BCE). Modern chemical weapons came into widespread use during World War I.

Chemical warfare agents may be delivered by spray tanks, smoke generators, bombs, land mines, floating bombs, and missiles. Some weapons contain the entire weapons system (detonator, agent, and fuel assembly, if necessary). In contrast, binary weapons contain two relatively nontoxic chemicals in separate chambers that, when combined, react rapidly to form a highly toxic chemical agent. Chemical warfare agents may be in gaseous, liquid, or solid states. Their effects may be incapacitating or lethal. Chemical weapons are typically classified and discussed in terms of their target organ (e.g., nerve, blood, lung, skin, or psychological) or type of effect (choking, harassing, or blistering).

▪ NERVE, BLOOD, AND PSYCHOLOGICAL AGENTS

Nerve agents work by attacking the central nervous system. Nerve agents can be lethal. They are the most prevalent chemical warfare agent. Exposure to a small amount of a pure nerve agent, via inhalation or ingestion, can lead to death within minutes. Examples of nerve agents are sarin (also known by its U.S. code, GB), tabun (GA), soman (GD), and VX. These agents all belong to the same chemical family, organo-phosphorus compounds. This same class of compounds is used in insecticides. Blood agents block the uptake and delivery of oxygen in the blood, leading to oxygen starvation (anoxia) and death. Blood agents include hydrogen chloride, arsine, and cyanogen chloride. Psychological or psychotomimetic agents impair thought processes, induce hallucinations, or mimic the symptoms of psychoses. Examples include BZ, phencyclidine, Agent-15, and LSD. In large doses, psychotomimetic agents can be fatal.

▪ BLISTER, CHOKING, AND HARASSING AGENTS

Blister agents, also known as mustard agents or vesicants, are corrosive to tissues, causing burns and blisters on the skin or throughout the respiratory tract. Blister agents are extremely painful and can be lethal. Examples of blister agents include sulfur mustard (H and HD), mustard (HT), lewisite (L), and mustard-lewisite mixtures. The effects of mustard agents can be delayed. Victims may not be aware of their exposure to mustard agents until hours later, when symptoms begin to appear. Choking agents attack the respiratory system and can be lethal. Chlorine, phosgene, and diphosgene are examples of choking agents. Harassing agents are typically used in riot control and are not considered lethal under normal conditions. Harassing agents include tear gases (e.g., CN, CS, and CR) and vomiting agents (e.g., DA, DC, and adamsite).

Although multinational agreements prohibiting the use of chemical weapons date back to the first International Peace Conference in 1899, chemical weapons were used with devastating effects during various wars and conflicts of the twentieth century. On November 30, 1992, after two decades of intense negotiations, the Convention on the Prohibition of the Development, Production, Stockpiling and Use of Chemical Weapons and on Their Destruction (Chemical Weapons Convention) was adopted by the United Nations General Assembly. The convention was signed in Paris in 1993 and entered into force on April 29, 1997.

The Chemical Weapons Convention is the first multinational disarmament agreement that provides for the complete elimination of an entire category of weapons, prohibiting their development, production, acquisition, stockpiling, transfer, and use. The convention also prohibits assisting or encouraging other states to engage in such activities. Parties to the Chemical Weapons Convention are required to destroy all of their chemical weapons and chemical weapons production facilities. In addition, the parties are to destroy any chemical weapons they have abandoned in other countries. As of October 2002, 147 parties—including the United States—have ratified the Chemical Weapons Convention. The convention is administered by the Organization for the Prohibition of Chemical Weapons (OPCW), located in The Hague.

Deadlines for demilitarization of chemical weapons under the convention include:

- April 29, 2000—destruction of 1 percent of the most dangerous (Category 1) weapons;
- April 29, 2002—destruction of 20 percent of Category 1 weapons and 100 percent of Category 2 weapons;
- April 29, 2005—destruction of 45 percent of Category 1 weapons;
- April 29, 2007—destruction of 100 percent of Category 1 weapons and destruction of 100 percent of chemical weapons production facilities.

Under the convention's "exceptional circumstances," a party may apply to the OPCW for an extension of these deadlines. The final deadline for destruction of chemical weapons stockpiles is April 29, 2012. The deadlines established under the Chemical Weapons Convention have met with varying degrees of success.

To monitor and ensure compliance with the demilitarization schedule, the Chemical Weapons Convention includes provisions for routine inspections by the OPCW. Parties to the convention may also petition the OPCW for challenge inspections of other parties suspected of noncompliance and for investigations of the alleged use of chemical weapons.

▪ IDENTIFYING THE ISSUES ▪

U.S. chemical weapons stockpiles consist of nerve agents VX, sarin, and tabun and blister agents mustard and lewisite. These stockpiles are located at eight army bases in the continental United States and, until recently, at Johnston Atoll in the Pacific Ocean. Incineration of the more than 400,000 chemical weapons stockpiled at Johnston Atoll was completed on November 29, 2000.

Even prior to the Chemical Weapons Convention, the United States began destroying its chemical weapons stockpile. In the early 1980s, the U.S. Army declared much of its existing stockpile to be obsolete and developed plans to destroy it. National Academy of Science studies found the risks associated with disposal to be much lower than the risks associated with continued storage. Among the risks associated with storing chemical weapons are leaks from aging containment vessels, fires, natural disasters, and security issues such as theft by terrorist organizations. The scenario used at the major sites to define maximum risk is a natural event (e.g., earthquake, hurricane) that breaches the storage site and detonates stored weapons. The fear is that the accidental or deliberate detonation of a single weapon could lead to the detonation of thousands of weapons stored in proximity.

While most Americans support the disarmament of chemical weapons, there is much controversy over the location, methods, and timing of their destruction. Much of the controversy has surrounded the selection of incineration as the "baseline" or preferred technology for the destruction of the U.S. chemical weapons arsenal. The controversy has cost the army's chemical weapons disposal program significant amounts of time and money. Cost estimates for the program have grown from just over $1 billion to more than $20 billion. Recent estimates suggest the United States will miss the convention's 2007 deadline for the destruction of chemical weapons stockpiles.

In the past, surplus and obsolete chemical weapons were destroyed by detonation, open burning, evaporation, burial, and ocean dumping. Today, two methods—incineration and chemical neutralization—are accepted for destroying chemical weapons. Each process consists of two steps: demilitarization followed by incineration or neutralization. Demilitarization consists of removal of the chemical agent from the weapon. After demilitarization, the individual parts of the weapon—the chemical agent, the explosive, the shell, and the packing material ("dunnage")—are handled and destroyed separately.

The United States used high-temperature incineration to destroy chemical weapons at the Johnston Atoll from 1990 to 2000 and at Toole, Utah, since 1996. Incineration is also being proposed for use at chemical weapons storage depots in Alabama, Arkansas, and Oregon. Opponents of incineration argue that the army's chemical weapons incinerators have a history of operational problems and design flaws. They also argue that incinerators are more susceptible to accidental releases of toxic gases than are neutralization systems. In addition, opponents maintain that the air emissions associated with incineration will routinely release heavy metals, dioxins, and other chemicals that will jeopardize the health of nearby residents.

Chemical neutralization facilities are being considered for the remaining U.S. chemical weapons storage sites, which are located in Colorado, Indiana, Kentucky, and Maryland. However, chemical neutralization has yet to be proven a viable alternative to incineration, and it has other risks associated with it. At this writing, the army is still investigating technologies for chemical neutralization. Technologies currently being examined include hydrolysis followed by biodegradation and hydrolysis followed by supercritical water oxidation.

Stockpiles of more than 70,000 metric tons of chemical weapons and more than 8 million munitions have been declared as falling under the Chemical Weapons Convention and inspected by OPCW inspectors. Currently, four parties—the United States, the Russian Federation, India, and one other state party—have disclosed possession of chemical weapons under the convention, and all have begun to destroy their stockpiles. The United States and the Russian Federation are the two largest known possessors of chemical weapons. The remaining holders of chemical weapons around the globe are largely unknown or unconfirmed except to the OPCW, which keeps confidential all disclosures under the convention. Countries suspected of having chemical weapons stockpiles or capabilities include China, Egypt, Iran, Iraq, Israel, Libya, North Korea, Pakistan, and Syria. Of these, Egypt, Iraq, Libya, and North Korea have not signed the convention. Israel has signed but has yet to ratify the convention. A number of Middle Eastern states have refused to sign the convention until Israel's suspected nuclear program is addressed.

At this writing, the Russian Federation is planning to use a chemical neutralization process, neutralization-bituminization, to dispose of its chemical weapons. However, the Russian program is experiencing extreme difficulties, missing the first milestones for destruction of weapons under the Chemical Weapons Convention. Russia has stockpiles of an estimated 44,000 metric tons of chemical weapons at seven depots. Most of the stockpiles, nearly 80 percent, consist of highly toxic nerve agents. The remaining stockpiles consist mainly of mustard agents and a smaller amount of phosgene. The total projected cost of the Russian chemical weapons disposal program is $7 billion. The main obstacle faced by the Russian chemical weapons demilitarization program is a severe lack of funds.

As mentioned, the Chemical Weapons Convention requires that member parties destroy chemical weapons they have abandoned in other nations. There are a number of special concerns that need to be addressed for abandoned chemical weapons. Most important is the handling of such weapons. Abandoned chemical weapons are particularly hazardous—they are likely to be in poor, deteriorated condition and require additional handling for retrieval and relocation to a disposal facility. Aging chemical weapons are at increased risk for accidental detonation, leakage, or contamination. It is also important to properly identify the chemical components of abandoned weapons. Different chemicals have different requirements for handling, storage, and disposal.

The storage, handling, and disposal of chemical weapons produce additional wastes. Secondary waste from chemical weapons disposal programs include trash, packing materials, wooden pallets, spent charcoal, and other materials—any of which may be contaminated. The ultimate disposal of secondary waste is an issue for all chemical waste disposal facilities. In the United States, some state and local agencies require an approved plan for the handling and disposing of secondary waste prior to the issuance of permits for chemical waste disposal facilities.

The ultimate success of the Chemical Weapons Convention remains to be seen. Critics argue that the convention is meaningless without the participation of all nations with chemical weapons capabilities. Such arguments center on the belief that fear of retaliation is the most effective deterrent to use. Verification of compliance with the convention is also an issue. While the convention includes comprehensive provisions for inspections, some of these provisions have yet to be exercised. For example, the United States has recently expressed a desire to call for challenge inspections of several parties to the convention. However, the United States has held off on its request, reportedly due to growing management and financial issues within the OPCW. Many believe that the convention will create a false sense of security in that chemical weapons could still be produced and deployed on a small scale by terrorist organizations with relative ease. One example of this is the release of the nerve agent sarin by the Aum Shinri Kyo cult in Japanese subways in 1995. A key goal of the U.S. program is to destroy our own aging weapons in order to avoid an accident that could kill or severely injure American troops and civilians.

▪ ADDRESSING THE ISSUES ▪

In order to address safety concerns at the U.S. chemical weapons disposal facilities and the surrounding areas, comprehensive worker safety and emergency preparedness plans have been developed. Security at the sites is high, with armed guards and physical barriers in place. The Federal Emergency Management Administration (FEMA) has developed Chemical Stockpile Emergency Preparedness Programs (CSEPPs) for each facility and its surrounding communities. Local CSEPPs include emergency response centers, specialized equipment and training for emergency responders, early warning systems (i.e., sirens), communication plans, and public education programs. These programs are designed to provide a level of comfort and reassurance to local communities as much as they are designed to ensure rapid and appropriate response to a chemical emergency at the facility.

Community and worker safety programs for chemical weapons disposal facilities have also been developed by the Centers for Disease Control and Prevention (CDC). CDC's role includes the development of risk-based exposure limits for the chemicals at the facility, monitoring to ensure that worker and community exposures remain below acceptable limits, and training of medical personnel in the affected communities.

At this writing, the United States has destroyed more than 23 percent of its chemical weapons stockpile. Progress is continuing, although the abandonment of incineration plans at a number of facilities has resulted in significant program delays. The National Research Council's (NRC) 1999 report, "Review and Evaluation of Alternative Technologies for Demilitarization of Assembled Chemical Weapons," evaluated four nonincineration technologies for possible use by the U.S. program. The NRC found that the four chemical neutralization technologies studied were 99.9999 percent effective at destroying certain chemical warfare agents, as is incineration. However, questions remained as to the safety of the by-products of decomposition. The report also noted that, as the technologies were new, potential problems associated with the processes were unknown. Additional studies by the U.S. government are ongoing and expected to conclude in 2002.

At the international level, the OPCW has conducted more than a thousand inspections at sites within the territories of fifty parties to the convention. Each of the four parties that has disclosed chemical weapons stockpiles to the OPCW has reportedly begun their destruction programs. The United States, India, and an unnamed state party have all met the April 2000 deadline for destruction of 1 percent of Category 1 chemical weapons. In addition, all of the Category 3 weapons held by these three parties were destroyed ahead of the convention deadlines. The Russian Federation program, which has experienced significant delays due to financial difficulties, is now getting under way thanks to foreign aid from the United States, Britain, Italy, and other countries. The Russian Federation has begun to eliminate its Category 3 agents, as well as munitions containing phosgene (a Category 2 agent). In a cost-saving move, the Russian government plans to recycle much of the phosgene for use in its plastics industry. The success of the Russian program will require continued international investment and OPCW acceptance of creative approaches to reduce program costs, such as the phosgene recycling plan.

▪ IMPORTANT POINTS FOR RESEARCHING A STORY ▪

- It is important to note that the definition of chemical weapons under the Chemical Weapons Convention is sufficiently broad to include chemical warfare agents, their precursors, and the unfilled weapons and equipment designed to deliver them. This definition prevents countries from developing binary weapons to circumvent the convention. (As noted earlier, binary weapons contain two relatively nontoxic chemicals that, when combined, react to form a highly toxic agent.)

▪ AVOIDING PITFALLS ▪

- The major pitfall for a reporter is to try to find the reality that exists within the rhetoric about this subject. Within the United States, there are strong opponents and proponents of incineration and other technologies. The claims made by both sides can lead to the false conclusion that these weapons cannot be safely destroyed and that they need to be left in place. In fact, as noted, a large proportion of the U.S. stockpile has been destroyed. For scientifically grounded information about this program, we recommend the reports issued by the National Research Council's Committee on Review and Evaluation of the Army Chemical Stockpile Disposal Program.

▪ INFORMATION RESOURCES ▪

- **GOVERNMENT/ACADEMIA**
- Centers for Disease Control and Prevention
  (www.cdc.gov/nceh/demil)
  Special Programs Group (F-16), National Center for Environmental Health, 4770 Buford Highway NE, Atlanta, GA 30341-3724
- Chemical and Biological Defense Information Analysis Center (CBIAC)
  (http://ss-cbiac.apgea.army.mil)
  Aberdeen Proving Ground—Edgewood Area P.O. Box 196, Gunpowder, MD 21010-0196
  (410) 676-9030; fax: (410) 676-9703
  E-mail: kingj@battelle.org
- Chemical Stockpile Emergency Preparedness Program Portal
  (www.csepp-planners.net)
  Innovative Emergency Management, Inc.
  8555 United Plaza Blvd., Suite 100, Baton Rouge, LA 70809
  (225) 952-8191; fax: (225) 952-8122
- Federal Emergency Management Agency (FEMA)
  (www.fema.gov)
  500 C St. SW, Washington, DC 20472
  (202) 566-1600
  emergency information and media affairs: (202) 646-4600; fax: (202) 646-4086
  E-mail: pao@fema.gov
- Monterey Institute of International Studies, Center for Nonproliferation Studies (CNS) (http://cns.miis.edu/index.htm)
  460 Pierce St., Monterey, CA 93940
  (831) 647-4154; fax: (831) 647-3519
  E-mail: cns@miis.edu
- National Academy Press (www.nap.edu)
  Source for reports issued by the National Research Council's Committee on Review and Evaluation of the Army Chemical Stockpile Disposal Program, including:
  - "Closure and Johnston Atoll Chemical Agent Disposal System" (2002) (http://www.nap.edu/books/0309084059/html/)
  - "Evaluation of the Army's Draft Assessment Criteria to Aid in the Selection of Alternative Technologies for Chemical Demilitarization" (2000) (http://books.nap.edu/books/NI000212/html/)

- "Occupational Health and Workplace Monitoring at Chemical Agent Disposal Facilities" (2001)
  (http://www.nap.edu/books/0309075750/html/)

- Organisation for the Prohibition of Chemical Weapons (www.opcw.nl)
  Johan de Wittlaan 32, 2517JR The Hague, Netherlands
  +31-(0)70-416 3300; fax: +31-(0)70-306 3535
- U.S. Army Soldier and Biological Chemical Command (SBCCOM) (www.sbccom.army.mil)
  Chemical Stockpile Emergency Preparedness Office
  Aberdeen Proving Ground, MD 21010-5423
  (410) 436-4292; fax: (410) 436-3179
  E-mail: jxyaquia@sbccom.apgea.army.mil

■ INDUSTRY

- NBC Industry Group (www.nbcindustrygroup.com)
  P.O. Box 2781, Springfield, VA 22152
- Raytheon Company (www.raytheon.com)
  141 Spring St., Lexington, MA 02421
  (781) 860-2386; fax: (781) 860-2520

■ NONPROFIT/CONSUMER ORGANIZATIONS

- Arms Control Association (www.armscontrol.org)
  1725 M St. NW, Washington, DC 20036
  (202) 463-8270; fax: (202) 463-8273
- Bonn International Center for Conversion (BICC) (www.bicc.de)
  An der Elisabethkirche 25, 53113 Bonn, Germany
  +49-228-911 96-0; fax: +49-228-24 12 15
  E-mail: bicc@bicc.de
- Chemical and Biological Arms Control Institute (www.cbaci.org)
  1747 Pennsylvania Ave. NW, 7th Floor, Washington, DC 20006
  (202) 296-3550; fax: (202) 296-3574
  E-mail: cbaci@cbaci.org
- Chemical Weapons Working Group (www.cwwg.org)
  c/o Kentucky Environmental Foundation
  P.O. Box 467, Berea, KY 40403
  (859) 986-7565; fax: (859) 986-2695
- The Henry L. Stimson Center (www.stimson.org)

11 Dupont Circle NW, Suite 900, Washington, DC 20036
(202) 223-5956
E-mail: info@stimson.org

- Stockholm International Peace Research Institute (SIPRI)
(www.sipri.se)
Signalistgatan 9, SE-169 70 Solna, Sweden
+46-8-655 97 00; fax: +46-8-655 97 33
E-mail: sipri@sipri.org

CHILDREN'S HEALTH (ASTHMA)

▪ BACKGROUND ▪

The American Lung Association estimates that asthma costs the U.S. economy $12.7 billion per year. An estimated 15 million Americans, including 4.8 million children, suffer from asthma. Asthma accounts for more pediatric hospital admissions and missed days of school than any other chronic condition and claims the lives of nearly 300 U.S. children each year. The Centers for Disease and Prevention (CDC) reports that asthma rates among children under the age of five increased 160 percent between 1980 and 1994. Scientists suspect that the drastic increases in asthma prevalence rates during the past twenty years are due to a combination of exposures to environmental factors, such as secondhand smoke, and genetics. Much of the current research is focusing on the role of indoor air pollution in asthma development.

Asthma is a chronic lung disease. Symptoms of asthma, including coughing, wheezing, and difficulty breathing, typically occur in intermittent episodes, or "attacks." During an asthma attack, three major changes in the lungs make breathing difficult: the muscles surrounding the airways tighten; the cells lining the airways become inflamed; and increased mucous production clogs the airways. Asthma attacks can be sudden and, without appropriate medication, can become life-threatening.

The pattern, frequency, and severity of asthma attacks vary significantly among children. Some children with asthma can remain relatively free of symptoms for long periods of time; others suffer mild to severe symptoms on a daily basis. There are four classes of asthma severity: mild intermittent, mild persistent, moderate persistent, and severe persistent. Children with mild intermittent asthma have attacks once a week or less that last from a few hours to a few days. Children

This brief is based upon information provided by Natalie C. Freeman, Environmental and Occupational Health Sciences Institute (EOHSI), Piscataway, New Jersey, and Dona Schneider, Edward J. Bloustein School of Planning, Rutgers University, New Brunswick, New Jersey.

with mild persistent asthma have symptoms more often than once a week but not daily. Children with moderate persistent asthma have symptoms on a daily basis that interrupt their sleep at least once per week. Children with severe persistent asthma have daily symptoms that frequently interrupt their sleep.

▪ IDENTIFYING THE ISSUES ▪

Scientists are uncertain about the specific causes of asthma development, or onset, in children. Scientists believe that some individuals are born susceptible to developing asthma. However, heredity and factors in the environment both appear to play a role. Parental history of asthma, maternal cigarette smoking during pregnancy, infection with respiratory syncytial virus (RSV), and exposures to house dust mites, secondhand smoke (sometimes referred to as environmental tobacco smoke [ETS]), and cockroaches have all been suggested as factors associated with childhood development of asthma.

While data are lacking on the causes of asthma development, scientists have identified a number of factors, or triggers, that can bring on an attack in an asthmatic individual. Major asthma triggers include allergens, a number of indoor and outdoor air pollutants, drugs, viral infection, temperature changes, exercise, and emotions. Children with asthma may be sensitive to one, a combination, or all of these triggers.

Allergens are substances that trigger an immune response in sensitive individuals. House dust mites, cockroach droppings and particles, pollen, mold spores, and the dander, urine, and saliva of household pets have all been shown to trigger or exacerbate asthma symptoms in allergic asthmatic individuals. Household dust is a major source of exposure to these allergens. Other allergic triggers of asthma include certain foods and preservatives, including sulfites, aspirin and other nonsteroidal anti-inflammatory drugs, and other medications, such as penicillin.

As mentioned, studies have shown that children exposed to secondhand tobacco smoke have an increased risk of developing asthma. Exposure to secondhand tobacco smoke can also trigger asthma attacks and exacerbate existing asthma symptoms. The U.S. Environmental Protection Agency (EPA) estimates that between 200,000 and 1 million asthmatic children have their condition made worse by exposure to secondhand smoke each year. Childhood exposure to secondhand tobacco smoke is also associated with a greater number of emergency room visits for asthma and asthma-related symptoms.

In addition to ETS, other indoor air pollutants have been shown to trigger asthma attacks. (See the brief on "Air Pollution [Indoor].") Exposure to formaldehyde emitted from new carpets and furniture and volatile organic compounds found in household cleaning products, room deodorizers, fresh paint, and certain perfumes and fragrances have been associated with attacks in sensitive asthmatic individuals. Other indoor air triggers include houseplants, cut flowers, and cooking odors. Exposure to high levels of nitrogen dioxide from poorly vented furnaces and stoves has been shown to increase airway responses to other chemical irritants and allergens.

Outdoor air pollutants, including ozone, sulfur dioxide, and particulate matter, act as irritants and are common triggers of asthma attacks. (See the brief on "Air Pollution [Outdoor].") Some experts believe that prolonged exposure to and/or exposure to high levels of these pollutants, particularly ozone, can escalate an asthmatic individual's response to other inhaled triggers. Cold weather is another asthma trigger associated with outdoor air. Cold air can irritate the airways, causing bronchoconstriction, triggering an asthma attack, or worsening asthma symptoms.

Emotions, exercise, and viral illnesses may be of particular concern for children because of their increased exposure and limited ability to control these triggers. Anxiety, emotional upset, and even laughter can trigger an asthma attack in some children. Some people with asthma experience symptoms after several minutes of strenuous exercise. Children who are not old enough or attentive enough to recognize the early symptoms of an asthma attack are at risk as they continue to play through an attack without the benefit of medication. Conversely, children with exercise-induced asthma are also at risk of adopting unhealthy sedentary lifestyles, as well-meaning but misinformed adults steer them away from physical activity. Finally, inhaled viruses—particularly RSV but also the common cold—have been associated with asthma attacks in children.

Asthma prevalence rates—the percentages of people with asthma—are increasing. According to the CDC, the self-reported asthma prevalence rate in the U.S. population increased 75 percent between 1980 and 1994. The highest increases were seen among children aged zero to four years (160 percent) and children aged five to fourteen years (74 percent).

Statistics consistently show racial and socioeconomic disparity in the prevalence and severity of asthma in the United States. The asthma prevalence rates for African Americans, children living in lower income households, and inner-city populations are all markedly higher than the national rates. Further, there are significant racial differences in emergency room visits for asthma, asthma hospitalization rates, and asthma death rates. African American children are four times more likely than white children to be treated for asthma in an emergency room and are hospitalized for asthma more than three times as often as white children. Most strikingly, the death rate from asthma among African American children in 1993 aged zero to four years was six times the rate among white children the same age.

▪ ADDRESSING THE ISSUES ▪

Scientists suspect that the drastic increases in asthma prevalence rates during the past twenty years are due to a combination of external exposures to environmental factors and genetics. However, because genetic changes in a population take place very slowly over generations, genetic susceptibility alone cannot account for the skyrocketing asthma rates. Much of the current research is focusing on the role of indoor air pollution in asthma development. Children are spending increasing amounts of time (up to 90 percent) indoors, where many of the factors associated with asthma development—house dust mites, secondhand tobacco smoke, cockroach particles—are found. In addition, modern buildings are "tighter" than they used to be, with fewer windows and lower volumes of outdoor air drawn into circulation, resulting in higher concentrations of these asthma triggers.

A number of factors are believed to contribute to the racial disparities seen in asthma-related visits to the emergency room, hospitalization, and death. There has been speculation that increased exposure to asthma triggers, including ETS, outdoor air pollutants, and allergens in indoor air (particularly house dust mites, cockroach particles, animal dander, and mold) may have a role in the racial differences in asthma outcomes. However, the outdoor pollutants that have been associated with asthma—ozone, particulates, and perhaps sulfur dioxide (SO_2)—tend to vary over a relatively large geographic scale. That scale is generally larger than particular communities, or often even counties, where there are racial disparities in population distribution. In New

Jersey, for example, ozone concentrations tend to vary little across the state. Therefore, the observed racial disparities in asthma outcomes are more likely related to racial and socioeconomic differences in access to medical care, patterns of use of medical care, and access to medical follow-up and long-term asthma management.

Adverse outcomes from childhood asthma attacks, and often the attacks themselves, can be avoided by following an asthma management plan developed with the child's physician. An asthma management plan identifies (1) a child's specific triggers for asthma attacks, (2) strategies for avoiding those triggers, (3) methods for monitoring the severity of an attack, and (4) the dose and frequency of medication(s) in the event of an attack and between attacks. The success of an asthma management plan depends upon the commitment level of the child and the parent to following the plan. Education of the parent and child, effective communication with the child's physician, and access to medical care and medications are key.

In some cases, the triggers of a child's asthma attacks are obvious. Triggers such as exercise, cold air, emotional upset, and pet allergy are easily identifiable. Other triggers, such as dust mite allergy, pollen allergy, air pollutants, and food preservatives, may be more difficult to identify. The approach taken to pinpoint asthma triggers depends upon the severity of the child's condition and the preferences of the parent and physician. The least invasive approach for identifying asthma triggers involves keeping a diary of the timing and circumstances of the child's asthma attacks. If food allergy is suspected, a detailed food diary may be kept and/or the child may be put on an "elimination" diet, where suspect foods are eliminated and then slowly reintroduced to the diet one at a time to test the child's reaction.

If multiple triggers are suspected, clinical allergy testing may be desired. Skin tests—scratch tests and intradermal tests—are the most common types of allergy tests used for children. Blood tests are also available. These methods allow multiple substances to be tested at the same time. It should be noted that an allergy test is not an "asthma test." That is, a positive result in an allergy test indicates the presence of an allergy, not what the child's response to that allergy would be. The allergic response may or may not trigger an asthma attack. Provocation, or challenge, tests include direct exposure to suspected allergens under controlled conditions. These tests identify the allergens and the patient's specific response to each allergen. However, this type of test can cause severe allergic reactions and is not commonly administered.

Limiting exposure to asthma triggers is a primary strategy to reduce the frequency and severity of asthma attacks in children. If pollen or high ozone levels are a trigger, the child should be kept indoors when weather reports indicate high outdoor concentrations. If animal dander is a trigger, pets and products containing feathers (such as comforters and pillows) should be removed from the home. If removal of the pet is impossible, the pet should be kept out of the child's room, and the bedroom door should be kept shut. Carpeting and upholstered furniture should be removed from the home or kept isolated from the pet.

Frequent, thorough housecleaning is essential in the homes, particularly the bedrooms, of children sensitive to house dust mites, cockroaches, and/or molds. Minimum control measures for house dust mites include washing sheets, blankets, and comforters weekly in hot water and encasing mattresses and pillows in dust-proof ("allergen-impermeable") zippered covers. A damp mop on a bare wood or linoleum floor is the preferred method for cleaning. However, if carpets are present or if vacuuming is preferred, a high-efficiency vacuum with a high-energy particulate absorption (HEPA) filter should be used. House dust mites may also be controlled by removing stuffed toys from the child's bedroom, removing bedroom carpets, and reducing indoor humidity to less than 50 percent. Keeping indoor humidity levels between 25 and 50 percent should also help to minimize the growth of molds. In damp areas, a dehumidifier may be needed.

To control cockroaches, food and garbage should not be left exposed, and eating should be limited to the kitchen and dining areas. Food storage, preparation, and eating areas should be thoroughly cleaned, especially in areas where food residues might be present. Once potential food sources are limited, poison baits, boric acid, and roach traps are preferred control methods over chemical sprays, which may be irritating to asthmatic children.

Because secondhand tobacco smoke is associated with both the development and aggravation of asthma, children should be provided with a smoke-free environment. At the least, children's sleeping, eating, and playing areas and vehicles should be off limits to tobacco smoke and other irritants, such as strong perfumes and cleaning agents and sprays. Similarly, measures should be taken to avoid exposure of children sensitive to fresh paint, unvented stoves or heaters, and wood-burning stoves or fireplaces.

▪ IMPORTANT POINTS FOR RESEARCHING A STORY ▪

- With proper management, including medication and the care of a physician, an asthmatic child can participate in most, if not all, of the daily activities of his or her peers.
- A diagnosis of asthma (or a missed diagnosis in children with asthma) can have severe impacts on quality of life for the affected child and his or her family. Diagnosis of a child with asthma can cause emotional upset within the family, particularly if the trigger is the beloved family pet or the smoking habits of a parent. Reactions of other family members can range from denial to guilt and even anger directed at the affected child. Along with addressing the trigger(s) and developing an asthma management plan for the child, it is important to consider and respond to the reactions and concerns of other family members.

▪ AVOIDING PITFALLS ▪

- There is no cure for asthma. However, with proper diagnosis and treatment, asthma can be effectively managed. Further, the development of new and more effective medications enable children and adults to have greater control over their asthma.
- Because allergens are a common trigger for asthma, it is a common misconception to equate the two. It is important to note that not all people with asthma are sensitive to allergens. Similarly, not all people with allergies become asthmatic.
- The public holds many misconceptions about allergies and asthma. Some of these misconceptions can be dangerous, giving parents false reassurance in exposing children to potential triggers or discouraging the use of essential medications. For example, inhaled corticosteriods are important tools in the treatment of asthma attacks in adults and children. Many parents hesitate to give these medications to their children, believing that inhaled steroids may affect growth and development. The short-term use of inhaled steroids to treat asthma in children is safe and highly effective.

▪ INFORMATION RESOURCES ▪

■ GOVERNMENT/ACADEMIA

- National Heart, Blood and Lung Institute (www.nhlbi.nih.gov)
  Communications Office
  (301) 496-4236
- U.S Environmental Protection Agency
  (www.epa.gov/children/asthma)
  Office of Children's Health Protection
  1200 Pennsylvania Ave. NW, Mailcode 1107A
  Room 2512, Ariel Rios North, Washington, DC 20460
  (202) 564-2188; fax: (202) 564-2733

■ NONPROFIT/CONSUMER ORGANIZATIONS

- Allergy & Asthmatic Network Mothers of Asthmatics
  (www.aanma.org)
  2751 Prosperity Ave., Suite 150, Fairfax, VA 22031
  (800) 878-4403 or (703) 641-9595; fax: (703) 573-7794
- American Academy of Allergy, Asthma and Immunology
  (www.aaaai.org)
  611 East Wells St., Milwaukee, WI 53202
  (414) 272-6071; fax: (414) 272-6070
  E-mail: onlinemgr@aaaai.org
- American Lung Association (www.lungusa.org/asthma)
  1740 Broadway, New York, NY 10019
  national: (212) 315-8700; press_contact@lungusa.org
  local: (800) 586-4872
- Asthma and Allergy Foundation of America (AAFA)
  (www.aafa.org)
  1233 20th St. NW, Suite 402, Washington, DC 20036
  (800) 727-8462 or (202) 466-7643; fax 202-466-8940
  E-mail: info@aafa.org

CHILDREN'S HEALTH (LEAD)

▪ BACKGROUND ▪

Lead has been called the nation's number one preventable environmental threat to the health of children. As many as one million U.S. children have elevated levels of lead in their blood. At highest risk are minority and low-income children who live in older or dilapidated housing painted with lead-based paint.

Lead is a soft bluish or silvery gray metal. It is an element that does not break down into other substances and is not biodegradable. Once released into the environment, lead accumulates in soil and sediments.

Lead has a long history of use, reaching back at least as far as ancient Rome, when it was used for making water pipes. More recently, lead has been used in gasoline, pipes, solder, paint pigments, ceramic glazes, insecticides, ammunition, and storage batteries. Lead is also used in shields against electricity, X rays, and radioactivity. In particular, the widespread use of lead in gasoline (which was phased out in the 1970s) has made it omnipresent in the environment. Environmental exposure to lead can occur in all areas of the United States—rural and urban.

Lead is highly toxic and can affect all organ systems. Once taken into the body, lead is stored in bones, where it accumulates. At high levels, lead exposure can result in coma, convulsions, and even death. Lead causes damage to the kidneys, liver, and nervous system and can cause anemia. Low-level lead poisoning, while capable of causing developmental and behavioral problems, has no discernable symptoms. The symptoms of moderate or midlevel lead poisoning are nonspecific and may include fatigue, irritability, difficulty concentrating, tremors, headaches, abdominal pain, vomiting, weight loss, constipation, hypertension, and muscle weakness. Because these symptoms are universal,

This brief is based upon information provided by Natalie C. Freeman, Environmental and Occupational Health Sciences Institute (EOHSI), Piscataway, New Jersey, and Dona Schneider, Edward J. Bloustein School of Planning, Rutgers University, New Brunswick, New Jersey.

the symptoms of lead poisoning are often not recognized as such until blood lead levels become dangerously high.

Children are more susceptible than adults to the health effects of lead because their bodies are still developing, their activities bring them into greater potential contact with lead, and their bodies retain more ingested lead than do adult bodies. Lead is more easily absorbed through the gastrointestinal tract in children. Further, in infants and very young children, the immature blood/brain barrier permits the transport of lead to the brain. Children under three years old tend to frequently put their hands and/or toys into their mouths, providing a direct exposure pathway for lead-containing dust, paint chips, or soil.

A small number of children who eat dirt do so because of the presence of a condition known as pica, or the practice of eating dirt. Children at risk for pica include those with poor nutrition or vitamin deficiencies and those living in poverty, as well as those with a family history of pica. The practice can also be related to ethnic customs in cultures where eating soil is practiced (such as in Africa and the southwestern United States). This cultural practice is referred to as geophagy.

The effects of lead poisoning in children vary with the age of the child and the amount of lead to which they are exposed. At low levels, lead is associated with decreased intelligence, reading and learning disabilities, hearing impairment, hyperactivity, and behavioral problems. The neurological effects of childhood lead poisoning are permanent.

■ IDENTIFYING THE ISSUES ■

Lead accumulation in the body is measured through laboratory testing of blood. Blood lead levels are measured in units of micrograms of lead per deciliter of blood (μg/dl). Adverse health effects have been found at lower and lower levels. In 1991, the federal government sharply lowered the threshold level for the amount thought to be safe for lead in blood from 25 μg/dl to 10 μg/dl. Some experts argue that 10 μg/dl is still too high. Recent studies have found subtle impacts on intelligence, as measured by standard IQ tests, in children with blood lead levels lower than 10 μg/dl.

Children may receive their first exposure to lead before they are even born. Lead stored in bones may be released during pregnancy along with calcium into the mother's bloodstream and pass through the placenta to the fetus. The significance of this potential exposure route is not known, as routine blood lead testing of pregnant women and/or neonates is not conducted.

The major source of lead exposure for children is lead paint chips and dust in older homes. Lead in residential paint was banned in 1978. However, an estimated 60 percent of all housing units in the United States contain some lead paint. This figure rises to 80 percent in homes built before the 1978 ban. Children are exposed to lead paint through direct ingestion of paint chips or indirect ingestion of lead-containing house dust by mouthing toys, teething on lead-painted window sills and other surfaces, or putting their fingers and hands into their mouths.

Lead-contaminated dust that can settle throughout the house can come from scraping or sanding old paint from walls, opening and closing of windows and doors painted with lead paint, and weathering of home exteriors painted with lead paint. Adult hobbies—ceramics, jewelry making, oil-based painting, soldering, and stained-glass making—may also contribute to lead-contaminated household dust.

Soil tracked into the home is another source of lead-containing dust. Soil throughout the United States may be contaminated with lead from past automobile exhaust (particularly near major roadways), weathered exterior lead paint, insecticides, and industrial emissions. While lead in gasoline was phased out in the 1970s, it persists in soil.

The risk of lead poisoning from lead paint is greatest among poor, urban children. Data from the Third National Health and Nutrition Examination Survey (NHANES III) show that 16 percent of low-income children living in homes constructed before 1946 have blood lead levels greater than 10 μg/dl. In comparison, 4.4 percent of all U.S. children have blood lead levels above 10 μg/dl.

Drinking water is another potential source of lead exposure to children. Pipes in older homes, schools, and public buildings may contain lead and/or lead solder. Lead leaches from the pipes and solder into standing water within the pipes. Soft water and/or hot water can speed this process.

Other sources of childhood lead exposure include lead paint on older playground equipment, vinyl miniblinds that include lead as a plastic stabilizer, and lead pigments in imported pottery and cookware, plastic food wrappers, and imported children's toys. Contaminated agricultural and garden fertilizers are also potential sources of lead exposure, either by direct contact with soils where they have been applied or by ingesting the food grown on the fertilized area.

Certain types of traditional Mexican folk remedies known as *greta* and *azarcón* contain high levels of lead that can make people who ingest them, especially children, very ill. *Greta* is sometimes used by Hispanic families as a treatment for stomachache or intestinal illness. It is a bright yellow powder that normally contains a very high concentration of lead. The Washington State public health laboratories tested samples of this remedy and found that it contained nearly 80 percent lead. *Azarcón* is a bright orange powder that is also known as *rueda, coral, Maria Luisa, alarcón*, or *liga*. Samples of *azarcón* studied by the Washington State public health laboratories contained 70 percent lead. *Greta* and *azarcón* are usually not available for sale in the United States. Often families bring the folk remedies with them from Mexico.

▪ ADDRESSING THE ISSUES ▪

Overall, blood lead levels in children have dropped significantly during the past few decades. In 1978, approximately 14.8 million children in the United States had blood lead levels higher than the current 10 μg/dl guideline. Today, the number stands at less than 1 million. Much of the decline is attributed to the phase-out of lead from gasoline, paint, and plumbing. However, the legacy of past practices will be with us for decades—old paint, lead in drinking water caused by old pipes and solder that are still in place, and very high levels of lead in dust and soil near roads and highways that are contaminated from past gasoline emissions. These sources continue to provide moderate exposures to large populations of children and adults.

Lead is still discovered in imported products. Imported pottery, candlewicks, crayons, children's backpacks, and even lollipop wrappers have all been found to contain lead during the recent past. The Consumer Product Safety Commission investigates reports of lead in domestic and imported consumer products and conducts special dockside surveillance of imported products that may present a risk for lead poisoning.

Specific lead pollution emitting sites (stationary point sources), such as smelters, continue to affect small, local populations, causing elevated lead levels. It is estimated that approximately 230,000 children live near enough to smelters to be exposed to smelting by-products.

For children with blood lead levels lower than 45 μg/dl, removal of the source of the lead is usually sufficient to lower blood lead concentrations. For highly elevated blood lead levels, chelation may be necessary. Chelation is a medical procedure in which EDTA—a compound to which the lead binds—is intravenously injected into the body. It is then flushed from the blood along with the lead and excreted in urine. Succimer is another chelating agent that is now being used, especially in treating small children. The advantages of succimer are that it can be delivered orally and, unlike EDTA, it is not toxic to the kidneys.

▪ IMPORTANT POINTS FOR RESEARCHING A STORY ▪

- Lead-poisoned children must be removed from the source(s) of exposure. Right now, children are being used as canaries in the mine—to identify sources of lead exposure. Only a small percentage of children known to be at risk are ever tested for lead poisoning.
- Removal of lead contamination is often difficult and can sometimes exacerbate the problem if not done properly. Improper removal of lead-based paint, for example, can result in greater concentrations of lead-containing household dust and significantly greater lead exposures than leaving it undisturbed. Removal of lead-based paint should be conducted by a certified lead abatement contractor in accordance with the Residential Lead-Based Paint Hazard Reduction Act of 1992, also known as Title X of the Housing and Community Development Act of 1992.
- Household dust and lead exposures can be reduced through regular, thorough housecleaning with wet mops and moistened dust cloths; wiping and/or removing shoes before entering the house; and removing carpets that cannot be sufficiently cleaned. Frequent washing of children's toys, pacifiers, bottles, and blankets; enforcing thorough hand-washing before meals; and eating with utensils as opposed to bare hands can also reduce children's exposures to lead-containing soil and dust. Windowsills are another significant source of lead exposure through paint chips and lead dust created in older windows that are opened and shut over and over again. Wiping these areas is important. However, all of these measures are temporary at best and are significantly less effective than lead abatement by a certified contractor.

▪ AVOIDING PITFALLS ▪

- The media and public are typically more interested in sensational environmental risks such as lead present at Superfund sites than in risks such as lead paint. However, with lead (and many other hazards), the individual risk from lead-based paint is much greater and more widespread than the lead emissions from a Superfund site or an incinerator. Certainly both deserve coverage, but the former is often shortchanged.
- While lead in water can be a contributing factor (the body burden is cumulative), it is rarely the controlling factor. More often it is lead paint related, followed by cultural exposures or proximity to smelting and other industrial operations. The source of lead contamination in drinking water is often the plumbing within the home and not the water distribution system, aquifer, or supplier. Using cold water for drinking and cooking and running the cold water for several minutes before using it can reduce exposure to lead from lead pipes and solder.
- It is incorrect to assume that lead poisoning is solely a blighted neighborhood issue. While low to midlevel lead poisoning is positively related with lower income status, there is a growing problem of acute lead poisoning in middle- and upper-income families who buy older homes for renovation or restoration.

▪ INFORMATION RESOURCES ▪

▪ GOVERNMENT/ACADEMIA

Some state health and environmental agencies have their own programs and regulations for lead abatement. Some local health departments offer lead inspections to homeowners.

- Centers for Disease Control and Prevention (CDC) Childhood Lead Poisoning Prevention Program
  (www.cdc.gov/nceh/lead/lead.htm)
  Lead Poisoning Prevention Branch
  Division of Environmental Hazards and Health Effects
  National Center for Environmental Health

1600 Clifton Rd., MS E25, Atlanta, GA 30333
(404) 498-1420; fax: (404) 498-1444

- The National Lead Information Center (www.epa.gov/lead/nlic) (www.hud.gov/lea)
  Office of Pollution Prevention and Toxics
  (800) 424-LEAD
- U.S. Consumer Product Safety Commission (www.cpsc.gov)
  Office of Information and Public Affairs
  4330 East-West Highway, Bethesda, MD 20814-4408
  (301) 504-0580 or (800) 638-2772; fax (301) 504-0862
- U.S. Department of Housing and Urban Development (HUD) (www.hud.gov)
  Office of Lead Hazard Control
  451 Seventh St. SW, P-3206, Washington, DC 20410
  (202) 755-1785

■ INDUSTRY

- National Lead Assessment and Abatement Council (www.nlaac.org)
  P.O. Box 535, Olney, MD 20830
  (800) 590-6522 or (301) 924-0804; fax: (301) 924-0265
- National Lead Service Providers' Listing Service (www.leadlisting.org)
  c/o QuanTech, 1815 Fort Myer Drive, Suite 908, Arlington, VA 22209
  (888) LEADLIST or (703) 312-7837

■ NONPROFIT/CONSUMER ORGANIZATIONS

- Alliance to End Childhood Lead Poisoning (www.aeclp.org)
  227 Massachusetts Ave. NE, Suite 200, Washington, DC 20002
  (202) 543-1147; fax: (202) 543-4466
- Coalition to End Childhood Lead Poisoning (CLEP) (www.leadsafe.org)
  2714 Hudson St., Baltimore, MD 21224
  (800) 370-LEAD (5323) or (410) 534-6447; fax: (o 534-6475
  ceclp@leadsafe.org
- Environmental Defense Scorecard (www.scorecard.org) or (www.environmentaldefense.org)

257 Park Ave. South, New York, NY 10010
(212) 505-2100; fax: (212) 505-2375

- For more information on pica, contact www.eating-disorder.org/pica.

See also:

- Stapleton, Richard M. 1994. *Lead Is a Silent Hazard.* New York: Walker.

CROSS-BORDER ENVIRONMENTAL ISSUES (U.S.-MEXICO)

▪ BACKGROUND ▪

The U.S.-Mexico border region is shared by two countries, ten states, and many counties. Border populations move fairly freely between the two countries. Clearly, people on both sides of the border share the same air and the same drinking water sources, as well as similar infrastructure, poverty, and political issues. Public health must be concerned with issues on both sides of the border because disease does not respect human-made borders.

The U.S.-Mexico border is a unique region of both the United States and Mexico. Spanning more than 2,000 miles, the border both divides and connects four U.S. and six Mexican states. These states are California, Arizona, New Mexico, and Texas in the United States and Baja California, Sonora, Chihuahua, Coahuila, Nuevo Leon, and Tamaulipas in Mexico. Although there are some restrictions on border crossings, the population is quite fluid, moving with relative ease from one side of the border to the other. In 1997, from Mexico into the United States, there were over 208 million legal passenger car crossings, over 3 million commercial truck crossings, and over 45 million pedestrian crossings. This movement of the population back and forth across the border occurs on a daily basis. People living in the border region are interconnected and cross the border in both directions to shop, work, visit family and friends, and obtain medical care.

Border communities have experienced rapid growth over the last twenty years, which has led to an increased, often overwhelming demand on both the physical environment and public services. The populations on both sides of the border are very poor, with nine of the ten poorest U.S. counties located along the border. The U.S. border population is growing three times as fast as the nation's, and the population

This brief was written by Theresa Byrd, Behavioral Sciences and Health Education, University of Texas–Houston, School of Public Health at El Paso.

of Mexico's border municipalities is predicted to double over the next twenty years. Migration to the border from the interior of Mexico accounts for about half of the population growth along the border. Much of this migration may be due to the growth of the *maquiladora* industry. *Maquiladoras* are mostly foreign-owned industrial plants that were developed after the signing of an agreement between Mexico and the United States in 1965 that created the Border Industrialization Program (BIP). The agreement allowed foreign-owned facilities in Mexico to send products back to the United States with reduced tariffs and barriers. Despite a 1972 agreement allowing these plants to operate in the interior of Mexico, most *maquiladoras* are on the U.S.-Mexico border. The majority of *maquiladoras* on the border are concentrated in the cities of Tijuana and Cd. Juarez, where there are over 600 and 300, respectively. Alcoa, Delphi, Automotive Systems, and General Electric are among the companies that have set up thousands of manufacturing plants along the border to take advantage of lucrative tax breaks and cheap labor. These companies import raw materials duty free into Mexico, process them into fully or partially assembled goods, and ship them back into the United States.

This rapidly expanding industrial zone has all of the problems associated with explosive economic growth, including enormous population growth and demands on the existing infrastructure that far outweigh its capabilities. One outcome of this tremendous population growth has been the development of substandard residential subdivisions on both sides of the border. These subdivisions are called *colonias*. They often lack piped-in water, sewerage, garbage collection, and paved roads. Many of these *colonias* are not subject to zoning regulations and may have nonstandard and unsafe electrical wiring, plumbing, and construction. Although there have been some improvements due to programs on both sides of the border, the basic infrastructure does not exist to provide safe drinking water and sewage removal to all residents. These conditions contribute to many health problems in the border region, including higher rates of infectious diseases such as diarrhea, hepatitis A, typhus, cholera, and tuberculosis.

▪ IDENTIFYING THE ISSUES ▪

Water is one of the biggest concerns in the area. Groundwater supplies are being used up rapidly, and fears of an eventual water shortage are very real. Underground aquifers in Cd. Juarez are projected to run out of water in twenty years, and Mexican officials fear U.S. efforts to channel more water from the Colorado River to California will further reduce water supplies in many towns. Often in the *colonias* there is not access to clean drinking water, and the lack of sewage treatment threatens the water that is there. Cd. Juarez, a city of nearly two million residents, has only just begun the development of a major sewage treatment plant. At present, only about 34 percent of the wastewater in Cd. Juarez is treated; the rest often finds its way into the shared drinking water sources of Juarez and El Paso, Texas. Waste water treatment plants set up in Mexciali have been overwhelmed by the enormous growth in population. As a result, they have spilled millions of gallons of raw and partly treated sewage into the New River that flows north into the United States. The U.S. Environmental Protection Agency (EPA) considers the New River to be one of the dirtiest rivers in the country.

One of the major environmental health issues on the U.S.-Mexico border is the lack of adequate infrastructure to provide water, sewerage, and solid waste removal. According to an assessment completed in 1999, 12 percent of the border population did not have access to clean drinking water, 30 percent did not have wastewater treatment facilities serving them, and 25 percent did not have access to solid waste removal and disposal facilities. A 1998 Texas A&M study reported that about 50 percent of the more than 350,000 *colonia* residents in Texas did not have access to clean drinking water.

The need for infrastructure is even greater on the Mexican side of the border, where many large communities lack facilities for clean water, sewerage, and solid waste disposal. Lack of funding due to the extreme poverty of the region and the resulting low tax base is one explanation for the poor infrastructure. In addition, there is a lack of reinvestment in border communities by U.S. industries.

Air quality is another concern. Residents in many border cities are exposed to air pollutants from a variety of sources, including emissions from trucks and other vehicles, dust from unpaved roads, open burning, fireplaces, wood-burning stoves, and industrial activity. According to the EPA, there were fourteen border cities that exceeded at least one of the air quality standards set by the federal government in 1999.

Hazardous waste disposal has also become an issue along the border. In Mexico, much hazardous waste is generated by the *maquiladora* industry. Although hazardous materials are supposed to be returned to their country of origin for disposal, there is evidence that some wastes are left in Mexico by U.S. industries and not disposed of properly. There have been cases of children finding and playing with toxic substances left by *maquiladora* plants in the *colonias* in Mexico. The Mexican National Institute of Ecology in 1997 estimated that only 2 percent of hazardous waste generated in Mexican border states was returned to the United States. Mexico itself has a lack of waste disposal sites located in the border areas. Because the government is centralized and all tax revenues are sent to Mexico City and distributed throughout the country, funds raised in the border region may not be used to build infrastructure there.

■ ADDRESSING THE ISSUES ■

Several initiatives have been developed to address the environmental health issues on the border. These include the Border Health Commission (BHC), the Border Environmental Cooperation Commission (BECC), the North American Development (NAD) Bank, the Border XXI Initiative, and various local initiatives.

In 1994, the United States–Mexico Border Health Commission Act became Public Law 103-400. From this legislation, an agreement was made with Mexico to establish the BHC. One goal of the commission is to provide a venue for discussion of U.S.-Mexico border health issues, including environmental health concerns.

The BECC was developed in 1993 under the North American Free Trade Agreement (NAFTA). The commission's primary function is to make sure that proposals submitted by border communities for environmental infrastructure projects are technically sound and financially feasible. Projects are also expected to be self-sustaining and supported by the public. The BECC provides technical assistance to border states in the development, implementation, and oversight of environmental projects related to water, wastewater, and solid waste disposal. The United States and Mexico provide money to cover the operating expenses of the BECC.

The NAD Bank was also developed in 1993 under NAFTA. The purpose of the bank is to facilitate financing for environmental infrastructure projects. Only projects that have been certified by the BECC are eligible for assistance. The bank makes loans, loan guarantees, and grants. The United States and Mexico contribute equally to the bank.

Many communities, especially small ones, have not been able to get funding through the NAD Bank, in part because the interests rates are too high. To date, most of the bank's participation in projects has come in the form of grants from the EPA.

The Border XXI Initiative, led by the EPA and the Secretaria de Medio Ambiente, Recursos Naturales, y Pesca (SEMARNAP), was initiated in 1995. The program involves both federal and state agencies. The goals of the program are to clean up the environment, protect public health, manage natural resources, and encourage sustainable development within the border area. The Border XXI Initiative has provided a means of dialogue but does not provide resources to solve problems that are discussed.

▪ IMPORTANT POINTS FOR RESEARCHING A STORY ▪

- It is important to talk to people on all sides of the issue. There are seldom only two viewpoints on the U.S.-Mexico border. Not only will there be several U.S. points of view, there will also be several in Mexico. For example, the *maquiladoras* provide Mexico with millions of jobs and make large annual contributions to their local governments to help pay for projects to improve local infrastructure. However, local officials and managers of the *maquiladoras* disagree over whether contributions by the *maquiladoras* equal the wealth being generated. Remember that health issues on one side of the border will eventually become health issues on the other. The border does not stop disease.

▪ AVOIDING PITFALLS ▪

- Environmental health issues on the U.S.-Mexico border can be quite politically charged. You may find people on both sides of the border willing to blame the other country for every problem (sometimes they are right), and this often leads to an impasse.
- Some environmental issues have become issues of outrage for communities, as they have tried to make changes and have been unsuccessful because of lack of resources and lack of interest from agencies. This outrage may make the actual health risk seem much greater than it is. The question of environmental justice is a real is-

sue for residents of border communities and should be addressed. (See the brief on "Environmental Justice and Hazardous Waste.")

▪ INFORMATION RESOURCES ▪

▪ GOVERNMENT/ACADEMIA

- North American Development Bank (www.nadbank.org/)
- U.S. Environmental Protection Agency, Border XXI Initiative (www.epa.gov/usmexicoborder/index)
- U.S.-Mexico Border Health Commission (www.borderhealth.gov/)

▪ NONPROFIT/CONSUMER ORGANIZATIONS

- Border Information and Outreach Service (www.us-mex.org/)
- Pan American Health Organization links to border health issues (www.paho.org)
- Texas Natural Resource Conservation Commission (www.tnrcc.state.tx.us/exec/ba/)

See also:

- General Accounting Office. 1999. *U.S.-Mexico Border: Issues and Challenges Confronting the United States and Mexico*. Report by the National Security and International Affairs Division. GAO/NSIAD-99-190.
- General Accounting Office. 2000. *U.S.-Mexico Border: Despite Some Progress, Environmental Infrastructure Challenges Remain.* Report by the National Security and International Affairs Division. GAO/NSIAD-00-26.
- Loustaunau, M. O., and M. Sanchez-Bane, eds. 1999. *Life, Death and In-Between on the U.S.-Mexico Border: Asi es La Vida*. Westport, Conn.: Bergin and Garvey.
- Power, J. G., and T. L. Byrd, eds. 1998. *U.S.-Mexico Border Health: Issues for Regional and Migrant Populations*. Thousand Oaks, Calif.: Sage Publications.
- Schmidt, C. W. 2000. Bordering on environmental disaster. *Environmental Health Perspectives* 108, no.7. (www.ehpnet1.niehs.nih.gov/members/2000/108-7focus)

DIOXIN

▪ BACKGROUND ▪

Dioxin has been called the most toxic chemical known to humans. While that characterization continues to be debated among the scientific community, it is safe to say that dioxin is the most politically contentious substance in recent history. In the 1970s, dioxin was linked to the herbicide Agent Orange and a host of adverse health effects among U.S. troops. In the 1980s, dioxin contamination resulted in the abandonment of Times Beach, Missouri. Most recently, the international community has called for the worldwide elimination of dioxin and other persistent organic pollutants (POPs).

Dioxin is an umbrella name for a class of chemical compounds that contain carbon, hydrogen, oxygen, and chlorine. Dioxins are part of the larger class of compounds known as polycyclic halogenated aromatics.

Dioxin is an unavoidable by-product of a variety of natural and synthetic processes. It is inadvertently formed in industrial processes involving the use of chlorine, including bleaching of paper and the production of certain chemical herbicides. Dioxin can also be released into the air when wood, coal, oil, or solid waste is burned. Low levels of dioxin are also emitted in cigarette smoke.

Dioxin is highly stable and insoluble in water. It adheres to clay and soot and dissolves in oil and organic solvents. Once released into the environment, dioxin remains for many years and is included in the group of chemicals known as POPs. POPs are chemicals that remain chemically unchanged in the environment for long periods of time. These chemicals become widely distributed throughout a region, or even across the globe, traveling long distances in air and water currents. POPs accumulate within the fatty tissue of living organisms and are toxic to humans and wildlife.

When dioxin is released into the atmosphere, it may be transported long distances and has been found in remote parts of the world. When released into water, dioxin concentrates in sediments, fish, and other aquatic organisms. Dioxin biomagnifies in animal food chains, including aquatic food chains. This means that increasingly higher concentrations of dioxin are found in the tissues of animals higher up in the food chain.

The toxicity of dioxin depends upon the species of animal exposed, the specific type of dioxin involved, and the route and duration of exposure. The most familiar form of dioxin is 2,3,7,8-tetrachlorodibenzo-p-dioxin, also known as 2,3,7,8-TCDD or simply TCDD. TCDD is extremely toxic. Scientists frequently discuss the toxicity of dioxin or mixtures of dioxins in toxic equivalents (TEQs) or by using toxic equivalence factors (TEFs), which describe their toxicity relative to the toxicity of TCDD.

The most well documented health effect from dioxin is chloracne, a severe skin disease with characteristic lesions on the face and upper body. Chloracne occurs after exposure to high concentrations of dioxin. Exposure to high levels of dioxin is also associated with skin rashes and discoloration, excessive growth of body hair, and liver damage. Based upon occupational studies, the World Health Organization's International Agency for Research on Cancer (IARC) has classified TCDD as a Group 1 carcinogen—having "sufficient evidence of carcinogenicity in humans."

Animal studies have demonstrated a wide range of effects of TCDD exposure at the biochemical, cellular, and organ levels. Some of these effects may be beneficial or adaptive (having little or no measurable negative impact), while others are clearly adverse. Effects with questionable significance include changes in enzyme activity and hormone levels. Adverse effects observed in animal studies include impacts on immune function, developmental delays, endometriosis, and impaired reproductive function.

▪ IDENTIFYING THE ISSUES ▪

Occupational health incidents involving dioxin have been recorded as early as the 1930s. However, dioxin first became the subject of public health debate as a result of the U.S. military involvement in Vietnam in the late 1960s. Agent Orange was used in Vietnam as a defoliant, and one of its chemical components, 2,4,5-trichlorophenoxyacetic acid (2,4,5-T), was contaminated with dioxin during manufacture. Veterans who were exposed to Agent Orange during the Vietnam War have experienced a variety of health problems that may be related to dioxin exposure, including chloracne, cancers, neurological damage, decreased fertility, and liver disorders.

The Veterans Administration (VA) provides benefits for a "presumptive list" of ten diseases that may be associated with dioxin exposure. The VA presumes that all personnel who served in Vietnam and have one of the listed diseases were exposed to Agent Orange and are therefore eligible for benefits. The following diseases are on the VA's Agent Orange list: chloracne, Hodgkin's disease, multiple myeloma, non-Hodgkin's lymphoma, porphyria cutanea tarda, respiratory cancers (lung, bronchus, larynx, and trachea), soft-tissue sarcoma, acute and subacute peripheral neuropathy, and prostate cancer. In addition to these diseases, benefits are provided to children of Vietnam veterans who have spina bifida, a congenital birth defect of the spine. In December 2001, the VA added adult-onset (Type 2) diabetes to the presumptive list of diseases.

As noted, dioxin is not intentionally manufactured. It is an unavoidable by-product of a number of chemical processes involving chlorine. For example, dioxin is formed during the bleaching of paper pulp with elemental chlorine. It has been a major issue for the paper industry. Some of the dioxin is released into the waste stream, while small amounts remain in the bleached paper products. Dioxin that is not removed from the waste stream during treatment is released into the environment in wastewater effluent. Fish with elevated levels of dioxin have been found downstream of paper pulp mills. Dioxin remaining in bleached paper products is a concern, particularly if those products are used in paper and cardboard food containers.

Dioxin is formed by the burning of plastic and organic materials and is often an issue in disputes over waste incineration projects. Concern centers on exposure to air emissions and ash that result from the burning of municipal or industrial waste. However, the major source of dioxin emissions today is thought to be uncontrolled burning of household trash by individuals.

The discovery of dioxin at a contaminated site is a lightning rod for public concern and political debate. Dioxin contamination has resulted in a number of government buyouts of contaminated residential areas, including the relocation of the entire town of Times Beach, Missouri, in 1983 and 358 families in Pensacola, Florida, in 1997. Public debate continues as to whether these relocations were motivated by public health or political concerns.

The U.S. Environmental Protection Agency (EPA) estimates that more than 95 percent of human exposure to dioxin occurs through food sources, particularly through consumption of animal fats where concentrated amounts of dioxin are found. In the late 1990s, there were several incidents where elevated dioxin levels in beef and chicken were traced back to contaminated feed products. Elevated dietary exposures to dioxin are a concern for persons with limited diets, such as subsistence fishermen and women and their families, and for babies and nursing infants. Because dioxin concentrates in fatty tissue, virtually all adults have some level of dioxin in their bodies. Dioxin from maternal fat stores is passed to babies in utero and through their mothers' milk. While meat and dairy products are the major sources of exposure for the general population, for individuals and populations who are heavy fish consumers, fish (and shellfish) may be a significantly greater source of dioxin exposure. This is particularly the case for consumers of fish and shellfish from areas with contaminated industrial sediments.

▪ ADDRESSING THE ISSUES ▪

The EPA reports that industrial dioxin emissions have fallen by almost 90 percent since 1980. One major change involved the paper industry, which largely shifted from using elemental chlorine as a bleaching agent to using chlorine dioxide, dramatically reducing the generation of dioxin. However, because of dioxin's persistence in the environment and continued presence in consumer and waste products, human and environmental exposures to dioxin continue to be a concern.

The United Nations Stockholm Convention on Persistent Organic Pollutants held in May 2001 calls for the elimination of twelve persistent organic chemicals, including dioxin. Intentionally produced POPs are slated for elimination as soon as the treaty is ratified. Elimination of dioxin and POPs produced as unintentional by-products is a long-term goal of the treaty, to be achieved through improvements in technology and environmental practices.

At present, there is no simple or inexpensive way to destroy dioxin-contaminated soil or waste. Disposal largely consists of physical containment or high-heat incineration. On-site incineration followed by on-site containment has been used to treat dioxin contamination at Times Beach and at a number of the EPA Superfund sites.

■ IMPORTANT POINTS FOR RESEARCHING A STORY ■

- There are more than a hundred different chemicals that fall under the umbrella of "dioxins," and their toxicities vary. Determine if tests have been done to identify the specific type of dioxin involved in the situation.
- Dioxins are typically not the only contaminant involved in a situation. Determine what other chemicals are present and what their properties are. Although dioxin may be the most toxic compound at a site, it may not be the most mobile. For example, water-soluble chemicals may travel faster to residential areas and be a more immediate concern for exposure.
- The toxicity of dioxin depends upon its bioavailability—whether plants and animals, including humans, can absorb the chemical from the environment. Laboratory tests are designed to extract virtually all of the chemical from the soil being tested. However, in the environment, the chemical may be so tightly bound to the soil that living systems and natural processes cannot remove it. In such cases, the dioxin would not be bioavailable and therefore would pose little threat. The bioavailability of dioxin and other pollutants depends upon its specific chemical form, the soil type, the method in which it was deposited, and the presence or absence of other contaminants.
- In 2001, the EPA amended SARA 313 rules (which require companies to submit a Toxic Chemical Release Inventory Form [Form R] for specified chemicals) in two areas to include PBT chemicals (persistent, bioaccumulative, and toxic chemicals substances and chemical categories), one of which is dioxin. The EPA says anyone burning oil or other fuels in large quantities can produce dioxin. This is based on measurements taken at large utilities companies. Since no one measures dioxin, it is most likely not present. The EPA, however, says companies must use these factors anyway. Therefore, dioxin may show up in SARA 313 reports.

■ AVOIDING PITFALLS ■

- Always be specific about which chemical compound is involved in a situation. While 2,3,7,8-TCDD is the most toxic of the dioxin compounds, it is typically found in much lower concentrations than other forms.

- Dioxins are not manufactured products; they are by-products of the manufacture of other compounds or of other processes. Dioxins are not produced intentionally.
- Dioxin has been referred to as the most toxic substance known to humans. This statement requires clarification. TCDD is the most toxic *synthetic* substance known in its effects on some test animals. The bacterial toxin that produces botulism, for example, is more acutely toxic to humans than is TCDD. Furthermore, the phrase "highly toxic" does not necessarily mean the effect is extremely bad but rather that the amount of exposure needed to produce the effect is extremely small.
- Agent Orange was contaminated with the dioxin TCDD. "Agent Orange" is not a synonym for dioxin or TCDD.

▪ INFORMATION RESOURCES ▪

▪ GOVERNMENT/ACADEMIA

- Agency for Toxic Substances and Disease Registry (ATSDR): Toxicological Profile for Chlorinated Dibenzo-p-dioxins (CDDs) (http://www.atsdr1.atsdr.cdc.gov/toxprofiles/tp104.html)
  Division of Toxicology
  1600 Clifton Rd. NE, MS E-29, Atlanta, GA 30333
  (888) 422-8737; fax: (404) 498-0057
- United Nations Environment Program—Chemicals—Persistent Organic Pollutants (POPs)(www.chem.unep.ch/pops/)
  Director's Office, UNEP Chemicals
  11-13 Chemin des Anemones,
  CH-1219 Chatelaine,
  Geneva, Switzerland
  (+41 22) 917 8183; fax: (+41 22) 797 34 60
  E-mail: pops@unep.ch
- U.S. Environmental Protection Agency—National Center for Environmental Assessment
  Dioxin and Related Compounds (www.epa.gov/ncea/dioxin.htm)
  1200 Pennsylvania Ave. NW, Washington, DC 20460

■ INDUSTRY

- Chlorine Chemistry Council (www.c3.org)
  1300 Wilson Blvd., Arlington, VA 22209
  (703) 741-5000
- International Paper (www.internationalpaper.com/media_hub)
  400 Atlantic St., Stamford, CT 06921
  Media Relations Manager
  (203) 541-8407; fax: (901) 763-7500
  Info Hotline (800) 223-1268 or (914) 941-5145

■ NONPROFIT/CONSUMER ORGANIZATIONS

- Center for Health, Environment and Justice (www.chej.org)
  P.O. Box 6806, Falls Church, VA 22040
  (703) 237-2249; fax: (703) 237-8389
  E-mail: chej@chej.org
- International POPs Elimination Network (IPEN) (www.ipen.org)
  Karen Perry, Physicians for Social Responsibility/IPEN Secretariat
  +1.202.898.0150 (x. 249)
  (202) 667-4260 (x. 249)
  E-mail: kperry@psr.org
- Natural Resources Defense Council (www.nrdc.org/media)
  40 West 20th St., New York, NY 10011
  (212) 727-2700; fax: (212) 727-1773
  E-mail: nrdcinfo@nrdc.org

DISPOSAL OF DREDGED MATERIALS

▪ BACKGROUND ▪

Natural processes such as erosion, sedimentation, and tidal forces constantly deposit sediments (e.g., rock, gravel, sand, silt, and clay) along the bottoms of rivers, channels, and estuaries. These sediments must be excavated, or dredged, to maintain and improve shipping channels, ports, and harbors for commercial, military, and recreational use. Each year in the United States, several hundred million cubic yards of sediment are dredged for these purposes.

One of the most pressing issues facing dredging projects is what to do with the dredged material. In the past, dredged sediments were discharged into adjacent waters, ocean disposal sites, or upland landfills. The vast majority of designated disposal sites for dredged materials in the United States are closed or approaching their capacity to accept additional material. Identification of appropriate disposal sites is often complicated by environmental issues.

▪ IDENTIFYING THE ISSUES ▪

Due to a long history of industrial discharges to waterways, the sediments of many water bodies are contaminated. (See the brief on "Surface Water Quality.") Sometimes the source of the contamination is local and can be identified. In these instances, the dredging may be part of an environmental remediation project. However, in many cases sediment contamination is the cumulative effect of myriad upstream discharges, past and present.

Sediments can be a reservoir, or sink, for chemicals that are hydrophobic. Hydrophobic chemicals are chemicals that have little or no affinity for water, low solubility in water, high solubility in lipids (fats), and a strong tendency to adhere to organic material in soil and sediment. As such, sediments can contain high concentrations of chemicals not detectable in the waters above them. Sediments may contain a variety of contaminants including nutrients (e.g., phosphate, nitrate, ammonia), heavy metals (e.g., arsenic, cadmium, lead, mercury), organic compounds (e.g., PCBs, dioxins, pesticides, petroleum hydrocarbons, polynuclear aromatic hydrocarbons), radioisotopes, and microorganisms.

Disposal options for dredged sediments are limited. Disposal options for contaminated dredged sediments are even fewer. Contaminated sediments may require expensive treatment before disposal. Highly contaminated sediments may require specialized handling, treatment, and disposal as hazardous waste in a designated facility.

Further contamination is also a concern during dredging operations. During excavation and disposal, sediments are disturbed, with some particles becoming resuspended in the water column. Suspended particles can be carried farther downstream, spreading the contamination, or they may be taken up by fish and other aquatic organisms. However, methods can be used (e.g., silt curtains or environmental buckets) that reduce or minimize the sediment "plume" during dredging. The same physical and chemical properties that make certain contaminants bind to sediments make them likely to bioconcentrate, or bioaccumulate, within the tissues of organisms exposed to them. Contaminants taken up and accumulated within fish pose health risks not only to the fish but also to the birds, animals, and people that eat them.

Sediment contamination is often a catch-22 situation. Dredging contaminated sediments may be controversial and expensive due to the exposure and disposal issues that must be addressed. However, leaving the sediments in place may not be an option. Sediments can be a continuing source of contamination within the water body, with contaminants being released at low levels almost continuously or at high levels during disturbances, such as storms. If sediment contamination affects aquatic life, regional fisheries may be placed at risk. Fisheries have been forced to close due to contamination and uptake by fish, at great economic loss to regional economies. Restrictions on navigation can result in huge economic losses, with the sediments posing a physical barrier to trade ships.

Dredging operations disrupt bottom-dwelling organisms within the water body. Some bottom-dwelling communities may reestablish themselves, but dredging can permanently alter local conditions and aquatic communities within the water body. Such effects may be most significant in estuaries, where deeper channels created by dredging may bring saltwater into the estuary. Increased salinity can adversely impact the estuary, nearby freshwater wetlands, and the vegetation, fish, and wildlife communities that inhabit them. Increased salinity in estuarine and wetland areas can also lead to saltwater intrusion into local surface and groundwater sources of drinking water.

Other issues associated with dredging operations include: the transportation of contaminated or possibly hazardous sediments, the noise and disruption associated with large dredging operations, and impacts on tourism during the operations.

■ ADDRESSING THE ISSUES ■

The handling and disposal of dredged sediments are highly controversial and highly regulated. The U.S. Army Corps of Engineers estimates dredged material disposal is governed by more than thirty environmental statutes, regulations, and executive orders. At the international level, the London Convention of 1972 governs ocean disposal of dredged materials. The major U.S. statutes covering disposal of dredged materials are the Marine Protection, Research and Sanctuaries Act of 1972, often referred to as the Ocean Dumping Act; the Federal Water Pollution Control Act Amendments of 1972 (the Clean Water Act, or CWA); and the National Environmental Protection Act. Permits for the disposal of dredged materials are issued by the Army Corps of Engineers, with oversight by the U.S. Environmental Protection Agency (EPA).

Because of the limited disposal space for dredged sediments, the current focus is on beneficial use of the material. Dredged material has a history of use as fill material to build or expand land for seaports, airports, and other commercial development. The range of accepted uses of dredged material has grown to include the capping of ocean disposal areas, shore protection, land improvement for flood control, the creation of habitat for fish and birds, restoration of wetlands, and use as topsoil and construction material.

■ IMPORTANT POINTS FOR RESEARCHING A STORY ■

- The chemical compounds of concern for dredging projects vary. Sediment contaminants are the result of (1) historical discharges and spills and (2) local and regional conditions and water chemistry. Environmental evaluation of sediments begins with a review of existing physical and chemical data for regional sediments, as well as a review of regional activities as possible sources of contamination.

- In order to be approved for ocean disposal, contaminated sediments must undergo a battery of biological tests (bioassays) to assess their potential risk to marine organisms. These tests are designed to identify contaminated sediments that would result in toxicity or bioaccumulation in exposed organisms. Bioassays are expensive and time consuming and may provide equivocal results. Opponents of ocean disposal criticize bioassays as unrepresentative of actual conditions at ocean disposal sites.

■ AVOIDING PITFALLS ■

- Offshore dredging for beach restoration or "nourishment" is highly controversial. Proponents argue that beach restoration is necessary to maintain local tourism and protect coastal housing. Critics argue that offshore dredging for beach restoration actually accelerates the erosion process by changing the dynamics of tidal and shoreline water and sediment flow.

■ INFORMATION RESOURCES ■

■ GOVERNMENT/ACADEMIA

- International Maritime Organization
  (www.londonconvention.org)
  4 Albert Embankment, London SE1 7SR, UK
  +44 (0)20 7735 7611; fax: +44(0)20 7587 3210
- National Dredging Team (www.epa.gov/owow/oceans/ndt)
- U.S. Army Corps of Engineers (www.hq.usace.army.mil/cepa)
  441 G St. NW, Washington, DC 20314
  (202) 761-0008
- U.S. Environmental Protection Agency, Office of Federal Activities
  (http://es.epa.gov/oeca/ofa/pollprev/dredge.html)
- U.S. Environmental Protection Agency, Office of Water, Oceans and Coastal Protection Division
  (www.epa.gov/owow/oceans/dmmp)

Office of Water (4101M)
1200 Pennsylvania Ave. NW, Washington, DC 20460

■ INDUSTRY/PROFESSIONAL ASSOCIATIONS

- General Electric/Hudsonvoice (www.hudsonvoice.org)
  (203) 373-2039
- The Port Authority of New York and New Jersey
  (www.panynj.gov)
  (212) 435-7777 (media inquiries only)
- Western Dredging Association (www.woda.org)
  WEDA Executive Office
  P.O. Box 5797, Vancouver, WA 98668-5797
  (360) 750-0209; fax: (360) 750-1445
  E-mail: weda@juno.com

■ NONPROFIT/CONSUMER ORGANIZATIONS

- CEASE (www.nodredging.com)
  P.O. Box 388, Hudson Falls, NY 12839
  (518) 791-2327
- Clean Ocean Action (www.cleanoceanaction.org)
  P.O. Box 505, Highlands, NJ 07732-0505
  (732) 872-0111; fax: (732) 872-8041
  E-mail: SandyHook@CleanOceanAction.org
- Coast Alliance (www.coastalliance.org)
  600 Pennsylvania Ave. SE, Suite 340, Washington, DC 20003
  (202) 546-9554
- Hudson River Foundation (www.hudsonriver.org)
  40 West 20th St., 9th Floor, New York, NY 10011
  (212) 924-8290; fax: (212) 924-8325
  E-mail: Info@hudsonriver.org

ENDOCRINE DISRUPTERS

▪ BACKGROUND ▪

The endocrine system regulates many of the body's functions, including growth, development, reproduction, metabolism, and digestion. The endocrine system is made up of glands (including the adrenal gland, pancreas, pituitary gland, thyroid, ovaries, and testes), hormones that are secreted by the glands, and receptors located in tissues and organs that recognize and respond to the hormones. When released at critical times, hormones trigger vital developmental milestones, such as the onset of puberty.

An endocrine disrupter, also called a hormonally active agent, is a chemical that interferes with the functioning of the endocrine system. Endocrine disruption can occur in several ways. The chemical may bind to a hormone receptor in place of the natural hormone. In this case, the chemical may mimic the action of the hormone and trigger a response in the receptor at the wrong time. Conversely, endocrine disrupters may block a hormonal response entirely. They can also overstimulate or block hormone production, or they can interfere with the natural breakdown of hormones by the body.

Well-known examples of endocrine disruption include the drug diethylstilbestrol (DES) and the chemical pesticide dichlorodiphenyl trichloroethane (DDT). DES was a synthetic estrogen prescribed to many women from the 1940s through 1971 to prevent miscarriage and promote fetal growth. Years later, DES was linked to reproductive abnormalities and vaginal cancer in adolescents and adults whose mothers had taken the drug during pregnancy. The pesticide DDT was widely used in the United States on crops and to control insects that carry malaria and similar diseases. It is still used and recommended for use in Third World countries for malaria control. Rachel Carson's 1962 book, *Silent Spring*, first reported on how DDT accumulated in the food chain, causing cancer, genetic damage, and reproductive dysfunction among exposed species. Birds exposed to DDT laid eggs with weak, thin shells that were easily broken, resulting in significant decreases in their population. In 1972, DDT was the first pesticide to be banned by the U.S. Environmental Protection Agency (EPA).

▪ IDENTIFYING THE ISSUES ▪

The ranges of normal hormone levels in the body vary widely, with some hormones operating at extremely low concentrations—in the parts-per-billion or parts-per-trillion range. Because even minor hormonal imbalances can result in significant adverse health effects, scientists are evaluating the endocrine activity of synthetic chemicals in the environment, even those that are released in small amounts. However, because of the difficulty in studying endocrine activity, the scientific evidence is still out. This is a future issue.

Chemicals known or suspected to act as endocrine disrupters include the drug DES, dioxins, polychlorinated biphenyls (PCBs), and organochlorine pesticides including DDT, aldrin, dieldrin, endrin, kepone, toxaphene, and 2,4,5-T. The EPA has already banned these particular chemicals in the United States. The international treaty on persistent organic pollutants (POPs) is addressing the continued use of some of these chemicals in other parts of the world. (See the brief on "Dioxins.") Other than DES, these chemicals are of particular concern because they accumulate in animal fat and are passed on to predators, including humans, who eat them. Chemicals that accumulate in the fat are passed along to offspring in the womb and through the mother's milk.

Because of the high level of interest in endocrine modulation, a large number of screening tests have been proposed, and even though none have been fully validated, these tests are now being widely used. Largely on the basis of such tests, many substances are now alleged to be endocrine modulators, including materials made by humans, such as insecticides, herbicides, fumigants, fungicides, detergents, resins, and plasticizers.

There are also naturally occurring substances with endocrine-modulating potential, such as phytoestrogens found in moderate to substantial amounts in plants including soya, beans, grains, vegetables, and fruit. In addition, there are pharmaceutical agents that are intentionally used because they have endocrine-modulating properties; the best known and most commonly used are oral contraceptives. What is not known is whether exposures to any of these substances, other than the pharmaceutical agents, at the low levels in which they are normally encountered have any impact on humans or the environment.

Accidental releases of endocrine-disrupting chemicals have had devastating effects on wildlife populations. For example, alligator populations living in Lake Apopka, Florida, declined after an accidental spill of DDT, dichlorodiphenyl dichloroethylene (DDE), and related compounds. Among other effects, the male alligators were found to be feminized—they had smaller than normal reproductive organs, higher estrogen levels, and lower testosterone levels.

Some scientists and environmentalists believe that one group of endocrine-disrupting chemicals—environmental estrogens (from external factors)—is responsible for a number of negative health trends in humans including declining male sperm counts, increased incidence of birth defects, increased incidence of breast and reproductive cancers, and declines in fertility. These trends have neither been confirmed nor conclusively linked to any environmental chemical exposure, nor are they likely to be.

There are many difficulties in studying the endocrine activity of environmental chemicals. First, there are the inherent limitations of extrapolating data (or applying the results) from animal studies to humans. Studies need to be conducted at artificially high doses in order to see a statistically significant response in a small population of study animals. Extrapolation of the results of these studies to extremely low level environmental exposures in humans leaves many uncertainties. In addition, there is the question of the exposure period of the study—a chemical may cause endocrine disruption at a very specific point during an animal's development. If the study does not include the critical developmental point in the animal's life cycle, the effect will be missed. Finally, humans are exposed to a wide range of chemicals in the environment, including many that are suspected endocrine disrupters. These chemicals may interact in the body, and their effects may be additive, synergistic (i.e., the effects of exposure to one chemical may be increased in the presence of another chemical), or antagonistic (i.e., the effects of exposure to one chemical may protect against the effects of another). The effects of endocrine disrupters could also be sequential (i.e., exposure to one chemical may sensitize an individual to the effects of subsequent chemical exposure). Animal studies that focus on exposure to a single chemical cannot account for any of these possible interactions.

▪ ADDRESSING THE ISSUES ▪

Individuals can limit their exposure to potential endocrine disrupters in a number of ways. The use of chemical pesticides and herbicides around the home can be limited or eliminated. Individuals can reduce their consumption of animal fats, trim excess fat from meat and poultry, and purchase organic produce. Those who fish for subsistence or sport should check with state and local authorities to ensure that waters they are fishing in are safe for eating their catch. Farmers can reduce or eliminate their use of agricultural chemicals by using integrated pest management techniques. Homeowners with shallow drinking water wells can test for the presence of potential endocrine disrupters that are currently regulated in drinking water or for pesticides that are used in the surrounding area.

The EPA has established an Endocrine Disrupters Screening Program (EDSP) to address the potential endocrine activity of pesticides and other industrial and environmental chemicals. The EPA is using a tiered approach to sort chemicals for testing based upon scientific evidence of possible endocrine activity. Organochlorine pesticides in the same family as DDT are to be among the first compounds evaluated for endocrine activity under the EDSP.

However, before the EPA can begin testing chemicals for endocrine activity, test methods must be scientifically validated. Currently, there are no approved laboratory methods for determining possible human endocrine disruption. The EPA is working to develop laboratory protocols and will then need to assess their effectiveness and reliability in different laboratories. For these reasons, the EPA does not anticipate that chemical screening under the EDSP will begin until 2003 at the earliest.

▪ IMPORTANT POINTS FOR RESEARCHING A STORY ▪

- Scientists, activists, and regulators use a number of terms to refer to chemicals with potential endocrine activity. The term "environmental estrogen" (estrogen linked to external factors) refers to chemicals that mimic the effect of hormones that control female characteristics (estrogens). Anti-estrogens are chemicals that block or cancel out the effects of estrogens. Anti-androgens block or cancel out the effects of male hormones. "Endocrine disrupters," "endocrine modulators," and "hormonally active agents" all refer to chemicals that have potential to alter the function of the body's natural endocrine system.

- Few studies have conclusively linked environmental estrogens, with the exception of the drug DES, or other endocrine disrupters with adverse health effects in humans. This does not mean that health effects are rare or have not occurred. It simply means that any widespread effects on human populations from endocrine disrupters in the environment have not been dramatic enough to be visibly noticed or measured.

▪ AVOIDING PITFALLS ▪

- Industry may argue that a specific chemical or group of chemicals has undergone extensive toxicity testing in the past. However, in the past, conventional toxicological tests were not specifically designed to evaluate potential endocrine activity, although some may have assessed effects that are the consequence of endocrine disruption. For example, endocrine disruption may occur at a stage in the life cycle that is outside the normal span of most toxicity tests. Some companies are now beginning to use some of the tests proposed for endocrine disruption assessment. However, additional testing may be required to fully characterize the potential for endocrine modulation.
- Much of the scientific data on endocrine disrupters are new, and the field is rapidly evolving. For many chemicals with suspected endocrine activity, there are no definitive data to link exposure to outcome, nor is there a well-understood mechanism of action. However, this lack of data does not mean that the chemical is not hormonally active or that the suspected effect is unimportant. The lack of data simply underscores the need for more research.

▪ INFORMATION RESOURCES ▪

▪ GOVERNMENT/ACADEMIA

- Tulane and Xavier Universities, Environmental Concepts Made Easy (www.som.tulane.edu/ecme/eehome)

Center for Bioenvironmental Research (CBR) at Tulane and Xavier Universities
1430 Tulane Ave., SL-3, New Orleans, LA 70112
(504) 585-6910

- U.S. Environmental Protection Agency Endocrine Disrupters Screening Program
(http://www.epa.gov/scipoly/oscpendo/)

▪ INDUSTRY/PROFESSIONAL ASSOCIATIONS

- American Chemistry Council (www.americanchemistry.com)
1300 Wilson Blvd., Arlington, VA 22209
(703) 741-5000; fax: (703) 741-6000.
- Chlorine Chemistry Council (www.c3.org)
1300 Wilson Blvd., Arlington, VA 22209
(703) 741-5000

▪ NONPROFIT/CONSUMER ORGANIZATIONS

- International POPs Elimination Network (IPEN) (www.ipen.org)
Karen Perry, Physicians for Social Responsibility/IPEN Secretariat
+1.202.898.0150 (x. 249)
(202) 667-4260 (x. 249)
E-mail: kperry@psr.org
- Natural Resources Defense Council (www.nrdc.org/media)
40 West 20th St., New York, NY 10011
(212) 727-2700; fax: (212) 727-1773
E-mail: nrdcinfo@nrdc.org

See also:

- Carson, R. 1994. *Silent Spring*. New York: Houghton Mifflin, 1962. Reprint, New York: Mariner Books.
- Colborn, T., D. Dumanoski, and J. Peterson Myers. 1996. *Our Stolen Future*. New York: Penguin Books. Updates at www.ourstolenfuture.org.

ENVIRONMENTAL JUSTICE AND HAZARDOUS WASTE

▪ BACKGROUND ▪

The processes of producing the goods and services that enhance our quality of life also produce by-products, including environmental pollutants and hazardous waste. Although the products may be shipped out and used elsewhere, the wastes and pollution from manufacturing are, for the most part, left behind for the originating community to deal with. In addition to potential environmental health risks from both operational and abandoned industrial facilities, many communities contain other potential sources of risk, such as landfills, incinerators, and sites for treatment and storage of wastes. While these sites affect all racial, ethnic, and socioeconomic groups, data suggest that people of color and lower-income groups are exposed to these hazards with greater frequency and magnitude. This phenomenon has come to be known as environmental injustice. Environmental justice therefore refers to a situation where segments of the population are not unequally exposed to hazards in the environment. The Washington-based Institute of Medicine's Committee on Environmental Justice examined the research on environmental justice and determined that while direct links between exposure and health are hard to verify, charges of environmental injustice are not unfounded and need to be taken seriously.

▪ IDENTIFYING THE ISSUES ▪

The issue of environmental justice involves disparities in the distribution of existing hazardous sites, including operational and abandoned sites, as well as disparities in efforts to locate new hazardous sites. The U.S. Environmental Protection Agency (EPA) defines environmental justice as:

> The fair treatment and meaningful involvement of all people regardless of race, ethnicity, income, national origin or educational level with respect to the development, implementation, and enforcement of environmental laws, regulations, and policies. Fair treatment means that no population, due to policy or economic disempowerment, is forced to bear a disproportionate burden of the negative human health or environmental impacts of pollution or other environmental consequences resulting from industrial, municipal, and commercial operations or the execution of federal, state, local and tribal programs and policies. (EPA 1998, 2)

Hazardous waste is produced in every state. However, since industry is its primary producer, it tends to be concentrated in major industrialized regions, which also tend to have a disproportionately larger and poorer minority population base. Here, industrial facilities are gathered for economies of scale, and abandoned industrial sites are left in their wake as industries move on. Disposal of waste generated by these facilities often requires the development of new hazardous waste sites that serve as temporary or permanent waste repositories. These locations are proposed on the basis of a number of factors, including their environmental integrity, but the lack of a vocal opposition in the receiving community may also be a factor in these decisions.

Though some hazardous waste sites clearly present serious hazards, most experts judge that many are unlikely to threaten public health. This may be little comfort to the community because even a site that poses little threat to health and the environment may still be a major threat to the value of one's home and quality of life. In addition, the stigma of living near a site is real, whether or not the hazard is real. The presence of hazardous waste at operational facilities or abandoned sites, as well as proposals to site new facilities, justifiably can generate enormous amounts of fear and anger (outrage) within a community.

Cleanup of hazardous waste sites is often a contentious issue. A laborious bureaucratic and legalistic cleanup process only exacerbates these feelings of outrage, and communities often demand total cleanup of the site. However, substantially reducing the dangerous sites' risk to both health and the environment is almost prohibitively expensive, and risks are typically addressed through containment and monitoring rather than cleanup. It is often impossible, and almost always expensive, to reduce the risk to almost nothing because we do not know, for example, how to clean soil down to the last molecule of contaminant. Policies and politics that force cleanup (especially "total" cleanup) increase the cost much more than they increase the measurable benefits.

The proposed siting of a new hazardous waste facility invariably causes controversy, pitting the developer of the facility against the facility's neighbors-to-be—the surrounding community. Although a few very small hazardous waste sites have been approved in the United States in the past couple of decades, no new large-scale, free-standing hazardous waste facilities have been sited anywhere in the nation since 1980. Hundreds of these facilities have been proposed and either failed to gain the necessary approvals or, in a few cases, been delayed. As the United States increases its production of hazardous wastes and implements laws to close inadequate, unsafe facilities, new and stronger pressure to find new sites for these facilities is emerging. As a case in point, the U.S. Energy Department in 2001 recommended that Yucca Mountain be used as a site for burial of radioactive nuclear waste from power plants and weapons manufacturing facilities after fourteen years spent studying proposed sites. The recommendation may still meet substantial technical, legal, and political challenges.

▪ ADDRESSING THE ISSUES ▪

Three important questions must be answered in making a determination regarding environmental justice: (1) whether communities with high concentrations of racial and ethnic minorities or low-income families experience poorer health status; (2) whether these communities are disproportionately exposed to a variety of environmental health hazards; and (3) whether there is a linkage between the exposure to environmental hazards and poor health status.

A large body of research has documented the existence of serious disparities in health status among people in the United States. People of color and individuals of lower socioeconomic status have shorter life expectancies, more health problems, more low birthweight babies, higher rates of infant mortality, higher rates of cancer, and higher overall mortality rates. Despite improvements in health status for all racial and ethnic groups in the United States, the gap in disparities has actually widened. Differences in socioeconomic status account for some of these disparities. For example, white Americans are more likely to earn higher incomes than other racial and ethnic groups, and they are therefore better able to access preventive health care. Differences in income, however, do not explain all observed disparities in health status between races.

Studies have found that minorities and lower-income communities also face higher levels of potential exposure to environmental hazards. One way of determining this is to look at the actual sites and their proximity to disadvantaged communities. This approach, which uses proximity to a site as a proxy for actual contact with the hazards produced at the site, was utilized in a report issued by the United Church of Christ Commission for Racial Justice in 1987. The report showed that communities with one or more commercial hazardous waste facilities had significantly larger racial minority populations than did communities without these facilities. The communities with hazardous waste facilities were also more likely to have lower per capita incomes. Other studies have found a similar pattern.

Another approach to examining exposure to environmental health hazards takes direct measurements or estimates of actual emissions from the hazardous source. This approach is considered more exact because it estimates the rate of release and the path of the material into and through the environment (either directly as airborne exposure or through infiltration of pollutants into the soil and subsurface water resources, or indirectly through the foods people consume).

Assessing levels of exposures is complicated. For example, studies have shown that in New York City, African Americans and Hispanics are much more likely to be hospitalized for asthma than people in the general population in New York. While data suggest that this and other examples of high rates of urban asthma are related to situations of environmental injustice, definitive conclusions are not possible because of wide variations in diagnostic methods; accuracy of diagnosis for different groups in the population; the wide range of toxic, allergenic, dietary, and infectious agents linked to asthma; and variations in susceptibility in different populations.

Once disparities in health status have been documented as well as disparities in exposure to environmental hazards, one still needs to determine if these differences in health status are the result of disparities in exposure. Establishing a causal relationship between exposure to hazards and negative health outcomes is difficult. Published research on many of the identified potential environmental hazards is limited, making it hard to draw conclusions linking the disparities in exposures to disparities in health. As a result, much of the research on exposures is based solely on proximity to potential sites. More research is needed to establish actual pathways for exposure and increase knowledge about disease processes.

Sound public health research must be the basis for addressing concerns about environmental exposures and environmental justice issues. This research must be conducted on two fronts: assessing the health status of the community and determining the level of contribution of specific environmental factors to that health status. Many factors make doing this research difficult, including the fact that the number of individuals affected and/or the incidence—the number of new cases of a disease in the population—may be small and the methodological complexity of measuring the contribution of various environmental factors.

Epidemiologists play an important role in this research. They must document the fact of excessive exposures (including the strength of the exposure and its pathway) and measure both susceptibility in the population and the actual health effects of one exposure relative to other potential factors present in the environment. Research to address environmental justice is often collaborative because it raises questions for toxicologists, epidemiologists, molecular biologists, clinicians, and social scientists.

Members of the community should be included in all stages of this research. Health researchers must pay close attention to the experiences and observations of community members. Often they come to suspect a problem exists long before the scientific or health community makes any connections. While professionals may know the general effects of particular toxic substances, they are likely to know less about the activities and places that lead to exposure. This can only be learned by talking with firsthand observers living in the community. An organized system of collecting this type of experiential information from the community is essential.

Participatory research involves members of the community in all stages of the research process, from planning to discussing the findings with scientists serving as a resource for the community. The community's role is to keep the research focused on issues of importance to the community so that it ultimately benefits from the findings of the research. This type of research produces challenges, which can lengthen the research process. The local community and representatives of the scientific community often speak different languages and live apart. The significance of the outcome is different for both groups, and this can lead to mistrust.

In 1990, the EPA formed the Environmental Equity Workgroup to assess the evidence that suggests that racial minority and low-income communities bear higher environmental risks compared with the general population. The group also considered what the EPA might to do about any identified disparities. It issued a report entitled "Environmental Equity: Reducing Risk in All Communities," in which it reported on several major studies that indicated the existence of environmental injustice. The Environmental Equity Workgroup's report also recommended that the EPA make environmental equity a priority.

The EPA created the Office of Environmental Justice (OEJ) in 1992 in response to public concerns and at the recommendation of the Environmental Equity Workgroup. The OEJ oversees the integration of environmental justice concerns into the EPA's policies, programs, and activities and serves as the contact for environmental justice outreach and educational activities. It also provides technical and financial assistance. The EPA's strategy to address environmental justice focuses on encouraging public participation and accountability, health and environmental research and data collection and analysis, protections for Native Americans, and enforcement, compliance assurance, and regulatory review. An Environmental Justice Coordinators Council was set up within the OEJ to bring together the community, industry, and state/local government groups to discuss "reinventing" solutions to environmental justice problems.

Executive Order 12898, "Federal Actions to Address Environmental Justice in Minority Populations and Low-Income Populations," was signed into law in 1994. It focuses federal attention on the environmental and human health conditions of minority and low-income populations with the goal of achieving environmental protection for all communities. Federal agencies must develop environmental justice strategies to help identify and address disproportionately high and adverse human health or environmental effects of their programs, policies, and activities on minority and low-income populations. Programs must provide minority and low-income communities access to public information on, and opportunities to participate in, matters relating to human health or the environment.

The EPA's efforts to help assure environmental justice include:

- Educating officials to recognize that certain populations who are disproportionately impacted by environmental pollution are excluded from the decision- and policy-making process;

- Providing environmental justice guidance for all staff;
- Devotion of resources to program implementation;
- Systematic review and integration of environmental justice priorities into activities;
- Establishment of pilot projects; and
- Development of measurement tools for accountability.

In an effort to help ensure that the EPA obtains adequate advice from stakeholders in implementing a national environmental justice program, the agency also established the National Environmental Justice Advisory Council (NEJAC) in 1993. This council provides independent advice to the EPA on all matters relating to environmental justice. It consists of twenty-five members appointed from stakeholder groups, including community-based organizations, business, academic institutions, state and local governmental agencies, and environmental groups. Membership is rotated to provide the greatest opportunity for a variety of individuals to serve on the council.

Specifically related to siting of new facilities, the Office of Solid Waste (OSW) formed the Resource Conservation and Recovery Act (RCRA) Siting Workgroup to review policy options related to siting of RCRA facilities. The workgroup holds meetings to evaluate technical issues related to the potential risk in various geographic locations, as well as to consider environmental justice issues raised by facility siting. The workgroup has met with NEJAC to discuss environmental justice concerns and potential solutions. As a result, environmental justice concerns have been incorporated into the annual OSW RCRA Guidance in the RCRA Implementation Plan (RIP). The RIP now calls for regions to develop implementation plans to address recommendations for environmental justice.

In 1999, the Institute of Medicine issued its report on environmental justice following an extensive study of the issue. Members of the Committee on Environmental Justice visited many poorer communities impacted by hazards in their midst and recommended that efforts among federal, state, and local public health agencies be coordinated to allow for better data collection and communication with the community. The research to untangle environmental justice concerns must involve affected communities, and the findings must be shared with stakeholders. These efforts must include educational efforts so there is an increased understanding of environmental health and justice issues. Where the basic science cannot provide definite answers, policy-makers should exercise caution on behalf of affected communities—especially those with limited access to health care and limited political and economic resources.

▪ IMPORTANT POINTS FOR RESEARCHING A STORY ▪

- When examining the presence of negative environmental sites within a community, it is important to recognize that a community also shares in the distribution of good environmental sites such as safe open spaces, good schools, convenient shopping, and community facilities. The presence of good environmental sites within a neighborhood is often overlooked and certainly underreported. Community residents are also very interested in the good environmental characteristics within their midst.
- Communities where environmental justice is raised as a concern bear double jeopardy: they experience higher levels of risk of exposure to environmental hazards or stressors in terms of both frequency and magnitude and they are less able to respond to these threats because they are less likely to have knowledge of the exposures and be active participants in the political process.
- While it is necessary to demonstrate that there are disparities in health status and disparities in exposure to environmental hazards, making a determination about environmental justice also requires demonstrating a plausible relationship between exposure to the hazard and negative health outcomes. Failing to link the two means that it is always possible that the relationship between exposure and health outcome is a spurious relationship—one caused by another as yet unidentified factor or set of factors.
- Siting decisions are complex. Find out why the site was located in close proximity to low-income or minority communities. Was the site selected because of the lack of a politically effective opposition, because land was less expensive, or some combination of these and other reasons? Was the makeup of the community the same when the site was first built—or did its composition evolve over time, as the result of changes in land values or job opportunities? Regardless of its history, however, if a site causes an environmental health threat and its impact is unfairly felt by some segments of the community, then it is important to assess its impact on health and look for ways to improve the situation.

- Environmental stressors that can influence human health include chemicals, biologics, allergens, and traditional toxicants as well as light, noise, odors, and particulate matter.
- Low-income and minority workers in the United States are disproportionately employed in jobs with higher levels of exposure to health hazards. As a result, they experience higher levels of work-related illnesses. This makes it more difficult to sort out the impact from exposures on the job and impacts from exposures in the community.
- The literature on environmental justice and related health effects is limited. There is a growing body of research looking at the siting of toxic waste facilities and effects on health. In most cases, however, adequate data are not available to fully explore the relationship among environmental, racial, ethnic, and socioeconomic factors that are linked with negative health outcomes.
- Communities impacted by issues of environmental justice include highly industrialized locations in the midst of major urban areas, communities located near industrialized sites that lack urban infrastructures, agricultural communities, and communities located near sites of past federal weapons manufacturing activity.
- In the EPA's massive study of public versus expert assessments of risk, hazardous waste cleanup was one area that the public considered much riskier than experts did.
- The distribution of risks as it relates to the distribution of benefits is an important aspect of fairness. For example, at a manufacturing facility, the risks—large or small—are concentrated in the immediate vicinity surrounding the facility. The benefits (rebates, reduced taxes) are usually not similarly concentrated. The people who live near the manufacturing facility in many cases tend to have lower incomes and less socioeconomic status than the people who live farther away. People living near the facility know the risks are not fairly distributed. This makes the risk a serious outrage and that, in turn, makes it a serious risk. (See the discussion of outrage in "The Language of Risk.")
- It is always hard to site controversial facilities. Communities, however, react differently based on how risks are presented to them. If a company comes into a community and says, "We're going to put our factory here, whether you want it here or not, and you can move if you don't like it," communities usually vigorously resist such a coercive approach. There is, on the other hand, no

guarantee of community acceptance for a company that chooses instead to say, "We'd like to put our factory here, but only if you want it here and if we can negotiate mutually acceptable terms—otherwise we won't build it." It is not possible to guarantee that voluntary siting processes will work or that coercive ones will likely fail. What is more certain is that the public will likely consider the factory a lot less risky if it does not feel as if it has been coerced. As noted in "The Language of Risk," "The right to say 'no' makes saying 'maybe' a much smaller risk."

▪ AVOIDING PITFALLS ▪

- While the environmental justice movement and brownfields initiatives share some common goals (eliminating environmental hazards and promoting health in the community), the two can diverge from one another in certain situations. Following remediation, many brownfields programs encourage industrial or commercial redevelopment of sites, offering little or no opportunity for community input into decisions regarding use of the site following remediation. The environmental justice movement, on the other hand, encourages greater community involvement in decisions regarding remediation as well as in decisions regarding use after cleanup. Environmental justice advocates can exercise considerable influence by actively participating in the permitting process.
- When presenting data regarding possible disparities in exposures, be certain of the method used to determine these disparities and the strengths and weaknesses of each. Most studies of environmental justice have looked only at proximity to potential sources of exposure. Only a small number have measured the rate of release and the path of the material into and through the environment.

▪ INFORMATION RESOURCES ▪

▪ GOVERNMENT/ACADEMIA

- National Environmental Justice Advisory Council (http://es.epa.gov/oeca/main/ej/nejac)

- U.S. Environmental Protection Agency, Environmental Justice in Waste Programs (www.epa.gov/swerosps/ej/)

See also:

- Anderson, D., A. Anderson, J. Oakes, and M. Fraser. 1994. Environmental equity: The demographics of dumping. *Demography* 31:229–248.
- Friedman-Jimenez, G., and L. Claudio. 1998. Environmental justice. In *Textbook of Environmental and Occupational Medicine.* 3rd ed. Edited by W. N. Rom. Philadelphia: Lippincott-Raven.
- The Institute of Medicine, Committee on Environmental Justice Health. 1999. *Toward Environmental Justice: Research Education and Health Policy Needs.* Washington, D.C.: National Academy Press. (http://www.nap.edu/books/030906407/html/121.html)
- United Church of Christ, Commission for Racial Justice. 1987. *Toxic Waste and Race in the United States: A National Report on the Racial and Socio-Economic Characteristics of Communities with Hazardous Waste Sites.* New York: United Church of Christ.
- U.S. Environmental Protection Agency, Office of Federal Activities. 1998. *Final Guidance for Incorporating Environmental Justice Concerns in EPA's NEPA Compliance Analyses.* Washington, D.C.: Government Printing Office.

FOOD IRRADIATION

▪ BACKGROUND ▪

Irradiating food with ionizing radiation to kill microorganisms and extend shelf life is not a new idea. The U.S. Food and Drug Administration (FDA) first allowed irradiation of wheat in 1963. Since then, a number of food items, including fruits, vegetables, tea, and spices, have been approved for irradiation. More recently, the FDA and the U.S. Department of Agriculture (USDA) approved irradiation of selected raw meat and poultry products. Food irradiation is permitted in more than forty countries.

Irradiation has been shown to be effective against a number of food-borne illnesses including cholera, E. coli infections, listeriosis, salmonellosis, shigellosis, gastroenteritis, septicemia, toxoplasmosis, and trichinellosis. The American Dietetic Association, the American Medical Association, and the World Health Organization endorse systematic irradiation of food to reduce the incidence of food-borne illness. Irradiation is lauded as a method of preserving and sanitizing foods shipped to developing nations and for famine relief.

Three different technologies may be used to irradiate food, depending upon the source and type of the radiation: gamma irradiation, electron-beam irradiation, and X-irradiation (X-ray). Gamma irradiation uses a radioactive form (isotope) of either cobalt (cobalt-60) or cesium (cesium-137), which emits high-energy photons, or gamma rays. Gamma rays can penetrate foods to a depth of several feet. Electron-beam technology uses a concentrated stream of high-energy electrons to irradiate food. The electrons can penetrate food only to a depth of about 3 centimeters (1.2 inches). X-irradiation is being developed as an alternate approach for food irradiation. X-irradiation uses a beam of electrons that can pass through foods. With each technology, the energy used for irradiation does not remain in the food, nor does it leave any residue.

Each irradiation technology has a history of other uses. Gamma irradiation, electron-beam technology, and X-irradiation have been used for many years to sterilize medical equipment. Gamma irradiation and X-irradiation are used in radiation treatment of cancer. X-ray photography, or radiography, has been an important diagnostic tool in medicine for the past century.

▪ IDENTIFYING THE ISSUES ▪

Scientists agree that food contamination continues to be a global problem. Even in the United States, where a high level of food safety has been achieved, the Centers for Disease Control and Prevention (CDC) estimates that there are approximately 76 million cases of food-borne illness each year, including 325,000 cases that require hospitalization and 5,000 deaths. Food irradiation has been identified as an important tool for use in reducing the incidence of food-borne disease.

Some critics argue that focusing on irradiation to destroy bacterial contamination distracts from what they say is the real issue—safe handling and sanitary practices within the meat and other food-processing industries. While these critics may agree that irradiation is effective in eliminating bacterial contamination, they argue that such contamination is preventable through improved housekeeping and handling practices among food processors. The food industry maintains that some level of contamination is unavoidable and that irradiation is meant to complement and enhance current efforts to ensure food safety. Industry representatives assert that irradiation will not result in a lowering of food safety standards among food processors.

Some scientists and groups opposed to food irradiation question the safety of the irradiating technologies, the generation of radioactive waste, and the possible risks to workers and the public. Such concerns are relatively minor for electron-beam and X-ray technologies, which do not involve the use of radioactive substances. However, gamma irradiation uses the radioactive isotope of cobalt (cobalt-60) or cesium (cesium-137) as an energy source and does present some safety and disposal concerns.

Critics cite accidental exposures of workers to radiation at facilities in other countries as evidence of the dangers of routine gamma irradiation of food. Critics also maintain that large amounts of ozone are produced as a by-product of gamma irradiation, placing workers and the environment at risk. (See the brief on "Air Pollution [Outdoor].")

The disposal and transport of radioactive waste are always contentious issues. Cobalt-60 has a limited lifetime—its radioactive half-life (i.e., the time it takes for half of the material to decay) is five years. Spent cobalt-60, in the form of a metal bar or "pencil," may be shipped back to a nuclear reactor to be recharged and then reused, or it may be disposed of as a solid radioactive waste. Cesium-137 has a much longer half-life (thirty-one years). Because it is solvent in water and cannot be recharged, spent cesium-137 must be sent to storage sites in special containment canisters. If the containment canister were compromised, cesium-137 could dissolve in water and be released into the environment.

Some scientists and groups opposed to irradiation question the safety of consuming irradiated foods, citing chemical changes in the food and decreased nutritional value. Irradiation does cause some chemical changes in foods, including the production of radiolytic products, or free radicals. Opponents of food irradiation maintain that free radicals present in recently irradiated foods may result in chromosomal abnormalities in consumers. Several small and controversial studies seem to support this claim and suggest that persons who are severely malnourished are at particular risk. Other studies have shown that these same free radical compounds are formed during other forms of food processing and preparation, including canning, cooking, freezing, steaming, and pasteurization. A number of studies have shown losses of vitamins A, C, and E and the B vitamins thiamine and riboflavin when foods are irradiated. The FDA and others maintain that any such nutrient losses, although measurable with modern technology, are too small to compromise overall nutrition. As irradiation is proposed as a method of preserving foods being directed to developing nations and for famine relief, some argue that the small nutritional losses may be significant for already malnourished consumers.

Food packaging also raises issues for food irradiation. In most cases, the food to be irradiated will already be packaged. Opponents charge that irradiation will result in chemical changes to packaging materials that will be transferred to the foods. This argument has recently been bolstered by reports of chemical releases from plastics contained in U.S. mail irradiated in response to the 2001 anthrax scare. As further evidence, irradiation opponents point out that the limited number of packaging materials approved for food irradiation has been an obstacle to widespread use of irradiation. According to the FDA, however, the limited number of approved packaging materials simply reflects the fact that few materials have been tested.

Labeling is also an issue for irradiated foods. Current regulations require that packages of single-ingredient irradiated foods (e.g., a cut of meat) be labeled with the international symbol for irradiation, the radura, and a phrase such as "Treated by Irradiation." Processed foods with multiple ingredients must indicate which ingredients, if any, have been irradiated in the ingredients list but are not required to have the radura logo on the package. Industry continues to lobby for less stringent labeling requirements, while consumer groups argue for increased reporting. Meanwhile, there have been some efforts by consumer groups to require disclosure by restaurants that use irradiated products.

A final issue concerns the perception and acceptance of irradiated foods by U.S. consumers. Both proponents and critics of food irradiation offer statistics that show the public is behind them. However, since irradiated foods are not yet widely available, the degree of consumer acceptance remains to be seen.

In order to allay public concerns, some industry groups have suggested that the phrase "cold pasteurization" be used instead of "irradiation" on food packages. This is really an oxymoron, since by definition, pasteurization is a heat-treatment process. It is impossible to have a "cold heat-treatment process." "Cold disinfection" or "radiant disinfection" would be more accurate euphemisms for irradiation, but this wording may be just as troubling to the public as the term "irradiation."

▪ ADDRESSING THE ISSUES ▪

Food irradiation is regulated by a number of U.S. government agencies and regulations. The FDA and the USDA's Food Safety Inspection Service regulate irradiation as a food additive. Under the oversight of these agencies, irradiation is clearly not intended to substitute for sanitary practices in food processing. Over the past several decades, elimination of food contamination during production and processing has become proactive, focusing on prevention. A number of countries, including the United States, have regulations requiring the development and use of risk management processes called Hazard Analysis Critical Control Point (HACCP) by food producers. Instead of relying upon food product inspections to ensure safety, HACCP requires that producers identify where contamination is likely to occur and then introduce preventive measures. HACCP regulations are designed to eliminate or at least significantly reduce the opportunity for food contamination. This would include setting minimum cooking temperatures and time requirements for cooked foods, such as hamburgers in fast food restaurants, to ensure elimination of harmful microbes. Irradiation is intended to supplement such food safety measures and provide an additional level of protection.

Food irradiation facilities within the United States are highly regulated to ensure worker and public safety. The Nuclear Regulatory Commission (NRC) regulates the licensing and operation of irradiation facilities that use radioactive sources. The FDA regulates electron-beam and X-irradiation sources used for food irradiation and other medical and industrial applications. The Occupational Safety and Health Administration (OSHA) has additional regulations governing worker exposure to sources of radiation. The U.S. Department of Transportation regulates the transport of radioactive energy sources used for food irradiation and their waste products.

The question remains whether food irradiation will see widespread adoption in the United States. Ultimately, consumer attitudes and acceptance will largely determine the fate of food irradiation. As an additional step in food processing, irradiation adds to the cost of food products. In order for irradiation to be widely accepted, the public needs to be convinced not only of its safety but also of its necessity. And consumers must be willing to pay more for irradiated foods.

▪ IMPORTANT POINTS FOR RESEARCHING A STORY ▪

- Irradiation does not eliminate the need for sanitary conditions on farms or at food-processing facilities. The level of irradiation necessary to eliminate bacterial contamination increases as the level of contamination increases. Effective treatment of highly contaminated food would require irradiation doses so high as to impact food taste and texture.
- Irradiation is not a substitute for proper food handling in the homes of consumers. Irradiated foods are not sterile and can be recontaminated by bacteria in refrigerators, on hands, and on food preparation surfaces.
- Scientists and groups on both sides of the issue refer to lists of studies to back up their claims of the dangers or safety of irradiation. It is important to scrutinize their sources. Some questions to ask: When were the studies conducted? If they were conducted

more than several years ago, have subsequent independent studies supported their findings? Have the studies undergone peer review? Were the studies published in reputable scientific journals? Are the findings of the study being accurately represented?

- Not all foods are suitable for irradiation.

▪ AVOIDING PITFALLS ▪

- Food irradiation is not a panacea or magic bullet to eliminate food-borne disease. Irradiation has been shown to be effective in eliminating a number of bacteria from certain foods. Food-borne disease is also associated with other sources not affected by radiation (e.g., chemical contamination) and with foods that are not approved or suitable for irradiation.
- Irradiation does not result in radioactivity in treated foods.

▪ INFORMATION RESOURCES ▪

▪ GOVERNMENT/ACADEMIA

- Centers for Disease Control and Prevention–National Center for Infectious Diseases/Food Safety Office (www.cdc.gov/foodsafety/)
  MS G24, Atlanta, GA 30333
  (404) 639-2213
- International Consultative Group of Food Irradiation (www.iaea.or.at/icgfi/)
  Food and Environmental Protection Section
  Joint FAO/IAEA Division of Nuclear Techniques in Food and Agriculture
  International Atomic Energy Agency
  Wagramerstrasse 5, P.O. Box 100, A-1400 Vienna, Austria
  E-mail: Official.Mail@iaea.org
- U.S. Department of Agriculture–Food Safety and Inspection Service (www.fsis.usda.gov)
  Congressional Public Affairs Office, Room 1175S
  1400 Independence Ave. SW, Washington, DC 20250-3700
  (202) 720-9113

- U.S. Food and Drug Administration–Center for Food Safety and Applied Nutrition (http://vm.cfsan.fda.gov/list.html)
  200 C St. SW, Washington, DC 20204
  print and online media: (202) 205-4144; fax: (202) 205-5169
  broadcast media: (301) 827-3434; fax: (301) 443-8512

INDUSTRY/PROFESSIONAL ASSOCIATIONS

- American Meat Institute Foundation (www.amif.org)
  P.O. Box 3556, Washington, DC 20007
  (703) 841-2400; fax: (703) 527-0938
- Food Marketing Institute (www.fmi.org)
  655 15th St. NW, Washington, DC 20005
  (202) 452-8444; fax: (202) 429-4519
  E-mail: media@fmi.org
- International Association for Food Protection (www.foodprotection.org)
  6200 Aurora Ave., Suite 200W, Des Moines, IA 50322-2864
  (515) 276-3344; fax: (515) 276-8655
  E-mail: info@foodprotection.org

NONPROFIT/CONSUMER ORGANIZATIONS

- The Center for Food Safety (www.centerforfoodsafety.org)
  660 Pennsylvania Ave. SE, Suite 302, Washington, DC 20003
  (202) 547-9359; fax: (202) 547-9429
  E-mail: office@centerforfoodsafety.org
- Organic Consumers Association (www.organicconsumers.org)
  6101 Cliff Estate Rd., Little Marais, MN 55614
  (218) 226-4164; fax: (218) 226-4157
- Public Citizen (www.citizen.org)
  1600 20th St. NW, Washington, DC 20009
  (202) 588-1000

GENETICALLY MODIFIED CROPS

▪ BACKGROUND ▪

Genetically modified crops have been called a lightning rod for a host of environmental, social, and political concerns. The controversy surrounding these products involves fear of new technology, distrust of government, hostility toward large multinational corporations, anxiety about food safety, concern for the sanctity of life, and even a science-fiction fear of mutant monsters. The issues are as complex as the technology, and the solutions are far from clear. The current debate will determine the future of the industry and the face of agriculture in the twenty-first century.

In genetic engineering of crops, genes from another plant or organism are transferred into the crop plant to produce a desired trait. While traditional plant breeding methods can take generations of trial and error to produce a desired effect, genetically engineered changes can be made in a single growing season. In addition, by enabling the manipulation of genes between different species and between plants and animals, genetic engineering allows changes that would never have been possible through traditional plant breeding.

Genetic engineering can be used to improve the color, flavor, size, or texture of a food crop or to increase the yield of the crop by protecting it against pests, chemicals, or disease. The majority of genetically modified, or transgenic, crops in use today are those engineered to tolerate certain chemical herbicides. The use of herbicide-tolerant crops allows farmers to spray the herbicide liberally without fear of crop damage. Herbicide-tolerant crops are intended to reduce the number of herbicides applied during a growing season and reduce the frequency of herbicide applications. Control of weeds with herbicides also lessens the need for plowing, thereby protecting against soil erosion.

The other major class of transgenic crops in current use are those

This brief is based upon information provided by Michael W. Hamm, Department of Nutritional Sciences, Rutgers University, New Brunswick, New Jersey.

engineered to resist insect pests. These crops include a gene from the soil bacterium *Bacillus thuringensis* (Bt) that produces a protein toxic to caterpillars. (Organic farmers have sprayed Bt directly on their crops as a natural pesticide since the 1940s.) Genetically engineered Bt crops reduce the need for chemical pesticide application since the pesticide exists within the plant itself.

■ IDENTIFYING THE ISSUES ■

The production and use of genetically modified crops have thus far resulted in controversy across the globe. Current issues surrounding genetically modified crops range from environmental impacts to health risks to consumers to potential impacts on the domestic and global economies.

■ ENVIRONMENTAL IMPACTS

Currently, the greatest environmental concern surrounding genetically modified crops is the potential for outcropping. Outcropping is the transfer of genes from crops to wild plants through pollen transport. The transfer of herbicide tolerance from genetically modified crops to related species of weeds, for example, could create "superweeds." Cases of outcropped resistance to the herbicide glyphosate have already been reported in wild varieties of ryegrass and mustard in Australia and Canada. Control of these wild varieties now will require the use of stronger herbicides. Outcropping is of particular concern in developing nations, where cultivated and related wild species of plants are often found together.

Another environmental concern regarding herbicide-resistant crops relates to the inherent use of the herbicides they are engineered to tolerate. Proponents maintain that herbicide-resistant crops will decrease the number and volume of field-applied herbicides. This may be true in the short-term in regions where herbicides and pesticides are already in use. However, the introduction of herbicide-resistant crops and their accompanying chemical sprays would comprise the first use of chemicals by many farmers around the world.

A number of environmental groups and scientists also believe that the use of genetically engineered Bt crops will ultimately result in a greater use of agricultural chemicals. These groups predict that Bt crops will accelerate the development of pesticide resistance among insects. Every population of insects exposed to a pesticide in the field has a few survivors. When these survivors breed, their resistance to the pesticide is passed along to their offspring, resulting in greater numbers of survivors in each successive generation. Over time, this phenomenon results in the need for stronger and stronger pesticides to control the insects. Farmers have been able to delay widespread resistance to Bt through integrated pest management (IPM), in which pesticides are applied judiciously. In IPM, insect populations are seldom exposed to Bt and are slower to develop resistance to it. In genetically engineered Bt crops, the pesticide is present throughout the plant, and the insects are exposed to it continuously. Because of this, Bt crops may accelerate the development of resistance in insects. Some entomologists predict pest resistance to Bt crops within three to five years of their widespread use. At that point, both genetically engineered Bt crops and field-applied Bt would become ineffective against pests. Widespread resistance to Bt would require the development and use of stronger pesticides and would rob organic farmers of an important tool.

▪ HUMAN HEALTH RISKS

The greatest concern among consumers is the potential for health risks associated with eating genetically modified foods. A common concern raised is the potential for the transfer of allergens into different foods. One case that is often cited involves the transfer of an allergenic protein from a Brazil nut into a soybean. Because nut allergies are relatively common and can be life-threatening, newly genetically engineered plants are routinely tested for them, and development of this particular product was halted before it reached the market. In September 2000, an antibiotechnology group detected a potentially allergenic genetically modified corn in taco shells purchased from a grocery store. The transgenic corn, called StarLink, was approved for animal feed but not for human consumption due to its potential allergenic properties. StarLink was subsequently found in several other brands of taco shells. The affected products were recalled by the food manufacturers, and the production of StarLink has been halted.

Consumer groups and some scientists are also concerned about the presence of marker genes in genetically modified foods. Marker genes help engineers in the laboratory to determine if the genetic material was successfully incorporated into the new organism. In addition, they typically transfer resistance to certain antibiotics to the genetically modified organism and remain fully functional in genetically modified plants. The concern is that genetically modified plants could transfer their resistance to antibiotics to bacteria present in the human gastrointestinal tract.

Increased human exposure to herbicides is also among the concerns raised by consumer groups. As the use of herbicide-tolerant crops increases, so will dietary exposure to residues of the specific herbicides used on these crops. Instead of relatively small exposures to residues from many different herbicides, consumers will be repeatedly exposed to residues of a few herbicides. Although these compounds have been shown to be safe at low levels, their safety will need to be reassessed as their concentrations in the typical diet increase.

▪ ECONOMIC IMPACTS

The development, testing, and marketing of genetically engineered products require significant investments of time and money. Accordingly, biotechnology companies are very protective of their products. This has led to a variety of ownership and patent issues. For example, in the United States, broad patents give biotechnology companies considerable control over farmers. Farmers may now buy seed for one-time use only and are required by the biotechnology companies to sign seed contracts that strictly forbid the saving of seed from the crop for future planting. Such patents present a problem for poor farmers and those in developing nations who rely on saved seed to meet their planting needs. Up to half of the soybeans grown in the developing world is planted with farmer-saved seed. Seed saving is also an important factor in maintaining crop diversity, as farmers save seed from plants that have performed well under local growing conditions.

Originally, biotechnology companies sent inspectors to their customers' farms to ensure that they were not saving seed. However, they have now engineered control measures directly into their products. These new technologies, whose sole purpose is to maximize profits and control, are at the height of the controversy over genetically modified crops. Gene-protection technology, popularly dubbed terminator technology, genetically engineers seed to produce a sterile crop. Nongovernmental organizations have been highly critical of this technology, citing potential losses in plant biodiversity, devastating impacts on small farmers, and threats to global food security. Another controversial technology, genetic use restriction technology, commonly referred to as traitor technology, inserts growth control genes into seeds. Traitor technology prevents seed germination, flowering, or fruit ripening unless chemicals, purchased from the seed's manufacturer, are applied at specific points in the growing season.

Biotechnology companies also have been aggressive in their efforts to identify and patent potentially useful genes in plant life. This has raised ethical debate concerning the patenting of living organisms, as well as issues of bioprospecting and biopiracy, as biotechnology companies secure patents on indigenous plant varieties around the world. Many of these varieties have long traditions of use in the developing nations where they are found. Once secured, such patents could be used to prevent exports of these products to the United States, threatening the livelihood of tens of thousands of small farmers worldwide.

There is also concern that the centers of crop production will be shifted entirely to industrialized nations as genetically modified crops begin to fulfill needs traditionally met by crops grown in developing nations. For example, the U.S. cosmetics industry has traditionally relied on imports of coconut oil to supply lauric acid, a principal ingredient in many soaps and cosmetics. In the Philippines, fully 30 percent of the population is employed in the production of coconut oil for export. The viability of this industry now is threatened by a rapeseed grown commercially in the United States that has been genetically modified to produce lauric acid.

▪ ADDRESSING THE ISSUES ▪

There are no simple solutions to the environmental issues surrounding genetically modified crops. To address the issue of insect resistance, the EPA requires producers of Bt crops to develop resistance management plans. As part of these plans, biotechnology firms are developing crops that incorporate pesticides other than Bt. These crops are to be put into production as insect resistance to Bt spreads. However, this is only a slightly different version of the current paradigm of developing increasingly toxic pesticides to combat increasingly resistant pests and does nothing to address the overall issue of insect resistance.

An alternative to this approach involves the planting of refugia—lands of nonresistant plant varieties planted between fields of Bt crops. The intent of the refugia is to slow the development of Bt resistance in pest populations. If the areas set aside as refugia are large enough, a large portion of the insect population will never encounter the Bt. Interbreeding of the insects feeding in the refugia with the insects feeding on Bt crops should slow the development of resistance in the insect population as a whole.

Many scientists believe that the biotechnology companies must abandon development of terminator, traitor, and similar technologies. These technologies have the potential to cause devastating and irreparable harm to farming in developing nations and to the global ecology. These technologies also have the more immediate effect of alienating the public and mobilizing public interest groups against even the most responsible uses of biotechnology. As an alternative, some groups are calling for a new system of patents that would protect the investment of the biotechnology firms but also recognize the need of poorer and subsistence farmers to save seed.

While agricultural biotechnology may help in relieving the world food crisis, it is not the sole solution. To be of any real value to the world's hungry, research is needed into the development of crops that could grow on marginal land with few external inputs. The economics of farming in developing nations needs to be considered in the development and marketing of genetically modified crops.

Genetic engineering is a revolutionary new technology. For the first time, scientists are able to circumvent the natural boundaries of kingdom, phylum, class, order, family, genus, and species and create new life forms. There is great uncertainty as to the consequences of genetic manipulation across these boundaries. Given this uncertainty, international and consumer groups are calling for adherence to the "precautionary principle." The precautionary principle dictates that adoption and spread of new technology be slowed, or even halted, to allow time to properly assess its local and global environmental, health, and socioeconomic impacts. Proponents of industry have criticized the precautionary principle as reactionary, antitechnology, and a barrier to economic growth. However, advocates of the precautionary principle maintain that the uncertainties are too great and the stakes too high to allow the use of biotechnology to grow unchecked.

Consumer rights activists are calling for the labeling of all foods containing genetically engineered products. Currently, the FDA mandates labeling of genetically modified foods only where the product differs significantly from the original version. For example, foods containing genetically modified ingredients must be labeled if their nutritional content has been altered or if they are known to have a potential to cause allergic reactions. The FDA also prohibits the labeling of products to indicate that they are free from genetically engineered ingredients. As a result, consumers have no means of differentiating genetically engineered from nontransgenic foods.

In response to strong consumer opposition to genetically modified foods, the European Union and Japan have put in place mandatory labeling requirements. As a result, many U.S. food companies plan to exclude genetically modified ingredients from their export products. Fearing similar consumer backlash at home, a number of companies are extending their self-imposed bans on transgenic ingredients to include products sold domestically. This voluntary ban on genetically modified ingredients by U.S. food companies may threaten the viability of the agricultural biotechnology industry.

At the international level, the United Nations has developed the Cartagena Protocol on Biosafety as part of the Convention on Biological Diversity. (See the brief on "Biodiversity.") The biosafety protocol was developed to address concerns regarding biotechnology, international trade, and possible risks to human health and the environment. It includes Advance Informed Agreement (AIA) procedures that must be followed prior to the initial export of a genetically modified organism that is to be introduced into the environment, such as seed. The protocol also includes procedures for information and technology exchange, risk assessment, and public education. The biosafety protocol will become legally binding once it has been signed and ratified by fifty governments. At this writing, the United States has not signed the biosafety protocol.

▪ IMPORTANT POINTS FOR RESEARCHING A STORY ▪

- There are two major categories of genetic engineering techniques: interspecies and intraspecies. Interspecies genetic engineering, where genetic material is removed from and recombined with DNA from members of the same species, is most closely related to traditional plant breeding. In intraspecies genetic engineering, the donor and host organisms are of different species or even different kingdoms. One experiment resulted in a genetically engineered tomato that included a flounder gene to enhance frost resistance.

In another experiment, a potato was engineered to include a chicken gene for bacterial resistance. Although they are not typical of the genetically engineered foods on the market today, the drama of these so-called frankenfoods captures the public's imagination and causes the greatest outcry against biotechnology.

- Unless engineered for appearance, it is virtually impossible to distinguish genetically modified seed or crops from the original varieties.
- Many organizations and individuals have taken extreme positions on the issue of genetically modified crops, and many have vested interests in the outcome of the debate. Even the USDA, which is charged with regulating the field-testing of genetically engineered plants, has a vested interest in the success of biotechnology. The agency holds several patents on genetically engineered crop traits, including terminator technology. The biotechnology firms that develop and control genetically modified crops are huge multinational corporations whose holdings typically include pharmaceutical, agrochemical, and even petrochemical companies. Given these competing interests, it is important to know your sources and their biases.

▪ AVOIDING PITFALLS ▪

- "Panic talk" and anecdotal information are being pushed on both sides of the issue. Be sure to check your information with recognized authorities from both camps. The sources listed at the end of this brief are a good starting point.
- Proponents hail genetically modified crops as the solution to the world food crisis because of their potential to develop high-yield and nutritionally enhanced crops to feed the developing world. However, the primary trait being genetically engineered today—herbicide tolerance—is of little use to subsistence farmers in developing nations. These farmers cannot afford the expensive genetically modified seed, let alone the herbicides they are designed to tolerate. The crop traits needed by farmers in the developing world—drought resistance, saline tolerance, and low nutrient requirements—are very complex and are not being aggressively pursued by the biotechnology companies.

- Not all uses of genetic engineering are controversial. There are many transgenic pharmaceuticals in use today, including genetically engineered human insulin. In the food industry, genetically engineered enzymes are used in 60 percent of all cheese produced in the United States.

▪ INFORMATION RESOURCES ▪

▪ GOVERNMENT/ACADEMIA

- National Agricultural Biotechnology Council
(www.cals.cornell.edu/extension/nabc/)
419 Boyce Thompson Institute, Tower Rd., Ithaca, NY 14853
(607) 254-4856; fax: (607) 254-1242
E-mail: nabc@cornell.edu
- United Nations Cartagena Protocol on Biosafety
(www.biodiv.org/biosafety/)
World Trade Centre, 393 St Jacques St., Office 300
Montreal, Quebec, Canada H2Y 1N9
+1-514-288-2220; fax: +1-514-288-6588
E-mail: secretariat@biodiv.org
- U.S. Department of Agriculture–Animal and Plant Health Inspection Service (www.aphis.usda.gov)
Legislative and Public Affairs Units
47 River Rd., Riverdale, MD 20737
(301) 734-7799; fax: (301) 734-5221
- U.S. Environmental Protection Agency–Office of Biopesticides and Pollution Prevention
(www.epa.gov/oppbppd1/biopesticides/)
Ariel Rios Bldg., Mailcode 7511C
1200 Pennsylvania Ave. NW, Washington, DC 20460
(703) 305-7090; fax: (703) 308-7026
- U.S. Food and Drug Administration–Center for Food Safety and Applied Nutrition
(http://vm.cfsan.fda.gov/list.html)
200 C St. SW, Washington, DC 20204
print and online media: (202) 205-4144; fax: (202) 205-5169
broadcast media: (301) 827-3434; fax: (301) 443-8512

INDUSTRY/PROFESSIONAL ASSOCIATIONS

- Biotech Knowledge Center (www.monsanto.com)
  Monsanto Company
  800 North Lindbergh Blvd., St. Louis, MO 63167
  (314) 694-1000; fax: (314) 694-3889
  E-mail: queries.media@monsanto.com
- Biotechnology Industry Association (www.bio.org)
  625 K St. NW, Suite 1100, Washington, DC 20006
  (202) 857-0244
- Council for Biotechnology Information (www.whybiotech.com)
  E-mail: inquiries@whybiotech.com

NONPROFIT/CONSUMER ORGANIZATIONS

- Campaign to Label Genetically Engineered Foods (www.thecampaign.org)
  P.O. Box 55699, Seattle, WA 98155
  (425) 771-4049; fax: (603) 825-5841
  E-mail: label@thecampaign.org
- Institute for Agriculture and Trade Policy (www.iatp.org)
  2105 1st Ave. South, Minneapolis, MN 55404
  (612) 870-0453; fax: (612) 870-4846
- Rural Advancement Foundation International (www.rafi.org)
  110 Osborne St., Suite 202, Winnipeg MB R3L 1Y5, CANADA
  (204) 453-5259; fax: (204) 925-8034
  E-mail: rafi@rafi.org
- Union of Concerned Scientists
  (www.ucsusa.org/agriculture/ag_biotres.html)
  2 Brattle Square, Cambridge, MA 02238
  (617) 547-5552
  E-mail: ucs@ucsusa.org

GLOBAL CLIMATE CHANGE

▪ BACKGROUND ▪

In March 2002, scientists reported on the extraordinary speed with which a piece of an ice shelf of Antarctica the size of Rhode Island disintegrated. Experts attributed the phenomenon to the buildup of greenhouse gas emissions that are warming the planet.

The "greenhouse effect" refers to the insulation provided by certain gases in the earth's atmosphere. Like the glass in a greenhouse, naturally occurring gases allow the sun's radiant energy to pass through the atmosphere and warm the earth's surface while at the same time slowing the escape of heat back into space. It is this natural greenhouse effect that makes life as we know it possible on earth. Without the insulation provided by these greenhouse gases, the average surface temperature of the earth would be approximately zero degrees Fahrenheit.

Human activities release additional amounts of naturally occurring and synthetic greenhouse gases into the atmosphere. Unfortunately, the buildup of these gases is a case of "too much of a good thing." As more and more greenhouse gases accumulate in the atmosphere, they trap additional heat, raising the earth's average temperature in an "enhanced greenhouse effect." The National Academy of Sciences (NAS) has confirmed estimates of a measurable increase (0.3–0.6 degrees Celsius) in the earth's temperature over the past hundred years. During this period, glaciers have retreated, floating ice in the Arctic Ocean has decreased, and the mean sea level has risen by 10 to 25 centimeters (3.9–9.8 inches).

At first, scientists debated whether the observed increase in temperatures was just part of the natural fluctuations in the earth's temperature. However, computer models suggest that the observed warming

This brief is based on a brief on "Ozone" in the second edition of *The Reporter's Environmental Handbook*. Additional information and comments were provided by Bernard Goldstein, M.D., Dean of the School of Public Health, University of Pittsburgh.

trend is too great to be part of natural variability. The vast majority of scientists now believe that the recent increase in the earth's surface temperature is due, at least in part, to the growing concentrations of greenhouse gases in the atmosphere. Scientists also believe that continued production of these gases will accelerate the rate of temperature increase. What remains uncertain is how much the temperature will increase, how fast it will increase, and what the local impacts will be. Also uncertain is the extent to which feedback loops may be operating. For example, surface warming will increase the levels of water vapor (a natural greenhouse gas) in the atmosphere. Increased water vapor, in turn, will contribute to further increases in temperature, in a cycle of positive feedback. The role of the oceans in global warming is also not clearly understood. Scientists believe the oceans will absorb some increases in atmospheric carbon dioxide and some of the increases in temperature. This would delay increases in the earth's surface temperature, but scientists cannot accurately predict the timing of the delay.

The natural greenhouse gases include water vapor, carbon dioxide, methane, ozone, and nitrous oxide. It should be noted that while there are several nitrous oxides, only one—NO_2—plays an important role as a greenhouse gas. Together, these gases comprise less than 1 percent of the earth's total atmosphere. However, this small amount is sufficient to maintain the average surface temperature of approximately 15.5 degrees Celsius (60 degrees Fahrenheit). Because of its relationship with temperature, water vapor is by far the most important of the natural greenhouse gases. Human activity introduces additional amounts of the naturally occurring greenhouse gases into the atmosphere. Emissions of carbon dioxide comprise the greatest human contribution (60–75 percent) to the enhanced greenhouse effect.

Carbon flows in a global cycle—it is exchanged naturally between carbon dioxide in the atmosphere and huge reservoirs (sinks) of carbon in the oceans and living things. Plants exchange carbon dioxide with the atmosphere through photosynthesis and respiration and slowly release carbon dioxide to the atmosphere through decay. Large amounts of carbon dioxide are also rapidly released to the atmosphere through the burning of fossil fuels, solid waste, and wood. Second to the combustion of fossil fuels, the most significant source of carbon dioxide is the intentional burning of tropical and temperate rain forests.

Carbon dioxide levels began to increase during the nineteenth century, with the Industrial Revolution and increasing deforestation. While population growth in general is highly correlated with poverty and low levels of energy consumption, population and wealth are major factors in energy consumption. During the past 200 years, atmospheric carbon dioxide levels have increased by approximately 31 percent. According to the United Nations Intergovernmental Panel on Climate Change, the present concentration of carbon dioxide in the atmosphere has not been exceeded during the past 420,000 years and perhaps not during the past 20 million years. Based upon current global trends, carbon dioxide concentrations in the atmosphere will double preindustrial levels by the year 2065.

Methane is responsible for 15 to 20 percent of the current enhanced greenhouse effect. Methane gas is emitted during the production and transport of fossil fuels. Decomposition of organic waste in municipal solid waste landfills, animal waste, the raising of ruminant (cud-chewing) livestock, swamps, and rice paddies also result in the release of methane gas. Atmospheric methane levels have more than doubled since the beginning of the nineteenth century, with the most rapid rise—approximately 1 percent per year—occurring during the last few decades. This rapid increase is due in part to increased waste disposal, increased mining, and changing agricultural practices, all of which produce significant amounts of methane.

Natural vegetation gives off large quantities of nitrous oxide (N_2O). However, the current increases in the concentration of this gas (approximately 0.3 percent per year) are thought to come from agricultural and industrial activities, biomass burning, and the combustion of fossil fuels.

Human activity also introduces the insulating effects of artificial gases—halocarbons, sulfur hexafluoride, and ozone—into the atmosphere. The role of ozone is complex. At the most basic level, ozone can be discussed in terms of "good ozone" and "bad ozone." Ozone exists mainly in the high upper atmosphere, the stratosphere. In the stratosphere, naturally occurring ozone is essential—it absorbs most solar ultraviolet radiation, preventing it from reaching the earth's surface where it is harmful to life. This stratospheric ozone is the "good ozone." (See the brief on "Ozone Depletion.") As a result of human activities, ozone also exists in the lower atmosphere, the troposphere. In the troposphere, ozone is formed when sunlight strikes nitrous oxides and volatile organic compounds that come from motor vehicles and industrial and power plant emissions. Tropospheric ozone plays a significant role both as a greenhouse gas and as a pollutant. This tropospheric ozone is the "bad ozone." (See the brief on "Air Pollution [Outdoor].")

The halocarbons include chlorofluorocarbons (CFCs), which are by-products of foam production, refrigeration, and air conditioning. Halocarbons also include hydrofluorocarbons (HFCs), perfluorocarbons (PFCs), and sulfur hexafluoride, which are generated by industrial processes. In the stratosphere, CFCs contribute to the depletion of the earth's protective layer of "good ozone." Since 1990, HFCs and PFCs have been phased in to replace the stratospheric ozone-depleting CFCs. However, HFCs and PFCs, along with sulfur hexafluoride, act as powerful greenhouse gases in the troposphere because they absorb infrared radiation in a region of the spectrum where there is little absorption by other gases. The atmospheric concentrations of these compounds are increasing by approximately 4 to 5 percent per year.

▪ IDENTIFYING THE ISSUES ▪

Climate models predict that if current emissions of greenhouse gases continue unchecked, the global temperature will rise by an estimated 1.4 to 5.8 degrees Celsius by the end of the twenty-first century. Some scientists conclude that the earth has not experienced a temperature increase of more than 1 degree Celsius during the past 10,000 years. Other scientists point to evidence that suggests global average temperatures during the Holocene Climatic Optimum (about 6,000 years ago) were 1 degree Celsius greater than in recent centuries.

There are many uncertainties about the specific impacts of global climate change, particularly at the regional level. Variables that contribute to the uncertainty include the levels of future emissions of greenhouse gases, the impacts of feedback loops, and the capacity of the oceans to absorb some of the change in atmospheric temperature. Further complicating the models are industrial emissions of sulfates that are precursors to sulfate aerosols from sources such as coal- and oil-fired power plants and ships that reflect sunlight back into space, resulting in localized cooling. Other types of aerosols such as carbonaceous aerosols (soot) that come from incomplete combustion of fuels and biomass are also thought to cause warming.

Climate change is predicted to bring about an estimated rise of 9 to 88 centimeters (3.5–34.3 inches) in average sea level by the year 2100.

Further, the oceans will continue to rise for centuries after greenhouse gas levels are stabilized. Coastline features, differences in tidal patterns and salinity, and changes in ocean currents will result in great regional variations in the rise of sea levels. Areas at most risk from rising sea levels include low-lying islands and coastal regions, especially densely populated fertile river deltas. Studies done by the United Nations Environment Program (UNEP) have identified the ten most vulnerable countries to rising sea levels: Bangladesh, Egypt, the Gambia, Indonesia, Maldives, Mozambique, Pakistan, Senegal, Surinam, and Thailand.

Rising sea levels will erode beaches and result in the loss of coastal wetlands and estuaries. These effects will be intensified in developed areas, where bulkheads, dikes, and other structures may prevent the creation of new wetlands. Saltwater intrusion into rivers, bays, and groundwater tables associated with rising sea levels will impact fisheries and potable (drinking) water supplies. Particularly at risk are shallow coastal aquifers—water-bearing formations that supply groundwater. A rise in sea level of 60 centimeters (23.6 inches) could result in the complete loss of some of these aquifers due to saltwater intrusion. Another predicted impact of global warming is increased flooding. In the United States, the Federal Emergency Management Agency (FEMA) has estimated that a rise in sea level of 30 centimeters (11.8 inches) would increase the size of the nation's 100-year floodplain by almost 18 percent and increase flood damages by 36 to 58 percent.

It is likely that agricultural production will see winners and losers due to global climate change. Agriculture in tropical and subtropical regions will be threatened by additional heat, shifting monsoons, and reduced soil moisture. On the other hand, regional climates in the higher latitudes in Canada and Europe, for example, may become more favorable to agriculture. However, soil types in these regions will limit intensive agriculture or livestock production. It has also been suggested that insects and plant diseases will migrate with global warming, resulting in greater crop loss in the temperate zones.

Carbon dioxide (CO_2) fertilization is thought to have enhanced the biological productivity of the earth as a whole and is expected to increase agricultural productivity. This effect is superimposed on the effect of changing climate. This is one factor in estimates of changes in agricultural productivity. At present, an increase in plants and soils (carbon storage) appears (from inference from atmospheric composition) to be occurring at a significant rate; the leading hypothesis for why this is happening is CO_2 fertilization.

The fates of ecosystems will lie in their ability to adapt to rapid global climate changes. Climate change is projected to outpace the ability of tree species to migrate. Global warming will likely result in the loss of tree species, changes in forest composition, and, in some regions, the loss of entire forests. These changes would, in turn, contribute to the greenhouse effect by adding large amounts of carbon into the atmosphere as these forests decay. Large vegetation losses would also affect local climate in terms of ground temperature, cloud formation, and precipitation.

The world's desert areas are expected to become hotter but are not expected to see increased precipitation. Higher temperatures will result in the loss of species in desert regions, particularly among those species that currently exist near their limits of heat tolerance. The shapes and boundaries of uplands, grasslands, and other ecosystems will change as a result of global warming. Some ecosystems may experience significant changes in species mix, as climate conditions begin to favor certain species over others. Those species unable to adapt to the rapidly changing conditions will inevitably become extinct. Along with global warming itself, all of these secondary changes have the potential of significantly affecting the earth's biological productivity.

Threats to human health associated with global climate change include the increased spread of diseases. For example, much of the population of central Africa lives in highlands that are only slightly above the altitude at which malarial mosquitoes thrive. Higher temperatures will allow mosquitoes to extend their range into these population centers. Similarly, warmer temperatures and reduced water supplies would impact water quality and sanitation, resulting in the spread of waterborne diseases such as cholera, salmonellosis, and giardiasis.

Global climate change is predicted to produce more frequent and more extreme weather events—violent storms, flooding, drought, and severe heat waves. These are events that have direct impact on human health and the availability of food. Other potential health impacts associated with global warming include increased rates of cardiovascular and respiratory disease due to changes in pollen formation and air pollution.

Some scientists believe the major human health issue associated with climate change will be population shifts. Sea level rise, agricultural failure, and drought, especially in the developing nations, would likely result in large migrations of population. Some sources predict that global warming will result in population shifts that could lead to war in what are now stable areas. In contrast, there are those who say that the impact of global climate change on human settlements will be negligible—that the pace of human technological response is so rapid that problems will be managed as they arise.

While scientists cannot accurately predict the regional consequences of global climate change, it is likely that large populations, economies, and infrastructures will be severely affected. The ability to accurately predict such impacts, however, may not precede their arrival. Regional variation and natural fluctuations make detection of warming trends difficult in the short term. Further, the lifetime of greenhouse gases in the atmosphere, combined with the action of feedback loops and the oceans, will result in continuation of global climate changes long after emissions of greenhouse gases are reduced. Attempts to reduce the emissions of greenhouse gases will require great expenditures on the part of industry and significant lifestyle changes for populations around the world. In the meantime, questions remain: What should be done in the face of scientific uncertainty about local and regional impacts? How much sense does it make to act without clear answers as to impact? How much worse will things be if we wait for more certain predictions before we act?

■ ADDRESSING THE ISSUES ■

Amid increasing scientific evidence of global warming and growing public concern over global environmental issues, the Intergovernmental Panel on Climate Change (IPCC) was created in 1988. The IPCC was established by the World Meteorological Organization (WMO) and the UNEP to assess scientific information on climate change, its potential impacts, and possible response strategies.

In 1990, the IPCC issued its First Assessment Report, confirming the scientific evidence for climate change. The report provided a scientific basis for negotiations on a global treaty on climate change. The United Nations Framework Convention on Climate Change (FCCC) was adopted in 1992. Today, 181 governments (including the United States) and the European community are parties to the convention. Annual Conference of Parties (COP) meetings are held to review and support the FCCC and to continue discussions on strategies to combat global climate change. The COP is the primary legal forum for future international actions to address climate change.

The FCCC set an ultimate goal of stabilizing atmospheric concentrations of greenhouse gases at safe levels. This is to be accomplished within a time frame that would allow ecosystems to adapt naturally to climate change, ensure the safety of global food production, and allow sustainable economic development. The FCCC did not establish specific emissions reduction targets or timetables to meet this goal. Instead, the parties gave a general commitment to address climate change and report to the COP on their actions.

The first COP was held in Berlin, Germany, in April 1995. The outcome of COP-1 was the Berlin Mandate, which stated that the commitments for developed nations contained in the FCCC were inadequate. Talks were launched to determine stronger, more specific commitments for these countries. The following year, the IPCC published its Second Assessment Report. This report is best known for its conclusion that "the balance of evidence suggests that there is a discernible human influence on global climate change." The report identified the availability of "no regrets" options and other cost-effective strategies for combating global climate change.

In December 1997, in Kyoto, Japan, the objectives of the Berlin Mandate were realized in the adoption of the Kyoto Protocol. The Kyoto Protocol commits the developed nations to reduce their collective emissions of six greenhouse gases—carbon dioxide, methane, nitrous oxide (N_2O), hydrofluorocarbons, perfluorocarbons, and sulfur hexafluoride—by a total of at least 5 percent. Each country's individual emissions reduction target must be achieved by the period 2008–2012. These targets would result in 30 percent lower greenhouse gas emission rates from developed countries in 2010 than would have been expected without the protocol. The 30 percent reduction applies only to developed countries, not to global emissions. In order to enter into force, the Kyoto Protocol must be ratified by fifty-five parties to the convention, including developed nations representing at least 55 percent of the total 1990 carbon dioxide emissions from this group. While some developing countries may have ratified the Kyoto Protocol, they do not have commitments under this protocol.

The thirty-eight developed countries often referred to as Annex B countries are: Australia, Austria, Belgium, Bulgaria, Canada, Croatia, Czech Republic, Denmark, Estonia, Finland, France, Germany, Greece, Hungary, Iceland, Ireland, Italy, Japan, Latvia, Liechtenstein, Lithuania, Luxembourg, Monaco, Netherlands, New Zealand, Norway, Poland, Portugal, Romania, Russian Federation, Slovakia, Slovenia,

Spain, Sweden, Switzerland, Ukraine, United Kingdom of Great Britain and Northern Ireland, and the United States.

The United States has not joined the eighty-four parties who have ratified the Kyoto Protocol. Major roadblocks preventing U.S. ratification of the protocol include its positions that developing countries also make the same commitments to limit greenhouse gas emissions as industrialized nations; that a global system of emissions trading be implemented where nations could purchase the unused emissions allotments of other nations; and that nations be allowed to count the carbon dioxide absorbed by forests and farmlands toward their emissions reduction targets.

In 2002, the George W. Bush administration developed a "Clear Skies" initiative, which calls for mandatory 70 percent cuts in emissions of three major pollutants by 2018 using a cap-and-trade system. The plan, however, would not require reductions in carbon emissions from power plants and factories linked to global warming.

While global climate change will impact the economies of all nations, developing nations will be most vulnerable. Policies for reducing greenhouse gas emissions will also have economic impacts. Cost-benefit comparisons are difficult to make. However, there are opportunities to minimize the costs of climate change policies and to promote sustainable development. For example, many economists agree that energy efficiency gains of 10 to 30 percent can be achieved over the next several decades at a zero net cost or even with economic gain. In the long term, raising energy efficiency can make industries and countries more competitive. Such "no regrets" strategies make economic and environmental sense even without the prospect of global climate change.

Given the major sources of greenhouse gas emissions—energy production and use, transportation, agriculture, and deforestation—achieving sufficient reductions in these emissions will require significant changes in developing and developed nations alike. Possible strategies (both actual changes as well as policy shifts) for reducing emissions of greenhouse gases include:

- Promoting the use of new technologies to reduce fugitive emissions from energy extraction and fuel transport;
- Converting existing power plants to include newer, more efficient technologies;
- Promoting the use of technologies, such as combined cycle power plants and cogeneration plants;

- Research and development of low-emitting technologies;
- Switching to less carbon-intensive fuels, an option that may be limited by finite global reserves of natural gas;
- Limiting and taxing emissions;
- Adopting systems of tradable emissions-based permitting, where industries would trade unused emissions with other industries, thereby allowing growth of new industry without increasing the total permitted emissions within the region;
- Increasing the use of renewable energy sources such as wind, solar, and small hydroelectric power;
- Promoting the construction of more end-use energy-efficient buildings;
- Promoting the development of more fuel-efficient vehicles, including hybrid vehicles that use a combination of fuel-fired engines and electric motors;
- Providing safe and efficient public transportation systems and promoting their use by limiting automobile access;
- Establishing "user fees" on older vehicles or offering credits for switching to more fuel-efficient vehicles;
- Adopting policies to ensure sustainable forest management;
- Establishing forests on degraded or nonforested lands;
- Changing agricultural processes to increase productivity and limit carbon release from soils;
- Using additives in livestock feed to increase feed efficiency and improve animal growth rates, resulting in lower methane emissions per unit of meat produced;
- Changing irrigation and fertilization practices in wet rice cultivation; and
- Changing the timing of fertilizer use in agriculture to optimize crop use of nitrogen.

The implementation of some of these strategies could be quite expensive, and some will not be applicable in specific situations. Some may have a greater impact than others. For many low-cost options, there are barriers (e.g., regulations and lack of financing) that have blocked some of these options. Implementing these and other strategies to achieve sufficient reductions in the emissions of greenhouse gases will require global cooperation. Developing nations have more immediate needs. It is difficult for them to forego economic development to avoid global climate change. These countries will need low-cost access to new, environmentally sound technologies. Developing countries are not bound by formal emission requirements under the Kyoto Protocol, but many are taking steps to rein in greenhouse gas emissions. One mechanism envisioned in the Kyoto Protocol to be an aid in encouraging the participation of developing countries is the Clean Development Mechanism (CDM). The CDM aims to help developing countries achieve sustainable development through greenhouse gas-reducing projects financed by industrialized countries. Credits generated from project activities may be used by industrialized countries to achieve compliance with their emission reduction or limitation requirements.

▪ IMPORTANT POINTS FOR RESEARCHING A STORY ▪

- Attempts to reduce emissions of greenhouse gases require economic sacrifices and lifestyle changes around the world. Developing nations will face the dilemma of how to promote economic growth and at the same time control global warming. At the individual level, choices will need to be made between issues of personal freedom versus public good. Current lifestyle trends in the United States involving large homes and large vehicles are in direct conflict with greenhouse gas reduction. The toughest question, however, is not necessarily what will be the local impacts of global climate change but what to do in the face of uncertainty? What are the environmental, social, and political costs of action or inaction?
- The goal of the United Nations is not to halt global climate change. It is accepted that global climate change will continue to occur. The FCCC hopes merely to slow the rate of change to allow ecosystems and agriculture time to adapt. Similarly, the FCCC goals do not include the cessation of greenhouse gas emissions but rather aim to cut the rates of increase of emissions.
- Investigate the economic and social aspects of proposals to reduce the threat of climate change, especially proposals in the international arena.
- While the mainstream scientific community now accepts global climate change as real, the general public remains skeptical. The public is even more skeptical about the impact of individual lifestyle choices on efforts to reduce greenhouse gas emissions.

▪ AVOIDING PITFALLS ▪

- Avoid equating global climate change solely with carbon dioxide emissions. The issue is much broader.
- The issues of global climate change and stratospheric ozone depletion are often confused. Ozone and CFCs are involved in both issues. In the lower atmosphere, ozone and CFCs act as greenhouse gases. (See the brief on "Air Pollution [Outdoor.]") In the upper atmosphere, CFCs break down the natural ozone layer that shields the earth from harmful ultraviolet radiation. (See the brief on "Ozone Depletion.")
- There remains a wide range of opinion about the science of global climate change, especially in the United States. Avoid taking a single point of view.
- Temporary extremes in temperature and weather cannot necessarily be used as direct evidence of global climate change. The widespread reporting of the presence of open water at the North Pole in August 2000 is a case in point. The observations of two scientists who had crossed the pole while on a tourist cruise were widely reported as evidence of global warming. Ten days after the story first appeared, it was retracted. Further investigation indicated that, while measurable increases in Arctic temperatures have occurred over the past thirty years, the presence of open water at the pole was neither a new event nor was it particularly alarming to scientists who study climate.
- Avoid focusing on solely technical solutions without acknowledging that many are untried. They, too, may cause climatic or other problems.

▪ INFORMATION RESOURCES ▪

▪ GOVERNMENT/ACADEMIA

- United Nations Framework Convention on Climate Change (www.unfccc.de)
  Secretariat of the United Nations Framework Convention on Climate Change
  Haus Carstanjen, Martin-Luther-King-Strasse 8, D-53175 Bonn, Germany

(49-228) 815-1000; fax: (49-228) 815-1999
E-mail: secretariat@unfccc.int

- U.S. Environmental Protection Agency (www.epa.gov/globalwarming/)
Office of Atmospheric Programs, Climate Protection Division
501 3rd St. NW, Washington, DC 20005
(888) 782-7937 or (202) 564-1471

■ INDUSTRY

- Alliance for Responsible Atmospheric Policy (www.arap.org)
2111 Wilson Blvd., Suite 850, Arlington, VA 22201
(703) 243-0344; fax: (703) 243-2874
- IPIECA (International Petroleum Industry Environmental Conservation Association)
2nd floor-Monmouth House
87-93 Westbourne Grove
London W2 4VL Great Britain

■ NONPROFIT/CONSUMER ORGANIZATIONS

- Climate Action Network (www.climatenetwork.org)
1367 Connecticut Ave. NW, Suite 300, Washington, DC 20036
(202) 785-8702; fax: (202) 785-8701
E-mail: nathalie@climatenetwork.org
- Environmental Defense (www.environmentaldefense.org)
257 Park Ave. South, New York, NY 10010
(212) 505-2100; fax: (212) 505-2375
- Global Warming Information Page (www.globalwarming.org)
The Cooler Heads Coalition
c/o Consumer Alert
1001 Connecticut Ave. NW, Suite 1128, Washington, DC 22036
(202) 467-5809; fax: (202) 467-5814

GROUNDWATER POLLUTION

▪ BACKGROUND ▪

Groundwater is water that flows beneath the earth's surface. Groundwater flows through pores between sand, gravel, or silt particles and through fractures, channels, and caverns in rock. These geologic formations and the groundwater that they hold are called aquifers.

Aquifers are replenished by the downward movement of water from rain and melting snow through soil and sediments (the unsaturated zone) into the aquifer (the saturated zone). This process is called aquifer recharge. The top of the aquifer—the water table—may be shallow, found just below the ground surface, or it can occur hundreds of feet below ground. The height of the water table may vary with weather or season, rising during periods of extended rainfall and falling during periods of drought.

Groundwater can reach the land surface in several ways. Groundwater may be connected to a surface water system, providing base flow to a wetland, estuary, lake, or stream. It can also be brought to the surface through a well. A well is simply a pipe drilled into the aquifer that fills with groundwater. Groundwater wells vary in design, depending on the geologic formation and purpose of the well. Water-withdrawal wells typically require a pump to bring groundwater to the surface. However, this is not true in all cases. In some areas, aquifers may be confined beneath thick, impermeable layers of clay or silt. These confining layers place the aquifer under pressure. Because of this pressure, the water level in a well may rise higher than the top of the aquifer. Such wells are called artesian wells. In some cases, water may even flow from an artesian well without pumping. Monitoring wells, drilled to measure the depth, flow, and/or quality of groundwater, may or may not have a pump, depending upon the depth of the aquifer.

This brief is based on information provided by Christopher Uchrin, Rutgers University, New Brunswick, New Jersey.

■ IDENTIFYING THE ISSUES ■

Groundwater provides a quarter of all the freshwater used in the United States. The major use of groundwater in the United States is for irrigation and electric thermoelectric power. The next largest use of groundwater is for public and domestic supply. Fully half of the total U.S. population, including 95 percent of the country's rural population, depends on groundwater for drinking, cooking, and bathing. Three-quarters of all U.S. cities depend on groundwater for part of their drinking water supply. A number of major cities obtain all of their water supply from groundwater. Groundwater is also an important source of freshwater for industrial and livestock operations.

In its 1999 report, "Safe Drinking Water Act, Section 1429, Ground Water Report to Congress," the U.S. Environmental Protection Agency (EPA) states that groundwater quality in the United States is "generally good." However, some estimates indicate that up to 25 percent of usable groundwater supplies in the United States are contaminated. It is difficult to make general statements regarding the overall quality of groundwater in the United States. Assessments of groundwater quality are most typically conducted when contamination is suspected or in areas where contamination would most likely be found. Extrapolation of results from such targeted assessments to overall groundwater quality would, therefore, be inappropriate.

Because of their yield of natural impurities, not all areas have usable aquifers beneath them. There are a number of factors that can make aquifers more or less susceptible to contamination. In general, the higher the water table, the easier it is to get the water out but the harder it is to keep the water unpolluted. Similarly, aquifers that are quickly recharged are generally more vulnerable to pollution than those recharged at a slower rate. Unconfined aquifers (where materials above the aquifer are permeable) are more susceptible to contamination than are confined aquifers. Aquifers in bedrock formations with large fractures provide pathways for surface contaminants to reach groundwater. Natural protective barriers such as thick clay units prevent groundwater contamination in many areas.

Groundwater contamination is typically a localized problem, with contaminants remaining in slow-moving plumes. Groundwater moves very slowly from several inches to a few feet each year. This is a mixed blessing. The good news is that the slow movement of groundwater keeps the pollution from spreading rapidly throughout a region. The bad news is that the pollution remains much more concentrated than it would in faster moving, more turbulent surface waters. The concentrations of pollutants in groundwater may be hundreds or thousands of times higher than those found in surface water. In addition, the cold temperature of groundwater can slow the decomposition of otherwise degradable pollutants. The combination of these factors can result in groundwater contamination that, untreated, would remain for years.

Groundwater pollutants come from both natural and human-made sources. Natural contaminants come from the geologic formations through which groundwater flows. Natural groundwater contaminants include inorganic chemicals such as aluminum, arsenic, chromium, iron, and lead; radioactive isotopes; and suspended and dissolved particles. A major natural contaminant is salt. While naturally occurring, these contaminants can render groundwater unsuitable for human consumption or agricultural or industrial use. Groundwater contaminants from human-made sources range from biological agents (bacteria, viruses, protozoa, and parasites) found in human and livestock waste to inorganic and organic chemicals released from human activities such as agriculture, power generation, industry, waste disposal, and travel. Major sources of groundwater pollution in the United States include improper handling and disposal of industrial waste on the ground, leachate from municipal solid waste landfills, infiltration and runoff of agricultural chemicals, infiltration from septic systems and cesspools, and leaking underground storage tanks and pipelines.

Methyl *tert*-Butyl Ether (MTBE) is one synthetic compound that has recently received much attention as a groundwater pollutant. MTBE is an oxygenate—a compound added to increase the oxygen content—in reformulated gasoline. MTBE was first added to fuels in the 1970s as a substitute for lead. The amount of MTBE in gasoline increased in the 1990s when reformulated fuels were required under the Clean Air Act to reduce ozone pollution in nonattainment areas. MTBE in gasoline enters groundwater through surface fuel spills and leaking underground storage tanks. It has been found in groundwater wells nationwide at very low levels. Compounds such as MTBE have fewer natural microorganisms to degrade them and in many cases can have longer, more extensive plumes. Very low levels of MTBE can render water undrinkable, giving it a taste and odor similar to turpentine. The human health effects of ingesting MTBE-contaminated drinking water are equivocal. The EPA's current guidelines suggest that MTBE levels in drinking water should be kept below EPA's taste and odor thresholds (40–60 parts per billion [ppb]) and that adverse health effects are unlikely at such levels. Groundwater and drinking water standards for MTBE set by individual states vary widely; current values range from 20 to 500 ppb. Some data suggest that MTBE may cause cancer at high doses.

▪ ADDRESSING THE ISSUES ▪

Industry and regulators have cooperatively developed and implemented a groundwater restoration strategy that prioritizes contamination discoveries into acute, chronic, and very low risk issues. There are three general approaches to groundwater pollution problems: containment, treatment, and prevention.

▪ CONTAINMENT

It is difficult to entirely isolate a contaminated plume in groundwater. Containment technologies include barriers to prevent pollution migration from contaminated soils into groundwater and to prevent the spread of pollutants within an aquifer system.

▪ TREATMENT

Conventional groundwater treatment consists of pumping the polluted groundwater to the surface, treating and/or cleaning it (either physically, biologically, or chemically), and pumping it back into the aquifer. This option can be very expensive; depending on the site, treatment systems can sometimes cost more than $5 million for design and installation, although some cost considerably less. In addition, the long period of time typically required to effectively pump and treat groundwater can lead to high costs to maintain the treatment system.

Newer groundwater treatment technologies are being developed and field-tested at federal and state cleanup sites. Many of these technologies require significantly less labor and maintenance than conventional groundwater treatment and therefore, once brought into wider usage, may offer considerable cost savings for groundwater remediation. For example, a new technology called a Permeable Reactive Barrier (PRB), once installed, is an entirely passive treatment system in which groundwater flows naturally through the treatment medium.

The total cost for design and installation of a PRB is generally less than \$1 million.

■ PREVENTION

Prevention of groundwater contamination is critical. Pollution prevention is far less costly to society, in the long run, than trying to mitigate the effects of pollution. Although pollution prevention may require upfront expenditures, responding to major pollution problems after the fact can bankrupt companies, take limited public funds from other uses, and disrupt citizens' lives and the economic health of a state. By their nature, preventive activities can be planned so that facilities can budget time and money in a way that minimizes cost while maximizing protection.

Pollution prevention efforts in the United States are increasing. These efforts include improved management of household and industrial wastes, underground storage tank protection programs, improved management of pesticides, and the establishment of regional groundwater protection programs.

Groundwater protection and remediation fall under a number of state and federal regulations and programs. Federal laws addressing groundwater include the Clean Water Act; the Safe Drinking Water Act; the Resource Conservation and Recovery Act (RCRA); the Comprehensive Environmental Response, Compensation and Liability Act (CERCLA, or Superfund); and the Federal Insecticide, Fungicide and Rodenticide Act (FIFRA). Programs under these laws have traditionally focused on groundwater remediation.

More recently, the trend appears to be moving toward programs aimed at protecting groundwater. A number of states have developed the EPA-approved Comprehensive State Ground Water Protection Programs (CSGWPP). These state programs typically include mechanisms for improved land-use management, the coordination of regulatory offices, and the establishment of well protection zones.

Aquifers sometimes have the capacity to naturally contain the spread of a contaminant plume and eventually restore themselves through various attenuation processes, primarily bioremediation. Natural attenuation, which relies on natural processes to clean up or attenuate pollution in groundwater, takes place at almost all polluted sites where the right conditions exist underground. When the environment is polluted with chemicals, nature works in several ways to help clean it up. Tiny bugs or microbes living in the groundwater use some chemicals for food. When they are completely digested, the chemicals can be changed into water and harmless gases. Chemicals can sometimes stick to surrounding soil, which holds them in place. While this does not clean up the pollution, it keeps the pollutants from moving into the groundwater and leaving the site. As the pollutants move through the groundwater, they mix with clean water, which reduces or dilutes the pollution.

If these natural processes can be shown to remove pollutants before they can affect public health or the environment, then costly engineered remediations can be avoided. In some cases, actively monitoring the progress of this type of natural restoration may be all that is required to protect human health and the environment. In other cases, limited source area treatment/containment or enhancing natural attenuation can be used as a restoration strategy. When scientists monitor or test conditions to make sure natural attenuation is working, this is referred to as monitored natural attenuation (MNA).

■ IMPORTANT POINTS FOR RESEARCHING A STORY ■

- Groundwater pollution sources are regulated as either point or nonpoint. A point source consists of a single discharge location, such as a home, business, industrial facility, leaking underground storage tank, or spill. Nonpoint sources typically cover broad areas and cannot be as easily pinpointed as a discharge pipe or single discharge event. Examples of nonpoint sources of groundwater pollution include runoff or infiltration from agricultural land, highways, and industrial areas.
- All water needs testing—even water used in chemical plants for making chemicals needs testing. The amount of testing depends on the end use. Routine water quality testing of public drinking water supplies is required by the EPA and state departments of health. Requirements for testing for private water supplies are less rigorous. In some areas, testing may only be required at the time of property transfer.
- Under the Safe Drinking Water Act, the EPA has issued maximum contaminant levels (MCLs) for more than eighty chemicals in drinking water. Complete analyses of groundwater samples for these compounds are expensive and generally unnecessary. It is

typically recommended that private water supplies be tested routinely for total coliform bacteria, nitrates, and lead. Where a suspected source of contamination exists, groundwater analyses can be targeted to suspected contaminants. For example, where a leaking underground storage tank is suspected, the contents can dictate the analyses—volatile organic compounds such as benzene, toluene, and MTBE for gasoline tanks or heavier semivolatile compounds for heating oil tanks.

- Knowing the specific groundwater contaminants can help in tracking down potential sources. Some examples: MTBE is associated with gasoline tanks and spills; tetrachloroethylene (also known as percholorethylene, or PCE) is a solvent historically associated with dry cleaning; fecal contamination may be associated with septic systems, leaking sewer lines, or animal feeding operations; and pesticides and nitrates are typically associated with agricultural sites.
- Laboratory reports for groundwater analyses are highly technical and notoriously difficult to interpret. The best reports will list the contaminants tested, the limits of detection, the concentrations detected, and relevant health and environmental standards. The reports typically list all the contaminants targeted by the analysis, regardless of whether they were detected in the groundwater sample. Depending upon the contaminant, results are reported in milligrams of contaminant per liter of water (mg/l), which is equivalent to parts per million (ppm), or in micrograms of contaminant per liter of water (μg/l), which is equivalent to parts per billion (ppb). Other values are reported in units specific to the test (e.g., pH, hardness, conductance, and turbidity). A professional environmental engineer may be needed to interpret these results.
- When evaluating laboratory reports, it is important to compare the detection limit—the lowest concentration of a contaminant that could be found by the analysis—with the drinking water standard for each compound.
- The cost of water pollution investigations can be very high. Therefore, government agencies and the responsible parties will develop most information themselves. Find out who (if anyone) is actively investigating a site. Work with them to understand the local circumstances. Verify analyses with other experts.
- The U.S. Geological Survey's National Water Quality Assessment Program (NAWQA) monitors more than fifty major river basins

and aquifers covering nearly all fifty states. The NAWQA collects and interprets data about water chemistry, hydrology, land use, stream habitat, and aquatic life. The U.S. Geological Survey manages water information at local and regional offices located throughout the United States. Although all offices are tied together through a nationwide computer network, each collects data and conducts studies in a particular area. Local information is best found by contacting the local offices.

▪ AVOIDING PITFALLS ▪

- A great deal of uncertainty is associated with groundwater contamination. Stories should avoid hiding this uncertainty. The identification, investigation, and mitigation of groundwater pollution are expensive, lengthy, highly technical, and often uncertain undertakings. The top experts may disagree in complex sites. These may be honest differences of opinion.
- Pollution sources may be old, with no remaining records or evidence at the site except the pollution that remains behind. The responsible sources for some well pollution incidents are never found.
- The taste, smell, or color of water is not necessarily an indicator of water quality. Water may be aesthetically unpleasant and yet not actually harmful to drink. Likewise, groundwater that to all appearances is pure could contain carcinogens in high concentrations. The only way to be certain of the quality of groundwater is to test it.
- Chemicals differ enormously in the health risks they present. Know what chemicals have been found and their concentrations. Some chemicals have thresholds below which no health effect is expected, while others are primarily a concern during prolonged exposure. Be careful in your use of health effect terms. Also, health effects may be debatable. Use more than one source of scientific information, and make sure that your source actually has expertise in the appropriate field. For every standard, there is a fact sheet outlining health effects available on the Internet.
- Focus on the good pollution stories as well as the bad. Many companies have taken drastic steps to clean up production waste, thereby making contamination of groundwater less likely. Indus-

try efforts to police itself should be covered by the environmental reporter, possibly with assistance from the business reporting staff.

- It is important to realize nothing in the subsurface moves rapidly by most relative standards. Groundwater pollution migrates slowly. It takes a year to move inches to a few feet. It is a common mistake to imagine an underground river that will spread pollution into the neighboring county in a few days.
- Groundwater quality is a localized issue. Use extreme caution in presenting national trends in water quality. The data may have little or no relevance to the actual regional situation.

▪ INFORMATION RESOURCES ▪

■ GOVERNMENT/ACADEMIA

- U.S. Department of the Interior, U.S. Geological Survey, National Water Quality Assessment Program (www.nawqa-who@usgs.gov)
- U.S. Environmental Protection Agency, Office of Ground Water and Drinking Water (www.epa.gov/water)
  401 M St. SW, Washington, DC 20460-0003
  (800) 426-4791 (Safe Drinking Water Hotline)
  E-mail: hotline-sdwa@epa.gov
- U.S. Geological Survey, Office of Ground Water (http://water.usgs.gov/ogw/)
  Office of Media Relations
  Reston, VA 20192
  (703) 648-4732

■ NONPROFIT/CONSUMER ORGANIZATIONS

- The Groundwater Foundation (www.groundwater.org)
  5561 South 48th, Suite 215, Lincoln, NE 68516
  (800) 858-4844 or (402) 434-2740; fax: (402) 434-2742
  E-mail: info@groundwater.org
- The Groundwater Protection Council (http://gwpc.site.net)
  13208 N. MacArthur, Oklahoma City, OK 73142
  (405) 516-4972; fax: (405) 516-4973

NATURALLY OCCURRING AND TECHNOLOGY-BASED DISASTERS

▪ BACKGROUND ▪

Environmental disasters are events in which a community is exposed to severe danger for a concentrated period of time, resulting in significant loss to the community. A disaster disrupts the social structure of the community and prevents it from being able to carry out essential functions. These extreme events are the result of environmental hazards that could be primarily naturally occurring events or events that are socially constructed, involving technological misapplications or malfunctions. For example, earthquakes are extreme naturally occurring environmental events, while accidental releases of chemicals and terrorism involving germ warfare are the result of socially constructed misapplications of technology. Both kinds of hazards are capable of producing disasters.

Today there is heightened awareness of disasters on the part of the public. The events of September 11, 2001, demonstrated that the United States is not immune to mass casualty disasters. It is likely that disasters—particularly terrorist-related disasters—will remain high on the public policy agenda for some time. Opportunities for addressing issues related to disaster reduction will increase with the enormous attention being given to the subject.

Disasters make news. These rapid-onset events directly threaten human life and the environment on a community-wide scale. Historically, disasters have been considered as either/or cases: as either natural disasters or socially constructed disasters. Reporters need to understand both kinds of disasters, as well as the growing possibility of an alignment of the two—a socially constructed disaster compounded by the occurrence of a natural disaster.

▪ IDENTIFYING THE ISSUES ▪

Extreme natural events that cause death or damage to large numbers of humans are referred to as natural hazards. Natural hazards can be divided into those of biological origin, such as malaria or schistosomiasis, and those of geophysical origin, such as earthquakes, severe storms, temperature extremes, wildfire, floods, drought, and volcanoes. The latter can be further categorized into events that take place rapidly and those that occur over periods of millions of years, such as long-term climate changes and glacial melting. Only rapid-onset geophysical events are considered in this brief.

The Worldwatch Institute reports that over two billion people were affected by natural disasters in the 1990s. Today, more people are displaced by natural disasters than by conflict, and the economic losses of such disasters totaled more than $608 billion. Poorer countries are especially hard hit, having fewer resources with which to cope and more uninsured losses. For example, Honduras and Nicaragua bore the brunt of Hurricane Mitch in 1998, suffering damages in excess of $8 billion—more than their combined gross domestic products.

While natural hazards traditionally have been considered as harmful aspects of the physical environment produced by forces outside of the control of humans, people often play a role in creating these hazards. More and more the resulting devastation from natural disasters is the consequence of ecologically destructive human practices and the growing numbers of people who live in harm's way. Humans have disturbed the ecological safety net through deforestation, changes in river flow, and filling in of floodplains. Natural defenses have been destroyed, and populations are less well protected against disasters. Flooding, for example, is often the result of weather events made worse by human activities such as deforestation, soil erosion, and land drainage. According to the Worldwatch report, one person in three now lives in harm's way—within 100 kilometers (62 miles) of a coastline. Thirteen of the world's nineteen largest cities—with populations in excess of ten million people—are located in coastal zones.

While people often play a role in exacerbating natural hazards, they often also have some ability to prevent them from occurring. For example, the loss of lives associated with tornadoes can be mitigated somewhat by use of early warning systems. Zoning ordinances that prohibit development of wetlands and floodplains are designed to avert costly disasters down the road.

Technology-based disasters are socially constructed disasters that involve technology gone awry—triggered by either inadvertent human error or deliberate human choice. Technology-related disasters range from unforeseen mechanical failures to intentional terrorism. These rapid-onset events often occur in technological areas that impact public safety, such as the collapse of large structures, public transportation disasters linked to mechanical failure, or manufacturing processes—including the manufacturing of biologicals, power production, and transport of hazardous materials. In any case, technology-based disasters result in life-threatening releases of energy and/or materials. For example, energy is released in a chemical form when a tanker car carrying hazardous chemicals explodes, or life-threatening materials are released when anthrax is sent through the mail.

Early hazard research focused primarily on naturally occurring events such as floods, droughts, and severe storms. In the 1970s and 1980s, however, following such disasters as Bhopal, Three Mile Island, and Chernobyl, attention shifted to large-scale, socially constructed disasters. Technology-based disasters are not new, however. History offers many examples, including the 1889 Johnstown flood in which 2,209 people drowned when the dam burst above Johnstown, Pennsylvania, or the sinking of the *Titanic* in 1912, to name only a few.

While technology-based disasters themselves are defined in terms of the role played by human error or deliberate choice, they, too, can be made worse by shortsighted human actions, just as in the case of natural disasters. For example, the location of potentially hazardous manufacturing facilities in densely populated areas can greatly increase the losses that result in the event of a technological disaster. Hence, the U.S. Nuclear Regulatory Commission (NRC) does not permit nuclear power reactors to be located in densely populated areas, although some nuclear power reactors are now in densely populated areas because of population growth.

Keith Smith's 1992 study of technological disasters of the late twentieth century shows several important trends in disasters such as those that occurred at Chernobyl and Bhopal. They are no longer confined to developed countries and are now likely to impact poorer populations vulnerable to extreme events and to have implications for larger areas.

Most natural disasters differ from those with a basis in technology in several important ways. Technology-based disasters have a greater likelihood of producing a longer lasting or permanent impact in terms of both human health and the environment when compared with naturally occurring disasters. Radiation leakages or releases of other toxic substances can affect future generations. These disasters also have a greater likelihood of producing a more global impact than most naturally occurring disasters. Volcanoes are one of the few natural events that have the potential for major global consequences. Natural disasters are almost always visible, while some technology-based disasters have the potential to be both invisible and lethal (e.g., radiation exposures).

While natural disasters and technology-based disasters are often considered separately, in reality they are often dynamically intertwined. Oil and chemical refineries and storage facilities and nuclear reactors may be located near active fault lines and made vulnerable during a natural disaster. Heavy rains and flooding may threaten hazardous waste storage facilities. Offshore oil rigs may be destroyed when they are in the path of approaching tropical storms. Natural events like earthquakes cause buildings and bridges to collapse. Natural hazards may actually cause, compound, or intensify technological ones. The earth's natural systems often help distribute hazards created by technology over large areas. Wind patterns blow releases, and rains flush particulate material out of the atmosphere. And sometimes technology is used to reduce or eliminate the hazards of naturally occurring events, as in the case of dams built so that people will be able to live in areas previously flooded.

▪ ADDRESSING THE ISSUES ▪

In industrial society, risks grow exponentially. Disasters endanger larger segments of the population and have the potential for increasingly more severe effects. In many ways, the future will be shaped by our ability to plan for and respond to disasters. Preparing for disasters or acting to reduce their impact is usually less expensive than the cost of recovery afterward. Disaster mitigation is sound investment according to the Worldwatch Institute, which estimates on average that every $1 spent on disaster preparedness saves $7 in disaster recovery costs. Investing in mitigation, however, requires governments and communities to shift their sights and plan toward the long term.

Although risks are potentially preventable, in reality this is impossible because of chance factors, human error, and politics. Totally risk-free design and construction that would eliminate all possibility of structural failure are unlikely as well as costly. The questions become "How safe is safe?" and "Safety at what cost?"

Predicting natural disasters proves challenging. A study at Princeton University in 2002 mapped areas in the United States at risk of natural disasters such as flooding, earthquakes, and tornadoes. The mapping was done to raise awareness of "predictable consequences of high risk land use." The study pointed to a thirty-year cycle of hurricane tracks that suggest big storms may track more to the east and north in the future. The study also confirms that costs of such disasters may be higher in the future due to population increases in areas likely to be affected.

The greatest potential for prevention exists with technology-based hazards, rather than natural events, since the former result from faulty engineering and/or human failings. Because human flaws (both unintentional and deliberate) are difficult to guard against, prevention usually involves modifications in engineering. While modifying factors prior to a disaster is the goal, often designs are changed only after events have occurred. For example, only following a number of disastrous oil spills (e.g., *Exxon Valdez*) did the Oil Pollution Act of 1990 begin to require full double hulls on oil tankers to be phased in starting in 1995.

Improvements in engineering design, advances in occupational safety, strict government regulations regarding fire and building codes, and greater awareness on the part of industrial managers and the general public have reduced some technological risks—but not all. Significant engineering changes have reduced the failure of dams. At the same time, the total number of people exposed to flood dangers has increased because of growth in the population and the numbers of people living in harm's way. Similarly, while airplane design has been greatly improved, air transport–related risks have increased as a result of the increase in plane size, the number of passengers, and the number of flights.

Trends in the twentieth century, such as growing energy demands, have tended to increase some technology-based risks at the community level, making community preparedness critical. For example, large modern chemical and petrochemical industries have been located near significant concentrations of population. The need to transport increasing amounts of hazardous materials creates risks for communities. Multinational companies have located facilities in communities within less developed countries where safeguards that protect the population are inadequate to handle these new situations. For instance, 2,000 people in Bhopal died from the release of methyl isocyanate.

The nuclear power industry has been involved in the development of community emergency response plans. Guidelines for the development of these plans were established by the Federal Emergency Management Agency (FEMA) and the NRC following the accident at Three Mile Island. Owners of all reactors are now required to develop and seek approval for emergency response plans as a condition for maintaining their operating licenses. These plans must include measures covering the need for indoor shelter (to protect the community against immediate release of radioneuclides), medical treatment (potassium iodide as a thyroid blocking agent), and evacuation.

■ IMPORTANT POINTS FOR RESEARCHING A STORY ■

- In the event of a natural disaster, remember to consider possible technology-based hazards that may be impacted that could increase damage to the environment and loss of life. These include the possible implications of a natural disaster for nearby engineering structures, transportation systems, and industries. Likewise, in the event of a technology-based disaster, remember to consider the possible role natural weather events could play in magnifying losses.
- It is important to distinguish between extreme events that are potentially predictable and those that are understandable but not predictable.
- Very different types of disasters—whether they are naturally occurring or technology-based—have very similar immediate consequences for decision-makers, such as emergency managers, military officers, or computer network operators. For example, response capabilities during disasters are often overwhelmed and resources are inadequate. New and unfamiliar problems emerge. Reliable information is hard to find, and a coherent view of the situation can be difficult to construct.
- Ability to forewarn can make a big difference. In the case of many technological disasters, however, there is little or no opportunity to issue warnings. Studies done by the U.S. Bureau of Reclamation on the effectiveness of warning systems found that for events where a warning of 90 minutes or more was possible the loss of

life was 2 people per 10,000 residents compared with 250 per 10,000 residents in cases where no warning or a warning less than 90 minutes was possible.

- Because disasters often reflect interactions between different types of systems, understanding them and responding to them require an interdisciplinary approach. For example, the terrorist events of September 11, 2001, required the response efforts of the Federal Bureau of Investigation (FBI), fire departments, local police, engineers, health officials, environmental specialists on air quality, and transport specialists, to name just a few.
- Don't assume terrorist-related disasters are the only possible mass casualty scenarios. Industrial accidents, transportation accidents, and natural disasters have the potential of resulting in thousands of deaths and injuries. In addition, simultaneous events can occur around natural events such as hurricanes or earthquakes.
- The response to the events of September 11, 2001, integrated use of military resources with emergency management and law enforcement, and their role in emergency management funding, planning, and operations is likely to increase as preparedness for terrorism becomes a major emergency management responsibility. These events, however, demonstrate that local first responders and community emergency managers will be the first line of response in disasters.
- Emergency management itself is rapidly becoming a high technology area. Reliance on technology, however, also increases the vulnerability of responding organizations, as was demonstrated at the World Trade Center when communication with the command center became difficult because of competing signals.
- An essential need in disasters is the ability to assess the health risks and ensure safety for first responders.

■ AVOIDING PITFALLS ■

- Some reporters too readily accept that disasters were accidents or unique events. Probe behind the accident to determine how it could have been prevented or, at the very least, its impact minimized through better land-use control and management of risks.

- People expect natural disasters—they don't expect technological ones. As a consequence, they respond differently to the risks involved. People hope natural disasters can be predicted—they don't expect them to be eliminated. Elimination of risks is applied more to technological events, and efforts to do so rely primarily on the application of more technology. Nevertheless, it is still a good idea to investigate what has been done to reduce risks imposed by natural disasters.
- It is tempting to think that socially constructed disasters can be eliminated through technology itself. As with any change, unintended consequences can sometimes wreak havoc. What appears to be a well-established and increasingly safe technology, such as dam building, sometimes becomes more hazardous because of changes in key environmental assumptions made during design and construction stages. New hazards are created when innovation outpaces our own ability to identify and understand the risks being generated. Don't fail to ask questions about the risks created by the use of more technology to eliminate the risk of disasters. Sometimes increased reliance on still further technologies (such as automation and computers) in efforts to address technological hazards raises concerns about possible yet-to-be-identified new hazards.
- While in-plant preparedness may be strong, the level of preparedness for chemical emergencies for the surrounding community and across communities as hazardous materials are transported through them is much lower. The level of preparedness of local emergency responders (police, fire, medical services, and transport) is what is critical to assess.

▪ INFORMATION RESOURCES ▪

▪ GOVERNMENT/ACADEMIA

- Disaster Research Center (www.udel.edu/DRC)
(originally located at Ohio State University)
University of Delaware, Disaster Research Center, Newark, DE 19716-2581
(302) 831-6618; fax: (302) 831-2091

- Environmental and Occupational Health Sciences Institute (www.eohsi.rutgers.edu)
  170 Frelinghuysen Rd., Piscataway, NJ 08854
  (732) 445-0200
  Environmental Health Division
  (732) 445-0193; fax: (732) 445-0784
  Environmental Policy Division
  (732) 932-0387 ext. 0; fax: (732) 932-0934
  Exposure Measurement/Assessment Division
  (732) 445-0150; fax: (732) 445-0116
- The George Perkins Marsh Institute (formerly the Center for Technology, Environment, and Development [CENTED])
  (www.clarku.edu/departments/marsh)
  Clark University, 950 Main St., Worchester, MA 01610-1477
  (508) 751-4622; fax (508) 751-4600
- The Institute for Crisis, Disaster and Risk Management (ICDRM)
  (www.seas.gwu.edu/~icdm/)
  George Washington University
  707 22nd St. NW, Staughton Hall, Washington, DC 20052
  (202) 994-6736
- Natural Hazards Center at the University of Colorado, Boulder
  (www.colorado.edu/hazards)
  University of Colorado
  482 UCB, Boulder, CO 80309-0482
  (303) 492-6818; fax: (303) 492-2151
- Office of Climate, Water, and Weather Services
  (http://205.156.54.206/om/hazstats)
  National Oceanic and Atmospheric Agency (NOAA)
  Office of Climate, Water, and Weather Service
  National Weather Service
  1325 East-West Highway, Silver Spring, MO 20910
  (301) 713-1726; fax: (301) 713-1598
- U.S. Environmental Protection Agency
  (www.epa.gov/children/asthma)
  Office of Children's Health Protection
  1200 Pennsylvania Ave. NW, Mail Code 1107A
  Room 2512, Ariel Rios North, Washington, DC 20004
  (202) 564-2188; fax: (202) 564-2733

▪ NONPROFIT/CONSUMER ORGANIZATIONS

▪ Worldwatch Institute (www.worldwatch@worldwatch.org)
1776 Massachusetts Ave. NW, Washington, DC 20036-1904
(202) 452-1999; fax: (202) 296-7365

See also:

- Abramovita, J. N. 2001. *Unnatural Disasters*. Worldwatch Paper 158. Washington, D.C.: Worldwatch Institute.
- Smith, Keith. 1992. *Environmental Hazards: Assessing Risk and Reducing Disaster*. New York: Routledge.

OCCUPATIONAL HEALTH

▪ BACKGROUND ▪

The workplace traditionally has been, and remains, a dangerous place because of the presence of hazardous substances; ergonomic stressors; physical agents such as heat, noise, and vibration; psychosocial factors such as stress and violence; and biological agents such as bacteria and viruses. Although many hazards exist in the workplace, they rarely come to the attention of the journalist unless there is an unusual precipitating event—a fire, a leak, or a cluster of illnesses or injuries. The ill effects of the environment on workers have been known for thousands of years. Workplace hazards or stresses can cause sickness, impaired health, or significant discomfort in workers. The degree of risk to workers from an exposure to a given substance depends on two things: the nature and potency of the toxic effects and the magnitude and duration of exposure.

▪ IDENTIFYING THE ISSUES ▪

Potential hazards workers may confront on the job include air contaminants; chemical, biological, physical, and ergonomic hazards; and occupational stress and violence. Air contaminants include particulates or gas and vapor contaminants. Common particulates include dust, fumes, mists, aerosols, and fibers. They are produced during industrial processes, for example, during the handling, crushing, grinding, colliding, exploding, and heating of organic or inorganic materials such as rock, ore, metal, coal, wood, and grain. Certain work processes produce particles of dust that are so fine they remain suspended in the air where they are either inhaled or ingested. These particles are considered hazardous until proven otherwise. Fibers such as asbestos are solid particles whose length is several times greater than their diameter.

Harmful chemical compounds can have a toxic effect in the workplace. They are found in the form of solids, liquids, gases, mists, dusts, fumes, and vapors. Some are toxic when inhaled, while others irritate the skin on contact. Workers who handle plants or animals or their products, those who handle food or are employed in food processing, and medical and laboratory personnel may be exposed to biological hazards such as bacteria and viruses, fungi, and other living organisms. Physical hazards include excessive noise, vibration, and lighting; extremes in temperature; and exposure to high levels of ionizing and nonionizing electromagnetic radiation.

Another serious safety problem in many jobs involves repetitive motion or ergonomic stress. Jobs that involve lifting, bending, and typing produce more than an estimated 1.8 million injuries annually. Injuries include neck sprains and irritation and inflammation of the tendon sheath of the hands and arms, a condition known as carpal tunnel syndrome. Technological changes that have resulted in assembly line speed-up, the addition of specialized work tasks, and increased repetition can produce ergonomic hazards such as excessive vibration and noise, eyestrain, repetitive motion, and heavy-lifting problems. Tools or work areas that are poorly designed can also produce ergonomic hazards. Repetitive motion over a prolonged period of time in jobs involving sorting, assembling, and data entry can cause carpal tunnel syndrome. Among the industries with the highest rate of ergonomic injuries are auto production, parcel delivery, meat and poultry packing, and nursing homes, where workers often lift heavy patients. Other workers with high rates include seamstresses, secretaries, and journalists. Rates are higher for women and Hispanic workers (who often accept the worst low-end jobs having a higher injury rate than other jobs).

Other hazards in the workplace may include psychosocial factors like stress, bullying, and violence.

▪ ADDRESSING THE ISSUES ▪

Potentially hazardous conditions are recognized and corrected as the result of a variety of precipitating events. Federal law assigns the responsibility for recognizing and controlling hazards to the employer. Public agencies respond only when this private responsibility has not been fulfilled. Many employers hire on-staff industrial hygienists who are specialists in occupational safety and health or retain them as consultants. They measure and identify exposures, problem tasks, and risks and examine how particular chemicals or physical hazards at a worksite might affect worker health. When situations are found to be hazardous to health, recommendations for appropriate corrective actions are made.

Workers may identify hazards in the workplace and, in some cases, be able to take steps to correct them. This can be accomplished by notifying the employer, a plant health and safety committee, a union, a local or state health agency, an attorney, or the Occupational Safety and Health Administration (OSHA) district office. Workers have the right to request a health hazard evaluation from the National Institute for Occupational Safety and Health (NIOSH), another agency that studies workplace health and safety issues nationwide.

The opportunity for recognizing workplace hazards has been enhanced by passage of the Federal Hazard Communication Regulation, administered by OSHA. This covers all employers and employees in the manufacturing sector. Some states have their own legislation, known as worker and community right-to-know laws. Both federal and state legislation require a certain amount of labeling and hazard disclosure and entitle employees to specific information regarding substances in the workplace. Under these laws, employers must reduce damaging exposures to toxic chemicals to permissible levels. Some workplaces are periodically monitored by industrial hygienists employed by local, state, or federal agencies to make sure potential exposures have been controlled. Periodic monitoring is spotty, however. Due to staffing limitations, it usually requires a complaint or an accident to trigger a government review.

OSHA's *Hazard Communication Standard* (Title 29, CFR, Part 1910.1200) requires manufacturers of hazardous materials to give Material Safety Data Sheets (MSDS) to purchasers of these materials. The MSDS provide employers with important health, safety, and toxicological information on chemicals used in the workplace as well as information on the risks to workers from exposure to them. The *Hazard Communication Standard* also requires that all containers of hazardous substances in the workplace be marked with appropriate warnings and identification labels.

Traditional procedures for controlling a hazard once it is recognized include substitution, engineering controls, personal protection, and administrative and regulatory controls. Often, a less toxic chemical or less hazardous process can be substituted for the one in current use without great expense. Sometimes substitution can be profitable for companies; other times, it is simply not feasible, but a company should always examine it as the first choice for hazard control.

Sometimes it is possible to isolate a process or chemical so that even though it remains toxic, either no one is exposed to it or the exposure is minimal. No exposure equals no risk. In many cases this is difficult to achieve without ceasing to use the compound entirely. For example, companies can modify existing ventilation systems to reduce airborne exposure to toxic chemicals. Increasing general ventilation dilutes toxic chemicals; installing local ventilation, such as laboratory hoods, removes the toxic substance from the air.

Work practice controls change the way in which workers carry out tasks. Some basic and easily accomplished work practice controls include (1) changing existing work practices to follow proper procedures that minimize exposures while operating production and control equipment; (2) inspecting and maintaining process and control equipment on a regular basis; (3) implementing good housekeeping procedures; (4) providing good supervision; and (5) mandating that eating, drinking, and smoking in regulated areas be prohibited.

A variety of protective clothing is on the market, including goggles, face masks, helmets, safety shoes, and respirators. The safety industry manufactures several different types of respirators for varying degrees of risk, including dust masks, canister respirators (mini gas masks with a filter and chemical-neutralizing substance), and air-supplied respirators, which use air hoses or a self-contained breathing apparatus carried in a metal tank on the user's back. The Occupational Safety and Health Act of 1970 requires that personal respirators must be coupled with ventilation and other engineering controls. However, the act allows use of respiratory protection alone on a temporary basis while engineering controls are being developed. Personal protective equipment must be properly fitted and worn. The equipment must also be regularly maintained and replaced as necessary.

Administrative controls include worker education, labeling, rotating workers, reducing overtime, and other procedures that do not directly address the issue of exposure. Those that do address controlling employees' exposure include scheduling production and tasks, or both, in ways that limit exposure levels. For example, employers might schedule operations with the highest exposure potential during periods when the fewest employees are present. When effective work practices or engineering controls are not feasible or while such controls are being put into place, appropriate personal protective equipment can be used to limit exposure.

Air sampling must be done to determine the quantity of specific chemicals in the workplace. Periodic medical evaluations of exposed workers, known as medical surveillance, are required in some but not all cases. These are complementary programs that assist in identifying hazards and controlling them.

The risks of biological hazards can be reduced for food handlers by preventing and controlling disease in the animal population and through the proper care of infected animals. Good personal hygiene (careful hand washing) and careful attention to minor cuts and scratches, especially on the hands and forearms, helps reduce risk to workers. Measures to protect health-care workers from biological hazards also include proper ventilation, use of personal protective equipment such as gloves and respirators, adequate infectious waste disposal systems, and control and isolation in situations of contagious diseases such as tuberculosis.

Ensuring worker safety in occupational settings where workers are exposed to ionizing radiation involves limiting the time workers are exposed, shielding (the greater the protective mass between a radioactive source and the worker, the lower the radiation exposure), and increasing the distance between workers and the source of exposure. Distance can be used to control exposure to both ionizing and nonionizing radiation.

Noise hazards can be reduced by the use of equipment and systems that are specifically designed to operate quietly. Other methods to control exposure to noise hazards include enclosing or shielding equipment (use of sound barriers or acoustical booths), assuring equipment is kept in good repair by replacing worn and unbalanced parts, mounting equipment on special mounts to reduce vibration, and the use of silencers, mufflers, or baffles. Some industries have successfully substituted the use of quiet work methods for noisy ones (e.g., welding parts rather than riveting them). Floor, ceiling, and wall treatments made of acoustical material can be used to reduce reflected or reverberant noise. Workers in noisy work settings are required by OSHA to be given periodical tests as a precaution against hearing loss.

Radiant heat exposure in factories such as steel mills can be a physical hazard that can be controlled using reflective shields and protective clothing.

By doing a thorough worksite analysis (which looks at the total physiological and psychological demands of the job), employers can correct or control ergonomic hazards by using appropriate engineering controls. This might involve redesigning work stations, improvements in lighting, use of different tools and equipment, teaching correct work practices such as proper lifting methods, shifting workers among several different tasks, reducing production demand, increasing rest breaks, and providing and mandating personal protective equipment. Well-designed, ergonomic work environments can result in increased efficiency, fewer accidents, lower operating costs, and more effective use of personnel.

Efforts to reduce ergonomic hazards on the job have received considerable attention in recent years. In 1999, legislation was passed requiring industries to send workers to a health care provider if they had symptoms of ergonomic injury related to repetitive motions. These regulations also required industries with ergonomic injuries to take certain ergonomic steps, such as reducing the amount of lifting. Citing the potential cost to businesses (estimated at $120 billion by business groups), the new legislation was repealed in 2000. Measures that seek voluntary steps on the part of high-risk industries replaced mandatory guidelines.

▪ IMPORTANT POINTS FOR RESEARCHING A STORY ▪

- Finding out information about occupational health can be difficult. Unlike infectious diseases or cancer, there is no registry of occupational illness, and only a few states make occupational diseases reportable the way they do infectious diseases. Just a fraction of worker compensation benefits are paid for disease (most payments are for traumatic injury), so court records are sparse. New Jersey leads the nation in that 7 percent of its worker compensation benefits cover disease, but that is mostly hearing loss. Employers are required by state labor departments and OSHA to keep a log of significant diseases and accidents, but these estimates are low at best. When a hazard is identified, OSHA issues bulletins to affected sites and posts the information on its website. For example, OSHA sent out a warning to dental labs about the risks to dental lab workers who might inhale beryllium dust while working on crowns and bridges.
- Determine how the hazard was discovered and by whom. There may be malfunctions in a manufacturing plant that brought the

hazards to light. Or perhaps a plant is aging. Human error is another factor to consider.

- Find out who is responsible for controlling the hazard, how the hazard will be controlled, and what the timetable is. Reporters should know who is responsible for investigating the hazard—even local health departments involved in the case should not be ignored. Public officials may know what is the health risk to workers and possibly even to the community.
- When the story involves a potential chemical hazard, find out what is the chemical hazard's toxicity relative to some well-known toxins such as ethanol (grain alcohol) and benzene. Be careful, however, in comparing carcinogens with noncarcinogens. Even comparisons between carcinogens can be tricky.
- Investigate the extent and duration of the exposure and how many people are known to have been exposed or could be exposed. There may be a particular group of workers at high risk from past exposure. Efforts should be made to locate these workers and their families and interview them. Learn what kinds of health effects have been identified. They could be diseases linked to a particular hazard, such as leukemia to benzene exposure, or there could be general symptoms that are attributable to many different types of chemical hazards that might be present.
- If the situation involves a possible exposure to a toxic substance, find out if OSHA has established legal limits for the substance and obtain equivalent estimates. For example, in the case of beryllium—a metal sometimes used in dentistry—OSHA has established a legal limit of 2 micrograms per cubic meter of air. OSHA has estimated that this is equivalent to dust about the size of a pencil tip spread throughout an area the size of the Statue of Liberty.

▪ AVOIDING PITFALLS ▪

- Reporters may misunderstand the urgency or "imminence" of a hazard. Correction may have to be done immediately, or, as in the case of chronic hazards, it may be achieved over a longer period of time in order to prevent irreversible disease or disability.
- There are always questions about the severity of the hazard. Reporters need to know just how toxic the material is. Low toxicity usually means low risk, but with extended exposure, the risk in-

creases. High toxicity at low or very short exposure may also result in low risk.

- Reporters must learn the precise size and nature of the workforce exposed. An office workforce may react strongly to a mild change in air quality that might go unnoticed by a factory workforce because their expectations are different. Better educated workers and workers who are more secure in their jobs are more likely to raise concerns about workplace hazards. Reporters should be aware that "undocumented workers" like migrant farmworkers often will not raise questions about even severe hazards.
- Don't overestimate or underestimate the strength of the scientific data. Scientists may not be firm with toxicity data, or they may be unsure of causal relations. Reporters should make every effort to find out whether symptoms reported by an affected group match symptoms regularly associated with a specific type of hazardous agent. Employers and even public agencies charged with doing an investigation of chemical hazards may assign a low priority to the project if the hazard is not imminent, the risk is low, the workforce is not very vocal, or the scientific data are shaky. In a society in which only a tiny budget supports occupational health and safety action on the state and federal levels, not all situations identified as hazardous can be addressed. This may turn out to be frustrating and a source of hostility for a particular workforce, who may seek an independent hazard investigation. Workers may turn to lawyers, journalists, physicians, or union leadership for help. Recognition of many significant hazards has been accomplished in this fashion. But there is a danger that vocal and well-organized workers will achieve public and regulatory attention for a small occupational risk while much larger occupational risks go uncorrected because affected workers may be less skillful at mobilizing attention.
- Occupational risks receive less media and public (and regulatory) attention than do environmental risks. Reporters should be alert to this tendency to dismiss as "the price of a good job and a good economy" a hazard that would be the material of editorial crusades if its victims were neighbors rather than workers. At the same time, reporters should be aware that a literally risk-free job environment is impossible.
- The dominant occupational risks are nonchemical: ergonomic problems, falls, vehicle crashes, and other types of industrial acci-

dents. Toxic chemicals are more insidious than accidents; their effects can take decades to show up, and they can be too easily ignored. On the other hand, once toxic chemicals in the workplace become an issue, the issue can generate a lot more outrage and public regulatory response than more conventional occupational risks, even though the latter may represent the greater hazard to workers.

- The role of workers in the reporting of occupational hazards can vary. Traditionally, workers have paid little attention to these issues, preferring to bargain on bread-and-butter issues instead. Many unions and many nonunionized workers still take this position. Getting employees to take precautions seriously and wear protective gear is a major issue in most hazardous workplaces. On the other hand, some unions (e.g., the Oil, Chemical, and Atomic Workers Union) have made toxic exposures a major bargaining and organizing issue. In other words, reporters cannot always measure the seriousness of the hazard by the seriousness with which employees are taking it.

▪ INFORMATION RESOURCES ▪

▪ GOVERNMENT/ACADEMIA

- U.S. Department of Health and Human Services/National Institute for Occupational Safety and Health (www.cdc.gov/niosh)
  (800) 35-NIOSH (356-4674); fax: (513) 533-8573
- Robert A. Taft Laboratories
  4676 Columbia Pkwy., Cincinnati, OH 45226
- Alice Hamilton Laboratory
  5555 Ridge Ave., Cincinnati, OH 45213
- U.S. Department of Labor/Occupational Safety and Health Administration (OSHA) (www.osha.gov).
  200 Constitution Ave. NW, Washington, DC 20210
  (202) 693-2000

▪ INDUSTRY/PROFESSIONAL ASSOCIATIONS

- The American Chemical Society (www.acs.org)
  1155 16th St. NW, Washington DC, 20036

(800) 227-5558 (U.S. only), (202) 872-4600 (outside the U.S.);
fax: (202) 872-4615
E-mail: help@acs.org

- CHEMTREC (www.chemtrec.org)
  1300 Wilson Blvd., Arlington, VA 22209
  (800) 262-8200, (800) 424-9300 (24-hour emergency response communication); fax: (703) 741-6037
  E-mail: chemtrec@americanchemistry.com
- Federation of American Scientists
  307 Massachusetts Ave. NE, Washington, DC 20002
  (202) 546-3300; fax: (202) 675-1010
  E-mail fas@fas.org <mailto:fas@fas.org>

See also:

- Lewis, Richard J., Sr., ed. 1999. *Sax's Dangerous Properties of Industrial Materials*. 10th ed. New York: John Wiley and Sons.
- NIOSH. 1997. *Pocket Guide to Chemical Hazards (NPG)*. It can be ordered or downloaded at www.cdc.gov/niosh/npg/npg.html.

OZONE DEPLETION

▪ BACKGROUND ▪

In early September 2000, the hole in the ozone layer above Antarctica covered a record area of approximately 28.4 million square kilometers (about 11 million square miles)—an area three times larger than the landmass of North America. Although the production of many ozone-destroying gases has been halted, concentrations of these gases in the earth's upper atmosphere (stratosphere) are only now reaching their peak. Because of their long lifetimes in the atmosphere, they will continue to deplete the ozone layer for several more decades. Ozone depletion is expected to reach its peak around 2010.

Ozone is a form of the element oxygen that occurs naturally in the stratosphere. The presence of ozone in the stratosphere is essential to life on earth. Stratospheric ozone absorbs a portion of the sun's radiation, preventing it from reaching the earth's surface. Most notably, ozone absorbs the type of ultraviolet radiation (UV-B) from the sun that can cause damage to living organisms and the environment. Ozone depletion refers to the decrease in stratospheric ozone due to the breakdown of ozone molecules by synthetic chemicals released into the atmosphere. The massive annual decrease of stratospheric ozone over the Antarctic in the polar spring has been termed the ozone hole by the popular press.

The ozone layer is an area of the stratosphere between 20 to 25 kilometers (12.4–15.5 miles) above sea level, where ozone is most concentrated. In considering the problem of ozone depletion, it is important to recognize that the ozone layer is far less tangible than the term suggests. The number of molecules of ozone in the atmosphere is relatively small. The highest concentrations of ozone in the stratosphere are only on the order of 10 parts per million. At standard temperature and pressure, the total amount of ozone in the atmosphere would form

This brief is based on an earlier version included in the second edition of *The Reporter's Environmental Handbook*. Additional information and comments were provided by Junfeng Zhang, Environmental and Community Medicine, Environmental and Occupational Health Sciences Institute (EOHSI), Piscataway, New Jersey.

a layer only 3 millimeters (0.11 inch) thick. This thin layer of ozone absorbs all but a small fraction of UV-B radiation from the sun.

The concentration of ozone in the stratosphere, even absent ozone depletion, is constantly changing. Ozone is continuously produced and destroyed in the stratosphere. Ozone is formed when short wavelengths of ultraviolet radiation are absorbed by oxygen molecules (O_2). The oxygen molecules split, and the individual atoms (O) recombine with other oxygen molecules to form ozone (O_3). In turn, when ozone absorbs ultraviolet radiation, it splits into one free oxygen atom (O) and one molecule of ordinary oxygen (O_2). The total amount of ozone overhead—the column ozone—varies naturally at different altitudes, at different latitudes, and at different times of the year. In the high latitudes, stratospheric ozone concentrations vary naturally by as much as 25 percent.

In the past, stratospheric ozone maintained a dynamic equilibrium—rates of production and loss of ozone were in balance. However, over the last several decades, the release and accumulation of chlorofluorocarbons (CFCs) and other ozone-depleting substances (ODS) in the atmosphere have resulted in significant losses of stratospheric ozone. In 1985, scientists identified the ozone hole—an area over Antarctica where ozone levels had fallen dramatically since the early 1980s. The ozone hole forms each Antarctic spring (September through November), when regional air circulation patterns, combined with chemical reactions triggered by the return of sunlight to the region, cause the stratospheric ozone level over the continent to drop to as low as 30 percent of its normal level.

The problem of ozone depletion occurs around the globe. Globally, ozone levels in the middle latitudes have fallen by an average of 5 percent per decade since 1979. Over the United States, column ozone has been depleted by a total of 5 to 10 percent, depending upon the season. During the winter of 1999–2000, researchers detected an ozone hole over the Arctic, where ozone levels were depleted by up to 60 percent. Until that point, ozone depletion in the Arctic had reached a maximum of 20 to 25 percent.

▪ IDENTIFYING THE ISSUES ▪

ODS are highly stable compounds that contain various combinations of chlorine, fluorine, bromine, carbon, and hydrogen. These compounds are also collectively referred to as halocarbons. CFCs are halocarbons that contain chlorine, fluorine, and carbon. Until recently, CFCs were widely used in refrigerants, in cleaning solvents for electronics, in foam and insulating products, and as propellants in spray cans. Once released into the atmosphere, CFCs remain unchanged and after one to two years make their way to the stratosphere. In the stratosphere, exposure to strong ultraviolet radiation breaks down CFCs, releasing single atoms of chlorine. The chlorine atoms destroy ozone molecules and are continually rereleased to destroy additional ozone molecules in a cycle that can continue for hundreds of years. Each CFC molecule that reaches the stratosphere can destroy up to 100,000 ozone molecules.

Another group of ozone-depleting halocarbons, the halons, are halocarbons that contain carbon, bromine, fluorine, and sometimes chlorine. Halons have been used extensively as fire-extinguishing agents. Other ODS include methyl chloroform (a solvent), carbon tetrachloride (an industrial chemical), and methyl bromide (a produce and soil fumigant). Like CFCs, the halons and other ODS are stable enough in the lower atmosphere to eventually reach the stratosphere. When broken down by strong ultraviolet radiation in the stratosphere, these compounds release either chlorine or bromine atoms, which react with and destroy ozone. Bromine, while less abundant than chlorine in the stratosphere, is much more reactive with ozone and accounts for up to 15 percent of ozone depletion.

Depletion of stratospheric ozone leads to higher levels (intensities) of UV-B at the earth's surface. In the Antarctic, surface measurements of UV-B are double their normal levels. Global satellite measurements taken over the period 1979–1993 showed significant increases in UV-B in the high and middle latitudes of both hemispheres.

Increased UV-B levels have significant implications for human health and the environment. In humans, UV-B exposure is associated with certain types of skin cancer, skin damage, premature aging of the skin, cataracts and other eye damage, and suppression of the immune system. Animal studies have shown decreased immune response to skin cancers and infectious agents with exposure to UV-B.

Aquatic life, particularly those organisms living close to the water surface, is also at risk of damage due to UV-B exposure. Scientists have shown reductions in phytoplankton production coinciding with increases in UV-B within the area covered by the Antarctic ozone hole. UV-B has also been associated with damage in the reproductive and early developmental stages of fish and shrimp. Even at current levels,

UV-B is a limiting factor for the reproductive capacity and larval development of these and other aquatic organisms. Increases in UV-B could have serious implications for these populations and the populations of animals that feed on them.

UV-B can also affect the growth rates of terrestrial plants. Some crop varieties are sensitive to UV-B and experience reduced yields with increased exposure to UV-B. Increases in UV-B may influence competition among wild plant varieties, with implications for changes in species composition and biodiversity. (See the brief on "Biodiversity.")

Increased UV-B levels may also affect the photodegradation of plastics and other synthetic polymers. Special additives are currently used in these products to protect them from sunlight in outdoor use. Increases in UV-B, however, may further limit the useful life of these products.

▪ ADDRESSING THE ISSUES ▪

The relationship between CFCs and stratospheric ozone was first brought to public attention in a research paper published in the journal *Nature* in 1974. The authors of the paper—two chemists from the University of California at Irvine, F. Sherwood Rowland and Mario Molina (now at the Massachusetts Institute of Technology)—reported that the chemical stability of CFCs would allow them to travel to the stratosphere. Rowland and Molina predicted that CFCs would then react with solar radiation and ozone, resulting in substantial declines in stratospheric ozone levels. Rowland and Molina received the 1995 Nobel Prize in Chemistry, along with Paul Crutzen of the Max Planck Institute for Chemistry Germany, for their pioneering work in atmospheric chemistry.

In 1977, the United Nations Environment Program (UNEP) and the World Meteorological Organization (WMO) hosted an international meeting on ozone depletion. The outcome of the meeting was a "World Plan of Action on the Ozone Layer." The action plan called for monitoring ozone and solar radiation; assessing the effects of ozone depletion on human health, ecosystems, and climate; and developing methods to assess the costs and benefits of control measures.

Initial efforts to combat ozone depletion focused on limiting CFC use in aerosols. In 1978, the United States, Canada, Denmark, Finland, Norway, and Sweden began phasing out the use of CFCs in nonessential aerosols. Two years later, the European Community enacted a freeze on its capacity to produce certain CFCs and a 30 percent reduction in the use of CFCs in aerosols. However, other uses of CFCs continued to expand amid growing international concern over their effects on the ozone layer.

International negotiations in the early 1980s led to the adoption of the Vienna Convention on the Protection of the Ozone Layer in March 1985. The Vienna Convention provided for international research, monitoring, and exchange of data regarding stratospheric ozone, CFCs, and halons. Through the convention, the framework for negotiations on emissions reductions was established. These negotiations resulted in the adoption of the landmark Montreal Protocol on Substances that Deplete the Ozone Layer in 1987. To date, a total of 175 countries are parties to the convention and the protocol.

The Montreal Protocol provides for periodic scientific assessments of the status of atmospheric ozone. Based upon the findings of these assessments, the protocol has undergone periodic amendments and adjustments to strengthen its provisions. The protocol contains a schedule to phase out all production and use of ODS, with the ultimate objective of eliminating these substances.

The search for acceptable substitutes for CFCs has not been easy. Demand for CFCs was initially met through reuse and recycling. Later, manufacturers developed substitute products, including hydrochlorofluorocarbons (HCFCs) and hydrofluorocarbons (HFCs). The HCFCs include hydrogen atoms in addition to chlorine, fluorine, and carbon atoms. These compounds have shorter atmospheric lifetimes than CFCs and much lower ozone-depleting potential (ODP) values. However, because they contain chlorine and have the potential to reach the stratosphere, HCFCs are only temporary replacements for CFCs. The Copenhagen Amendment to the Montreal Protocol establishes the year 2030 as the deadline for halting production of HCFCs. HFCs, on the other hand, do not contain chlorine and do not contribute to ozone depletion. However, some HFCs act as greenhouse gases, contributing to the problem of global climate change. (See the brief on "Global Climate Change.")

The most successful alternative to CFC use is the development of new processes and technologies that eliminate the need for CFCs and similar compounds. For example, new processes allow water-based cleaning in the manufacture of precision ball bearings, medical devices, and electronics components. Similarly, printed circuit boards are now manufactured using "no-clean" technology.

Results of the CFC phase-out have already been seen. The *Scientific Assessment of Ozone Depletion: 1998*, published under the auspices of the Montreal Protocol, found that the rate of ozone depletion at the middle latitudes has slowed and that total ODS in the lower atmosphere peaked in 1984 and was declining. However, due to the substance's atmospheric lifetime and time required to reach the stratosphere, the total amount of ODS in the stratosphere was not predicted to peak until the year 2000. The *Assessment* concluded that ozone depletion should reach its maximum within the first two decades of the twenty-first century, with possible recovery by midcentury. The authors of the *Assessment* were careful to note, however, that the recovery of the ozone layer will be influenced by other natural and human-produced factors, including atmospheric concentrations of certain greenhouse gases and global climate change.

▪ IMPORTANT POINTS FOR RESEARCHING A STORY ▪

- There are many natural processes and human activities that release chlorine into the lower atmosphere. The vast majority of these processes emit chlorine compounds that are soluble in water. These compounds "rain out" of the lower atmosphere in precipitation and do not reach the stratosphere. Large fires and certain types of marine life, however, do produce a stable form of chlorine that does reach the stratosphere. Scientists estimate that these natural sources are responsible for up to 15 percent of stratospheric chlorine.
- Large volcanic eruptions can temporarily affect ozone levels. Large volcanic eruptions, such as the eruption of Mount Pinatubo in the Philippines in 1991, release large amounts of hydrogen chloride and tiny particles called aerosols (unrelated to aerosol sprays). The hydrogen chloride released in such eruptions is rapidly converted to hydrochloric acid and "rains out" before it reaches the stratosphere. The aerosols, however, can be injected directly into the stratosphere by an eruption. While the aerosols themselves do not destroy ozone, their presence in the stratosphere temporarily enhances the rate of ozone depletion by chlorine-containing ODS.
- All CFCs manufactured to date will eventually escape and make their way to the stratosphere. Reuse and recycling of

CFC-containing products are considered preferable to their disposal, which would only serve to accelerate their release into the atmosphere.

■ AVOIDING PITFALLS ■

- Ozone has a dual role in the atmosphere. In the upper atmosphere, ozone absorbs ultraviolet radiation and is essential to life. In the lower atmosphere, ozone is the major component of smog. Many people confuse these two issues. It is important to note that these two phenomena are unrelated.
- The issue of ozone depletion is also often confused with global climate change. Ozone and global climate change are linked in a number of ways:
- CFCs, which contribute to ozone depletion, also act as greenhouse gases. (See the brief on "Global Climate Change.")
- Absorption of ultraviolet radiation by ozone heats the stratosphere. Ozone depletion, therefore, leads to a cooling of the stratosphere. Climate models indicate that cooling of the lower stratosphere (ostensibly due to ozone depletion) is already acting to delay the effects of greenhouse gases on atmospheric temperature.
- Global climate change is predicted to result in additional cooling of the stratosphere, as heat becomes trapped in the lower atmosphere. Cooler stratospheric temperatures are known to support conditions that accelerate the breakdown of ODS and result in enhanced ozone depletion.
- Increased UV-B radiation due to ozone depletion is predicted to reduce levels of marine phytoplankton. These phytoplankton are a major sink for global carbon. Significant losses of marine phytoplankton populations would result in the release of large amounts of carbon dioxide, a greenhouse gas, into the atmosphere.
- Many people continue to associate aerosol sprays with the problem of ozone depletion. First, it should be noted that CFCs used as propellants in aerosol sprays—not the sprays themselves—were the contributors to ozone depletion. Further, except for certain medical applications, CFCs in aerosols have long been replaced with non-ozone-depleting compounds.

▪ INFORMATION RESOURCES ▪

▪ GOVERNMENT/ACADEMIA

- British Antarctic Survey
(www.antarctica.ac.uk/Key_Topics/Ozone/Ozone.html)
High Cross, Madingley Rd., Cambridge, CB3 0ET, UK
+44 (0)1223 221400; fax: +44 (0)1223 362616
E-mail: science@bas.ac.uk or information@bas.ac.uk
- Internet FAQ Archives/Ozone Depletion FAQ (Frequently Asked Questions) (www.faqs.org/faqs/ozone-depletion/)
Robert Parson
Department of Chemistry and Biochemistry
University of Colorado
Boulder, Co 80309
(303) 492-6531; fax: (303) 492-5894
- Mario J. Molina (www-eaps.mit.edu/molina)
Massachusetts Institute of Technology
77 Massachusetts Ave., Cambridge, MA 02139
(617) 253-5081; fax: (617) 258-6525
E-mail: mmolina@mit.edu
- NASA Total Ozone Mapping Spectrometer (TOMS)
(http://toms.gsfc.nasa.gov)
GSFC Media Services, Mailcode 130, Greenbelt, MD 20771
(301) 286-8955, fax: (301) 286-1707
E-mail: gsfcmedia@pop100.gsfc.nasa.gov
- F. Sherwood Rowland
University of California at Irvine
Irvine, CA 92697
(949) 824-6016; fax: (949) 824-2905
E-mail: rowland@uci.edu
- United Nations Environment Program Ozone Secretariat
(www.unep.org/ozone)
The Secretariat for the Vienna Convention and the Montreal Protocol
P.O. Box 30552, Nairobi, Kenya
(254-2)62-1234 or (254-2)62-3851; fax: (254-2)62-3601 or (254-2)62-3913
- U.S. Environmental Protection Agency—Ozone Depletion
(www.epa.gov/docs/ozone)

USEPA, Global Programs Division
401 M St. SW, Mailcode 6205J, Washington, DC 20460
(202) 564-9101, (800) 296-1996 (Stratospheric Ozone Protection Hotline); fax: (202) 565-2096

▪ INDUSTRY/PROFESSIONAL ASSOCIATIONS

- Alliance for Responsible Atmospheric Policy (www.arap.org)
  111 Wilson Blvd., Suite 850, Arlington, VA 22201
  (703) 243-0344; fax: (703) 243-2874
- Alternative Fluorocarbons Environmental Acceptability Study (www.afeas.org)
  RAND Environmental Science and Policy Center
  1200 South Hayes St., Arlington, VA 22202-5050

▪ NONPROFIT/CONSUMER ORGANIZATIONS

- Friends of the Earth (www.foe.org/ptp/atmosphere/)
  1025 Vermont Ave. NW, Washington, DC 20005
  (202) 783-7400; fax: (202) 783-0444
  E-mail: foe@foe.org
- Ozone Action (www.ozone.org)
  1700 Connecticut Ave. NW, Suite 300, Washington, DC 20009
  (202) 265-6738; fax: (202) 986-6041
  E-mail: ozone_action@ozone.org

See also:

- Molina, M. J., and F. S. Rowland. 1974. Stratospheric sink for chlorofluoromethanes: Chlorine atom catalyzed destruction of ozone. *Nature* 249:810–814.

PESTICIDES

▪ BACKGROUND ▪

Pesticides are used in the home, workplace, and the outside environment. Immediate or short-term (acute) effects as well as long-term (chronic) effects are of concern. In the last five years, particular attention has been paid to the risk of pesticides to children. Children are a more sensitive group in the population due to their stage of development, activity patterns, and diet. Exposure, via diet or the environment, is often to several compounds. Assessment of aggregate exposure is now the focus of new federal regulations, most importantly, the Food Quality Protection Act (FQPA).

The term "pesticide" covers a wide variety of chemical compounds that control unwanted plants, insects, rodents, and other pests. There are over 600 active pesticide ingredients in over 50,000 formulated pesticide products. They fall into three categories of pesticides: herbicides, which kill plants; insecticides, which kill insects; and fungicides, which kill certain microorganisms.

Pesticides have made it easier to protect crops from insects, weeds, and diseases, enabling society to produce ever-larger amounts of fruits, vegetables, and grains free of blemishes and rot. The use of pesticides has served to dramatically increase crop yield and increase food production in an economical fashion. But as their use has increased, the hazards posed by these chemicals have become more apparent: pesticides have drained into streams and lakes, killing wildlife, and laboratory evidence has indicated that many pesticides fed to rats and mice are capable of inducing cancers. More recent evidence has suggested that trace levels of some pesticides on fresh food can become concentrated during the processing of such foods as jellies, ketchup, tomato sauce, and grain mixes.

This brief was written by Richard Fenske, School of Public Health, University of Washington, for the second edition of *The Reporter's Environmental Handbook*, with additions from Mark Robson, Division of Environmental and Occupational Health, University of Medicine and Dentistry of New Jersey School of Public Health, Piscataway, New Jersey.

In addition, pesticide use poses concern with regard to the buildup of crop resistance over time and the need to use ever-increasing doses. Weeds resistant to herbicides, for example, are threatening wheat fields around the globe and could become a problem in the United States.

In addition to agricultural pests, there are a number of household pests, such as fleas, roaches, and termites, as well as public health pests such as head lice, body lice, ticks that cause Lyme disease, and mosquitoes that carry West Nile virus.

▪ IDENTIFYING THE ISSUES ▪

There are five major pesticide health/environmental issues of concern: pesticide runoff into groundwater and surface water from farms and nonagricultural applications to lawns and golf courses; occupational exposures of farmworkers, commercial applicators, and others who work regularly with pesticides; pesticide residue on or in foods; exposures from drifting farm applications to adjacent communities; and children's exposure during residential use of pesticides. While all five are significant issues, technical experts would probably disagree on the importance of certain of them.

Many pesticides pose some form of risk to human health if not used correctly. Pesticides should be used only according to package directions. The most poisonous will be marked with a skull-and-crossbones symbol. Should these chemicals enter the body, they may cause illness, even death, in high concentrations. The chemical could destroy, for example, a liver cell and replace it with scar tissue. Some herbicides can cause illness, particularly chloracne, a skin eruption similar to regular acne.

If pesticides are present in the food chain—in meat, dairy products, grain, fruits, and vegetables—humans can be adversely affected. All mammals are affected in similar ways, so livestock can be made sick before they become part of the food chain.

Pesticides control vegetable and animal pests in different ways. For example, a common herbicide such as 2,4-D causes rapid growth in a plant until it dies. The insecticide malathion works on an insect's nervous system—the insect ingests the chemical, which then travels through the bloodstream and reacts with an enzyme that short-circuits the nervous system, causing death. Most insecticides in current use ultimately break down in the environment to the point at which they cause less harm to humans or livestock. However, this dictates that certain substances not be used on food crops just before harvest because the pest-control products need a given amount of time to break down in the environment.

The following are major groups of insecticides:

- Organophosphates contain carbon and phosphorus. They are usually used to kill insects and can affect the human nervous system in the same way. Early symptoms of poisoning in humans are flu-like symptoms, with a general malaise. The symptoms increase with the degree of exposure. In severe cases, there is a loss of bodily functions and other neuromuscular control, including pinpoint pupils of the eye. Some examples of organophosphates are chlorpyrifos (Dursban), diazinon, malathion, and parathion.
- Carbamates contain carbon and nitrogen and are similar to organophosphates in the way they affect the central nervous system of humans. The symptoms of poisoning are similar to those of organophosphates. Both break down relatively quickly in the human body but are acutely toxic, that is, symptoms occur within a few hours of exposure. Examples of carbamates are aldicarb (Temik) and carbaryl (Sevin).
- Organochlorines are organic compounds that have been chlorinated, usually with several atoms of chlorine per molecule. The organochlorines have been widely used in agriculture but are now mostly banned in the United States because of their persistence in the environment. Humans exposed to high levels of these chlorinated chemicals experience numbness and tingling of the mouth and face, dizziness, and tremors. They also report symptoms of memory and concentration loss as well as sleeplessness. The compounds remain in the body a long time, lodging in and damaging organs and fatty tissues. Some examples are aldrin, dieldrin, lindane, DDT, endrin, heptachlor, and chlordane. (See the brief on "Dioxin.")

Of particular interest are the organophosphate insecticides, commonly referred to as OPs. These are fast-acting, acutely toxic, broad-spectrum materials. They are potent neurotoxins and are particularly harmful to children if they are exposed at high levels.

The organophosphates and carbamates can cause immediate illness (acute toxicity). They may also have long-term effects (chronic toxicity), as can most other pesticides. Levels of pesticide exposure needed to create these long-term effects are not well understood by scientists. With the exception of known cancer-causing substances, there are levels of exposure at which no measurable harm occurs. In toxicology, this is called a threshold. The human body can potentially deal with exposure without negative effects. In occupational health, these are sometimes called Threshold Limit Values (TLVs).

Occupational thresholds are different from general public threshold levels because there is a wider range of tolerance and intolerance to substances in the general population than in a group of workers. Workers are usually healthier than nonworkers. In toxicology, a similar level is called a no adverse effect level (NOAEL). Federal and state agencies attempt to minimize risk for the general population by keeping exposures well below the NOAEL. Occupational and environmental standards also differ because of social values that hold that, because workers are compensated, they are expected to bear some risk, but bystanders are not compensated and therefore should be as risk free as possible.

The notion of a threshold—in particular, thresholds for carcinogens—is hotly debated. As a result, many pesticides are labeled as possible—not known—carcinogens, giving no indication of thresholds.

■ ADDRESSING THE ISSUES ■

In 1992, a federal court of appeals in San Francisco ruled that the U.S. Environmental Protection Agency (EPA) must remove from the market any pesticides that have the potential of causing cancer and that leave residues in processed foods. According to this ruling, such pesticides are covered under the Delaney Amendment—a provision of the Food, Drug, and Cosmetics Act that prohibits even trace amounts of any potentially carcinogenic additive in juices, breads, jellies, flour, and thousands of other processed foods. Previously, the EPA regulated pesticides under a separate law that allowed small amounts of cancer-causing chemicals to be present in foods if the chemicals' benefits to farmers and consumers outweighed the risk to health and the environment. The EPA has found that at least 67 of the roughly 300 pesticides used on food crops cause cancer in one or more laboratory animals. The 1992 court ruling affects at least 35 of these cancer-causing farm chemicals that also concentrate in processed foods.

In 1996, Congress unanimously passed landmark pesticide safety legislation supported by the Clinton administration and a broad coalition of environmental, public health, agricultural, and industry groups. Signed on April 3, 1996, the FQPA mandates a single health-based standard for all pesticides in all foods; provides special protections for infants and children; expedites approval of safer pesticides; creates incentives for the development and maintenance of effective crop protection tools; and requires periodic reevaluation of pesticide registrations and tolerances to ensure that scientific data supporting pesticide registrations will remain up to date in the future.

In some cases, safer pesticides have been substituted for more controversial ones, and the amount of pesticides used in agriculture has been reduced by the introduction of innovative approaches in agriculture, including integrated pest management (IPM). IPM refers to the introduction of natural predators into fields to control crop-damaging pests. Efforts have been made to restrict occupational exposures by requiring workers to wear gloves, coveralls, and respirators during applications, for example. In addition, measures have been taken to restrict runoff.

Genetic engineering (introducing genes that endow an organism with specific properties that might make wheat, for example, inherently pest resistant) is also being used by some agricultural chemical companies in an effort to curtail dependence on chemical pesticides. Proponents of biotechnology promise to mitigate pollution by decreasing dependency on agricultural chemicals; to create crops that require less processing, thereby cutting costs and curtailing the need for chemical additives; and to provide a means for addressing the dilemma of world population growth. (See the brief on "Genetically Modified Crops.")

▪ IMPORTANT POINTS FOR RESEARCHING A STORY ▪

- Always find out the name of the chemical involved in any exposure and whether the information regarding use of the chemical was obtained from an employer or an employee. Although farmworkers may be excluded under some states' worker and community right-to-know laws, the employer must make such information available to the consulting physician. In some cases, employers deliberately withhold pest control chemical information from workers.
- Determine whether a suspected victim of pesticide poisoning consulted a physician, and, if so, be sure to get the diagnosis. A

biological assay, such as measuring a certain enzyme in the blood and levels in the urine, can help confirm the diagnosis.

- Learn the extent of the exposure and how it happened. Find out the toxicity of the pesticide involved. The accuracy of this information is crucial in assessing risk to human health. Keep in mind that spraying occurs accidentally on occasion. The federal government has banned the use of certain pesticides because of concern over their impact on health. However, pesticides no longer used in the United States are often used overseas; in many cases, they are manufactured here, raising issues of colonialism and the double standard. In some cases, agricultural products sprayed with banned pesticides outside the country are then imported back to this country, raising the issue of a "circle of poison." Of course, it may make good cost-benefit sense for a Third World country with little cash and much hunger to use an effective, but hazardous, pesticide that the United States can afford to do without.
- The risk of pesticides goes beyond the human factor. Pesticides can greatly alter the ecosystem, wildlife and their food sources, and marine life. Newer pesticides are now required to be evaluated for their short-term and long-term effects on the environment.
- Each state has a lead agency, traditionally the pesticide control division in an environmental or agricultural agency, that has priority in investigating and bringing charges against companies that use banned pesticides, overexpose their workers, or pollute with pesticides. Several federal, state, and local health agencies may share jurisdiction over pesticides, including the EPA, the U.S. Food and Drug Administration (FDA), and the state agricultural office. Representatives of these agencies will keep extensive records on toxicity of pest-control chemicals.
- Toxicologists are an excellent resource on pesticides. They can be found in the state health department or at a local university.

▪ AVOIDING PITFALLS ▪

- The amount of chemical involved is important in communicating risk. There is an approved tolerance level, or limit, for pesticides to be used on food crops that is considered as safe for public consumption. Eating two peaches dusted with an insecticide is eminently less risky than swimming in a vat of the same substance for an hour.

- The standards for approving pesticides have become tougher. For many years existing applications were grandfathered. Now the government is reregistering long-approved pesticides and asking for new data to justify their safety, application by application. In many cases, pesticide manufacturers are declining to bother, not because they think the pesticide is hazardous but because the cost of reregistration research exceeds the commercial value of the product application. Thus the fact that a pesticide is already approved for use does not mean it is OK by today's standards—it might be grandfathered; conversely, the fact that approval is withdrawn does not mean that it is dangerous—reregistration might just be too expensive.
- Bruce Ames, who developed the Ames test for mutagenicity, has done research on natural versus pesticide carcinogens, essentially arguing that nature puts more carcinogenic pesticides in vegetables than agribusiness puts on vegetables. His point is not that vegetables are dangerous but rather that pesticide residues are safe. The irony here, if Ames is right, is that we are busy developing pest-resistant strains of plants so we will not need to apply so much pesticide; these strains may be more carcinogenic than the ones they replace. Thus, instead of residues on the apple (which can be washed off), we will wind up with carcinogens as part of the apple.
- Bioengineering is being used to develop both pest-resistant plants and pesticide-resistant plants (so we can use more pesticides without damaging the crops themselves). There is controversy over the process—gene splicing—and also over the goal. The deconstruction and reconstruction of DNA chains in edible plants and animals taps a wellspring of modern misgiving. The public is uneasy over genetic engineering, as are some food technologists. A telephone survey of public attitudes toward biotechnology, conducted by researchers at North Carolina State University in Raleigh in 1992, found that people favored genetic tailoring of plants, but crossing species lines, particularly using genes from animals, "got people nervous."
- Several years ago the pesticide Alar caused enormous concern. Alar is a chemical sprayed on apples to regulate their growth and color. Concerns were raised about health affects. The Alar controversy has had an impact on the scrutiny that pesticides receive from both the FDA and the EPA. Technically, Alar is a growth promoter rather than a pesticide. However, it is an example of

environmentalist overkill, since the risk was exaggerated in some of the anti-Alar propaganda and certainly misunderstood by some frightened citizens. On the other hand, the EPA had already determined that Alar was a significant enough hazard and an unimportant enough product to get it off the market—slowly. The real battle was between the slow, bureaucratic action versus fast, populist action to get rid of midsize risks. Many would argue that the threat of the latter has moved the FDA and the EPA a lot faster on pesticide issues since the Alar controversy.

▪ INFORMATION RESOURCES ▪

▪ GOVERNMENT/ACADEMIA

- ExtoxNet (http://ace.orst.edu/info/extoxnet)
  Cooperative effort of University of California at Davis, Cornell University, and Michigan State University
- National Environmental Education and Training Foundation (NEEFT) (http://www.neetf.org)
  1707 H St. NW, Suite 900, Washington, DC 20006-3915
  (202) 833-2933; fax: (202) 261-6464
- National Pesticide Information Center (http://npic.orst.edu/)
  Oregon State University, 333 Weniger, Corvallis, OR 97331-6502
  (800) 858-7378; fax: (541) 737-0761
  E-mail: npic@ace.orst.edu
- U.S. Environmental Protection Agency–Office of Pesticide Programs (http://www.epa.gov/pesticides)
  Office of Pesticide Programs
  Crystal Mall #2, 1921 Jefferson Davis Highway, Mailcode 7506C, Arlington, VA 22209
  (703) 305-7102; fax: 703-305-6244
  This site includes *Recognition and Management of Pesticide Poisonings* in both English and Spanish

▪ NONPROFIT/CONSUMER ORGANIZATIONS

Local hospitals and state poison control centers are other possible sources of information.

POLLUTION PREVENTION/ SOURCE REDUCTION

▪ BACKGROUND ▪

Industry defines pollution prevention as both "source reduction" and "end of pipe controls." The U.S. Environmental Agency (EPA), on the other hand, defines pollution prevention essentially as source reduction—"the use of materials, processes or practices that reduce or eliminate the creation of pollutants or wastes at the source." Thus pollution prevention is viewed by the EPA as an alternative to "end of the pipe" control of industrial waste. Instead of relying on treatment technologies to remove contaminants from industrial wastes as they leave the facility (through a pipe or stack), pollution prevention measures are changes that reduce or eliminate the amount of waste generated during production. This brief focuses primarily on the source reduction aspect of pollution prevention.

Pollution prevention approaches include reducing the use of water and chemical inputs, increasing efficiency in energy use, substituting less toxic raw materials, and changing maintenance procedures. A typical pollution prevention measure is switching to water-based materials from solvents.

Section 313 of the 1986 Emergency Planning and Community Right-to-Know Act (EPCRA) requires manufacturers to report environmental releases into the air and water of more than 600 toxic substances as defined by the EPA and state governments. The EPA compiles the data and maintains it in a publicly accessible national database called the Toxics Release Inventory (TRI). With access to TRI data, environmental and citizen groups have been quick to develop lists of the "worst" releases at the national, state, and local levels. The TRI database has become a strong incentive for industry to reduce its releases of listed chemicals.

This brief is based upon information provided by Michele Oschner, Assistant Director, Labor Education Center, Rutgers University, New Brunswick, New Jersey.

The Pollution Prevention Act (PPA) of 1990 established as national policy a hierarchy of waste management practices, with pollution prevention as the preferred method of reducing toxic emissions. The PPA also expanded TRI reporting to include data on the amounts of chemicals recycled, used for energy recovery, and treated on-site. In addition, facilities must now list their pollution prevention activities.

Two states, Massachusetts and New Jersey, also require covered facilities to submit facility-level materials accounting data for TRI substances. Material accounting is the process of tracking all inputs and outputs of a substance through a facility; the quantity of inputs entering must equal outputs leaving the facility in the form of products and/or production-related waste. In addition to the production-related waste information (reported on TRI as releases to the environment), materials accounting provides additional information on the total use of a substance at a facility, the amount chemically consumed during processing, and the amount shipped as or in a product. This information can be used to evaluate how efficiently a facility uses hazardous substances, provides clues as to the fate and transport of these substances in the environment, and provides consumers and environmentalists with information about hazardous substances in consumer products.

▪ IDENTIFYING THE ISSUES ▪

In addition to reducing toxic releases and improving public health, some (not all) pollution prevention practices can be cost-effective for industry by reducing raw material and energy costs and eliminating or reducing costs for the treatment and disposal of hazardous wastes. Other potential benefits to businesses include improved public image as TRI numbers fall, increased efficiency in manufacturing processes, decreased liability associated with handling less toxic chemicals and hazardous waste, and reduced worker and community exposure to toxic chemicals.

While pollution prevention activities can be as simple as changes in maintenance procedures, the most effective pollution prevention solutions are often neither simple nor easy to implement. Pollution prevention strategies typically require significant investments of time and money before they can be implemented. In addition to economic considerations, pollution prevention efforts can involve technical issues in toxicology and engineering and/or organizational structure and labor issues.

One approach to pollution prevention involves the substitution of chemicals that are on the TRI with chemicals that are not listed. On rare occasions, however, problems arise when new chemicals are used for which there is limited toxicity data. The use of a substitute chemical may reduce TRI emissions but raise questions concerning worker safety and health.

Another problem related to the absence of chemical toxicity data in the TRI is the tendency of the public and environmental groups to rank companies based upon the total amount of chemicals they release without regard to the chemicals' relative toxicity. This approach creates an incentive for industry to focus on reducing their highest volume emissions. While this approach improves their public image as they achieve huge reductions in the amounts of chemicals released, it may not necessarily provide the greatest protection of public health. The question remains: What is the relative public health benefit of reducing high volume emissions of compounds with low toxicity versus reducing low volume emissions of compounds with high toxicity?

▪ ADDRESSING THE ISSUES ▪

In 2000, the EPA began to address the issue of risk by lowering the TRI reporting thresholds for approximately fifty-five Persistent Bioaccumulative Toxic (PBT) substances. Substances that are persistent in the environment were given a 45.35-kilogram-per-year (100 pounds) reporting threshold, highly persistent substances received a 4.53-kilogram-per-year (10 pounds) threshold, and dioxin and dioxin-like compounds received a 0.1 gram-per-year (0.003 ounce) threshold. This is a significant reduction from the 4,535.9-kilogram-per-year (10,000 pounds) threshold, which previously applied.

Different methods for ranking the remaining TRI chemicals based upon their public health risk have been proposed by industry, policymakers, and environmentalists. At this writing, no single approach has been adopted. A few corporations and environmental groups have adopted their own systems for ranking relative risk. For example, Environmental Defense uses TRI data and a ranking system developed by researchers at the School of Public Health at the University of California at Berkeley to rank the potential health risks of industrial emissions. Public education about TRI data and their public health significance is crucial to directing pollution prevention efforts toward chemicals that pose the greatest threat to human health and the environment as opposed to those that are simply released in the greatest quantities.

Industries have undertaken initiatives to reduce source pollution. Toxic use reduction efforts are plant changes in production processes or raw materials that reduce, avoid, or eliminate the use of toxic or hazardous substances or generation of hazardous by-products per unit of product. These reduction efforts are done to reduce risks to the health of workers, consumers, and the environment without shifting risks between them. Toxic use reduction can be achieved by many techniques, including changing the raw materials of a product to use nontoxic or less toxic raw materials; reformulating or redesigning the end products to be nontoxic or less toxic upon use, release, or disposal; or product unit redesign or modification. For instance, an employer may use a nonhazardous substance to replace more toxic substances. The substance is safer for the environment and eliminates employee exposure to the hazard. The new procedure, however, may require an employee to enter and clean the inside of a tank to ensure it is fully cleaned, and this confined space entry may pose an even greater danger to the employee than the original exposure.

The EPA has undertaken an initiative referred to as the P2 program, which is intended to facilitate incorporation of pollution prevention concepts and principles into the operation of government agencies, businesses, nonprofit organizations, and individuals. For example, the Green Products initiative promotes safe labeling and consideration of environmental factors in purchasing and using products. The Business Practices initiatives aim to encourage changes in finance and business management.

Industry and academic partnerships, through programs such as the EPA's Green Chemistry Program, are developing new chemical products that are less hazardous to public health and the environment. Green chemistry and other technologies are approaching pollution prevention from the design side—it is far more cost effective to engineer pollution prevention into a process before construction than it is to retrofit or modify existing processes.

For existing facilities and processes, designing and implementing pollution prevention measures require commitment and input from all organizational levels, from machine operators to facility managers to corporate management. It is as essential to have machinery operators on board to learn new techniques and provide input for new ideas as it is to involve engineers with the appropriate expertise.

▪ IMPORTANT POINTS FOR RESEARCHING A STORY ▪

- There is considerable debate about which activities are included in pollution prevention. The EPA ranks pollution prevention activities in a hierarchy from most to least desirable. Reducing the use of toxic chemicals at the beginning of a process through design or product changes is the most desirable approach to pollution prevention. Reusing materials or recycling them in a closed loop within the process is next in desirability. The EPA's definition of pollution prevention does not include beneficial reuse (where one company's waste is another's raw material). Industry, on the other hand, takes the position that any activity that results in less waste, including beneficial reuse, is pollution prevention.

▪ AVOIDING PITFALLS ▪

- TRI data are not risk data or exposure data—they are simply the amounts of toxic chemicals released. TRI totals without risk assessment data can be misleading. The total amounts of chemicals released cannot be directly equated with environmental damage or health impact. Much depends upon the type of release. The highest volume releases of chemicals, for example, are often done through deep well injections into brackish (salty) water. Unless there is a leak in the pipe or in the aquifer, no one is exposed to the material. This is very different from releasing the same amounts of the same chemicals into a river immediately upstream of a water withdrawal point. In addition, some of the chemicals listed are more toxic than others. A news story that reports a release of 20,000 pounds of toxics from company A and the release of 10,000 pounds of toxics from company B does not necessarily show that company A put more people at risk than company B—it depends upon which chemicals were released, how and where they were released, and who, if anyone, was exposed.
- Environmental regulations are frequently characterized as economic costs and pollution prevention measures as economic bene-

fits. These generalizations do not always reflect the truth. Reported economic costs of environmental regulations are often based upon inflated projections specifically developed to oppose the pending regulation. Pollution prevention measures often require significant investments in time and money before they can be implemented. Often, the cost benefits of such projects are uncertain or require long-term investments. In many cases, environmental regulation becomes a necessary impetus to effect pollution prevention measures when the economic benefits are unclear.

■ INFORMATION RESOURCES ■

■ GOVERNMENT/ACADEMIA

- The Massachusetts Toxics Use Reduction Institute/P2 GEMS (www.p2gems.org)
  University of Massachusetts at Lowell
  1 University Ave., Lowell, MA 01854-2866
  (978) 934-3275 or (978) 934-3050
- Pollution Prevention Information Clearinghouse (PPIC)
  U.S. Environmental Protection Agency
  401 M St. SW, Room NEB606, Mailcode 7407, Washington, DC 20460
  (202) 260-1023; fax: (202) 260-4659
  E-mail: ppic@epa.gov
- U.S. Environmental Protection Agency—Office of Pollution Prevention and Toxics (OPPT) (www.epa.gov/p2/index)
  See also the Forum on State and Tribal Toxics Action (FOSTTA) within OPPT
  (See http://www.epa.gov/p2/resources/advisorygroups.htm)
- For state-by-state EPA information on agencies and organizations offering pollution prevention assistance, go to www.epa.gov/p2/resources/statep2

■ INDUSTRY

- ChemAlliance.org (www.chemicalliance.org)
  E-mail: johnsons@battelle.org

- Coordinating Committee for Automotive Repair (CCAR) (www.ccar-greenlink.org/ccar/index.htm)
  10901 Lowell Ave., Suite 201, Overlook Park, KS 66210
  1-888-GRN-LINK (476-5465)
  CCAR is a partnership of industry, education, and government
- National Metal Finishing Resource Center (www.nmfrc.org)
  (734) 995-4911

■ NONPROFIT/CONSUMER ORGANIZATIONS

- Environmental Defense (wwww.scorecard.org)
  257 Park Ave. South, New York, NY 10010
  (212) 505-2100; fax (212) 505-2375
- National Pollution Prevention Roundtable (www.p2.org)
  11 Dupont Circle NW, Suite 201, Washington, DC 20036
  (202) 466-7272; fax: (202) 466-7964
- The World Bank—New Ideas in Pollution Regulation (NIPR) (www.worldbank.org/nipr)
  The World Bank
  1818 H St. NW, Washington, DC 20433
  News bureau: (202) 473-7660; fax: (202) 522-2632

POPULATION GROWTH

▪ BACKGROUND ▪

In the year 1800, approximately 150,000 years after the first modern humans appeared, the global population reached 1 billion. The population doubled to 2 billion by 1930, and by 1960 the global population stood at 3 billion. In 1999, the world's population doubled again to more than 6 billion. The United Nations Population Division predicts that global population in the year 2050 will be between 7.8 and 10.9 billion, and scientists predict environmental, social, and economic consequences due to this growth in population.

Scientists attribute the rapid population growth over the past two centuries to advances in sanitation, medicine, and agriculture. In fact, the "population explosion" could be characterized also as a "health explosion." The twentieth-century population explosion was entirely the result of health improvements and the expansion of life expectancy—people are simply living healthier, longer lives than ever before. Advances significantly lowered infant mortality rates and increased average life expectancies in many nations by more than 50 percent, increasing from around thirty years in 1900 to the current average of around sixty-four years. Among the most significant advances accounting for the improvement in the human health situation were wastewater treatment, routine immunizations for childhood diseases, the use of DDT to prevent the spread of malaria, and the modernization of agriculture. Indeed, if it were not for other developments, discussed elsewhere in this brief and in other related briefs, the "health explosion" would have brought about an even greater growth of human numbers than actually occurred. Rough calculations, in fact, suggest that the world's population would be more than 50 percent larger than it is today if our century's revolution in survival chances had unfolded in the absence of other demographic changes.

The growing population combined with increasing consumption, propelled by new technologies and globalization, is bound to alter the planet on an unprecedented scale. Signs of environmental stress are everywhere. The question that now arises is: How can we ensure the well-being of growing human populations and still protect the environment? As pointed out in the United Nations Population Fund report *The State of World Population 2001*, the key policy issues are: how to use available land and water resources to produce food for all; how to promote economic development and end poverty; and, in doing so, how to address such environmental consequences of human activity as global warming and the loss of biological diversity.

▪ IDENTIFYING THE ISSUES ▪

Population and environmental issues are closely connected. Clear demographic trends and critical environmental issues are highlighted below.

▪ DEMOGRAPHIC TRENDS

Some scientists argue that global population growth is stabilizing and that the total population will level off at about nine billion by the end of this century. Differences in the predicted rates of population growth are due to differing assumptions regarding fertility rates, life expectancy, and migration. And there is great uncertainty in all of these assumptions. Future life expectancies are estimated based upon current trends in infectious disease, medical care, and food supply. For example, the future course of the AIDS epidemic must be considered in predicting life expectancy, particularly for African nations. Estimates for fertility and migration are even more uncertain.

It has been argued that the reason the world population currently totals about six billion—rather than nine billion or more—is that fertility patterns have also changed over the last century. Of all the diverse changes in fertility recorded over the past hundred years, undoubtedly the most significant has been secular fertility decline—the sustained and progressive reduction in family size due to the deliberate practice of birth control by prospective parents. Historically, secular fertility decline is a very new phenomenon, apparently not occurring in any society until about two centuries ago. It was during the period between the two world wars that, for the first time, fertility rates in industrialized countries dropped below the net replacement level, which is the level below what would be necessary for long-term population stability. However, the occurrence of these periods of subreplacement fertility appeared to be temporary and was neither sufficiently prolonged nor sufficiently large enough to bring on actual population decline in the countries affected. In the last quarter of the twentieth century, some observers note that fertility dropped to previously unimaginable peacetime lows in a number of prosperous countries. Given this decline, there is some speculation that as this new century begins, almost half of the world's population may be living in countries characterized by subreplacement fertility.

Scientists forecasting population stabilization predict that fertility rates in developing nations will drop as life expectancy increases. The assumption is that high fertility rates are based not in cultural tradition but in parents' need to ensure that enough of their children will reach adulthood to work on the family farm or business and to care for them in their old age—the so-called insurance effect. Population stabilization predictions assume that as life expectancies increase with improved access to food, water, and medical care, the need for large families to ensure survival will disappear and fertility rates will drop. These predictions almost universally assume that developing nations will embrace family planning as their socioeconomic situations improve and basic education levels rise.

Whatever the actual rate of increase, continued population growth for the foreseeable future is a certainty. This is particularly true in developing nations, where a large proportion of the population is just entering their childbearing years. In such countries, the birth rate will continue to increase due to the sheer numbers of women giving birth, although the numbers of children per family (i.e., the fertility rate) may decrease. This phenomenon is called population momentum.

■ ENVIRONMENTAL TRENDS

Most scientists agree that overpopulation already contributes to global environmental problems and threatens the sustainability of existing natural resources. Environmental trends impacting population growth include agriculture and food security issues, water scarcity, deforestation, urban/industrial problems, and carrying capacity/ecological footprints.

An estimated 1 billion people in the world today live in hunger. The U.N. Food and Agriculture Organization (FAO) reports that of the 1 billion people, 800 million are chronically malnourished. In many countries, population growth has raced ahead of food production in recent years. Over half of the world's populations, representing most of the people of the developing world—including virtually all of sub-Saharan Africa—live in "low-income, food deficit countries" as classified by the FAO. These countries do not produce enough to feed their people and cannot import sufficient food to close the gap. Low-income food-deficient countries face constraints in achieving food security, such as limited arable land, the shrinking size of family farms, land degradation, water shortages, irrigation problems, and waste.

Approximately a third of the world's population lives in countries with water stress. (See the brief on "Water Supply.") According to some estimates, this figure could grow to two-thirds by the year 2025. Water use has grown six-fold over the last seventy years. Globally, 54 percent of the annual available freshwater is being used, two-thirds of it for agriculture. By 2025, the figure could be 70 percent due to population growth alone. If per capita consumption of water everywhere reached the level of more developed countries, it would be 90 percent. In 2000, there were 508 million people living in thirty-one water-stressed or water-scarce countries. The number will grow to 3 billion in forty-eight such countries by 2025. By the same year, it is projected that 4.2 billion people (over 45 percent of the world total) will be living in countries that cannot meet the daily requirement of 50 liters (13.2 gallons) of water per person to meet basic needs. Lack of adequate food and water is leading to overconsumption of existing resources—overpumping and depletion of existing groundwater stores, overfishing, and conversion of forests and marginal lands for agriculture.

Deforestation is one of the most visible environmental effects of population growth. Scientists estimate that 9 to 16 million hectares (22.239–39.536 million acres) of forest were lost year during the 1990s. Causes of large-scale deforestation include conversion of lands for farming and grazing, commercial logging, and urbanization. In many developing nations, local populations who rely on subsistence farming and wood for shelter and fuel also contribute to deforestation.

With deforestation—particularly the loss of tropical rain forests—great numbers of species are lost to extinction. Scientists estimate that the earth is currently losing species to extinction at a rate of 17,000 to 100,000 per year—a rate unprecedented in human history. Some sources estimate that up to 20 percent of the world's species will become extinct within the next twenty years. (See the brief on "Biodiversity.")

Deforestation also has significant implications for global climate change. The clearing of forests by burning quickly adds large amounts of carbon dioxide to the atmosphere. Carbon dioxide is a greenhouse gas that traps radiation in the lower atmosphere, resulting in warmer surface temperatures. Deforestation also reduces the earth's ability to remove carbon dioxide from the atmosphere. (Plants remove carbon dioxide from the atmosphere during photosynthesis and convert it to organic matter.) Thus deforestation by burning not only contributes to global climate change, it also reduces the earth's natural defenses against it. (See the brief on "Global Climate Change.")

Deforestation often leads to desertification, when now-exposed fertile soil is washed away by storms. Desertification also occurs when agricultural land becomes salinized from long-term irrigation or is depleted of its nutrients from overgrazing or monoculture (i.e., the intensive farming of a single crop). An estimated 3.6 billion hectares (8.896 billion acres) of the world's arid lands (excluding preexisting deserts) have been lost to desertification.

Most scientists also agree that overpopulation already contributes to a host of other environmental problems. Increased energy needs, greater numbers of motor vehicles, and the industrialization of developing nations associated with population growth all contribute to air pollution, ozone depletion, and emissions of greenhouse gases. (See the briefs on "Air Pollution [Outdoor]," "Global Climate Change," "Ozone Depletion," and "Sprawl and Environmental Health.") These factors are linked to the growing urbanization that is occurring as the global population expands.

Urbanization in developing nations has increased dramatically over the past half century. At the start of the twenty-first century, more people will live and work in the urban centers of the world than in rural areas for the first time in history. Urban populations are currently growing substantially faster than the population as a whole. In addition to pollution problems, urbanization places greater demands on existing infrastructure, including sanitation facilities, public transportation, housing, recreation, health care, and education systems. Local governments (even those in wealthy nations) are often unable to finance improvements in infrastructure and services required by growing urban populations. The result is often a reduction in (or the elimination of) services and a lower standard of living.

Scientists do not know the earth's ultimate carrying capacity—the maximum number of people the earth can support. Estimates range from several billion to sixteen billion. Some argue that current rates of consumption of finite resources indicate that the earth's carrying capacity has already been exceeded. Another approach scientists use to measure people's impact on the environment is referred to as the ecological footprint indicator. The footprint estimates a population's consumption of food, materials, and energy in terms of the area of biologically productive land or sea required to produce those natural resources or, in the case of energy, to absorb the corresponding carbon dioxide emissions. Measurement is in "area units." One area unit is equivalent to 1 hectare (2.47 acres) of world average productivity. Footprint analysis captures the two most important dimensions of the challenge of sustainability—per capita consumption and population growth.

The ecological footprint indicator also identifies areas of high and low natural biological capacity and regions responsible for "ecological deficits," where resource consumption exceeds sustainable use levels. According to the World Wildlife Federation's *Living Planet 2000* report, global consumption in 1996 stood at 2.85 area units, 35 percent more than biological availability, calculated at 2.18 units. The individual countries in the Organization for Economic Cooperation and Development (OECD) had a total ecological footprint of 7.22 area units per person in 1996, more than twice the biological capacity of 3.42 units. Non-OECD countries had a total ecological footprint of 1.81 area units per person, slightly less than the corresponding biological capacity of 1.73 area units.

▪ ADDRESSING THE ISSUES ▪

Absolute population stabilization would require fertility rates to drop to replacement levels (i.e., two children per family). However, even if global fertility suddenly dropped to replacement rates, population momentum would continue population growth for several decades.

Most governments cannot mandate family planning and reductions in fertility. To do so violates basic human rights. In order to achieve reductions in fertility rates, governments, to varying degrees, are addressing the social and economic factors behind the high fertility rates such as:

- High infant mortality rates. High fertility rates are often linked to high infant mortality rates. In countries with high death rates among infants and children, parents tend to have larger families to ensure that they have enough surviving children to work the family farm or work the family business and to take care of them in their old age.

- Poor government services for the sick and elderly. As stated, one of the factors contributing to high fertility rates is parents' need to have enough children to support them in their old age—the insurance effect. Government programs that guarantee care for the elderly reduce this need.
- Low education levels among women and girls. High fertility is linked to low education levels among women and girls. Women with higher levels of education tend to marry later and have fewer children starting at an older age.
- Access barriers to health care and family planning. Women with access to health care, preconception planning, and birth control have fewer children. Anti-abortion activists have lobbied to withhold U.S. government funding of international aid organizations that provide family planning and reproductive health services that include abortion. At this writing, this controversy is delaying the U.S. contribution to the United Nations Population Fund (UNPF). (UNPF's Reproductive Health Program includes family planning and sexual health programs for women and girls but does not provide funding for or support abortion.)
- Limitations on women's rights. Women need to have power over their own bodies and their own reproduction.

Population stabilization will take many generations, particularly in developing nations that are experiencing population momentum. In the meantime, global population will continue to increase. Action needs to be taken to manage existing natural resources, to ensure food and water security, and to provide adequate standards of living for the growing populace. These efforts will require international commitments, not only to the goal of population stabilization but also to the principles of sustainable development.

At the 1994 International Conference on Population and Development (ICPD) in Cairo, 179 countries reached consensus on the relationship between population and development and set goals for 2015. Actions were agreed upon in several categories: population and development; reproductive and sexual health; gender equality, equity, and the empowerment of women; partnerships and collaboration; and mobilization of resources. Countries were urged to factor in population concerns in all development strategies and to take action to end gender-based violence. The ICPD endorsed universal education and elimination of the gender gap in primary and secondary education by 2005; efforts to reduce neonatal mortality and mortality rates for infants and children under five years of age; and provision of universal access to a full range of safe and reliable family-planning methods and related reproductive and sexual health services.

A five-year review in 1999 at a second conference referred to as ICPD+5 showed progress in meeting the goals of ICPD and reaffirmed their importance. Many governments have made changes in their health and population programs to conform more closely with the ICPD emphasis on individual choice and rights. Because the HIV/AIDS situation had grown in urgency, the ICPD+5 stepped up its recommendations with regard to access to preventive reproductive methods.

Action on population, environment, and development issues is both necessary and practical. The various international agreements and international consensus on population and development underline the need for broader and more extensive efforts.

■ IMPORTANT POINTS FOR RESEARCHING A STORY ■

- Do not overlook the role of population growth in other environmental stories. Population growth can be examined from the angle of almost every environmental topic discussed in this handbook and vice versa. Population growth may be a key contributing factor to local and regional environmental problems.
- Factors such as population size, growth, distribution, and movement help determine the relationship between people and their environments. Similar numbers of people can have very different impacts on the environment depending on various structural and institutional influences. The most basic determinant of the impact of human activity is scale. More than thirty years ago, Paul Ehrlich described this relationship in the now-famous equation: I = PAT. People's impact on their environment (I) is a product of population size (P), affluence (A, representing output per capita or the level of consumption), and technology (T, representing the per unit output or efficiency in production). While this equation is often used, it has its shortcomings, not least of which is that the factors in the relationship are not independent but rather are related

in complex ways. Nevertheless, the approach has been useful in demonstrating that population dynamics are central to environmental change.

- There are "environmental paybacks" from population-related investments, that is, programs addressing population issues, women's empowerment, and poverty eradication. Research in this area has focused primarily on policies that tend to reduce fertility, where the resulting slowing of population growth is seen as easing human stress on the environment. Some studies have tried to estimate the additional environmental impact of a single birth and its descendants. Several others have compared the expected environmental impacts associated with different demographic scenarios. Results from such studies need to be fed back to policy-makers who need information on the returns to investments (particularly public investments) in such programs in order to set priorities for resource allocation.

▪ AVOIDING PITFALLS ▪

- As with all statistics, population growth statistics can be misleading. For example, the relatively small percentage of the earth's surface that has been developed for human habitation might suggest that there is plenty of room for population growth. However, this would overlook the need for the earth to provide more than just standing room. Land is required for agriculture, the provision of raw materials for manufacturing, waste handling, and recreation, among other uses. Land and water are also required for the global circulation and renewal of nutrients. The question is not how many people can fit on the surface of the earth, but how large a population can the earth sustain before natural resources and quality of life are destroyed?
- Population growth is most often thought of as a problem for developing nations. These nations have the highest rates of growth and are the least well equipped to provide for their growing populace. However, wealthy nations consume significantly more resources per capita than do the developing nations. As such, comparatively smaller population increases in wealthy nations can result in proportionally greater environmental impacts. For example, the Worldwide Fund for Nature (World Wildlife Fund) estimates that

the United States, which accounts for 6 percent of the global population, consumes 30 percent of the world's resources.

- Some argue that there is plenty of food and water for current and future populations; we just have to get it to the populations who need it. Hunger and water shortages, however, are not simply problems of distribution; they are also problems of economics. Developing nations cannot afford to buy or distribute food and water to their growing populations.
- A number of observers have selectively stressed trends of aging and declining populations in some parts of the world in arguing that continued concern about global population growth is unwarranted. This is contrary to what the facts suggest. There will be as many people added in the next fifty years as were added in the past forty years. Further, the increase will be concentrated in the world's poorest countries, which are already straining to provide basic social services to their people.

▪ INFORMATION RESOURCES ▪

▪ GOVERNMENT/ACADEMIA

- The Center for International Earth Science Information Network (CIESIN) (www.ciesin.org)
  61 Route 9W, P.O. Box 1000, Palisades, NY 10964
  (845) 365-8988; fax: (845) 365-8922
- United Nations Population Fund (www.unfpa.org)
  220 East 42nd St., New York, NY 10017
- The World Bank (www.worldbank.org)
  1818 H St. NW, Washington, DC 20433
  (202) 473-7660; fax: (202) 522-2632

▪ NONPROFIT/CONSUMER ORGANIZATIONS

- Population Action International (www.populationaction.org)
  1300 19th St. NW, 2nd Floor, Washington, DC 20036
  (202) 557-3400; fax: (202) 728-4177
- The Population Institute (www.populationinstitute.org)
  107 Second St. NE, Washington, DC 20002
  (202) 544-3300; fax: (202) 544-0068

- Population Reference Bureau (www.prb.org)
  1875 Connecticut Ave. NW, Suite 520, Washington, DC 20009
  (202) 939-5407
- World Resources Institute (www.wri.org)
  10 G St. NE, Suite 800, Washington, DC 20002
  (202) 729-7600; fax: (202) 729-7686
  E-mail: front@wri.org
- World Wildlife Fund (www.worldwildlife.org)
  P.O. Box 97180, 250 24th St. NW, Washington, DC 20037
  (202) 293-4800; media can contact staff experts at
  (202) 778-9541; fax: (202) 293-9211
- Zero Population Growth (www.zpg.org)
  1400 16th St. NW, Suite 320, Washington, DC 20036
  (202) 332-2200; fax: (202) 332-2302
  E-mail: info@zpg.org

See also:

- Ehrlich, P. 1968. *The Population Bomb*. New York: Sierra Club/Ballantine.
- Ehrlich, P., with A. H. Ehrlich. 1990. *The Population Explosion*. New York: Simon and Schuster.

SPRAWL AND ENVIRONMENTAL HEALTH

▪ BACKGROUND ▪

Poorly planned, sprawling development is consuming increasingly larger amounts of land across the United States. The American Farmland Trust estimates that up to 20.25 hectares (50 acres) of prime farmland are lost to sprawl each hour in the United States. Sprawl increases traffic, contributes to air and water pollution, strains local infrastructure, and contributes to the decay of older urban centers. An alternative—"smart growth"—offers a new paradigm for development for the next century that promises to revitalize our urban centers and preserve open space.

Simply put, sprawl is development where it should not be—in rural and otherwise undeveloped areas. More specifically, sprawl is the noncontiguous outward movement of new development from central city areas. The result of fragmented land-use planning, sprawl is typically characterized by scattered, low-density development, with poor access between neighboring land uses.

What does sprawl look like? Sprawl is isolated developments of single-family homes surrounded by farmland. Sprawl is miles and miles of commercial strip malls. Sprawl is regional shopping centers and big box stores surrounded by undeveloped land. Sprawl is needing a car to get to the nearest grocery store. Sprawl is the realtor's sign on the farm that reads "Commercial Property," or "Zoned for Office/Retail/Commercial Use." Sprawl can be found in almost all nonmetropolitan areas of the United States and occurs in significant amounts in about a quarter of all U.S. counties.

This brief is based upon information provided by Robert W. Burchell, Center for Urban Policy Research, Edward J. Bloustein School of Planning, Rutgers University, New Brunswick, New Jersey.

■ IDENTIFYING THE ISSUES ■

Sprawl has its origins in the expanding number of suburban jobs that encouraged middle-class workers to leave the city and build homes on the outskirts of cities. The building of roads, highways, and bridges, subsidized by the federal government, enabled the exodus from the city. Tax subsidies to employers helped businesses relocate in suburban areas. Towns received short-term economic benefits from development and construction, and so planners have often looked past the negatives in poorly planned development. These become apparent only later as the demand for services such as roads, schools, sewer lines, and emergency services increases.

One of the main criticisms of sprawl is its consumption of large amounts of land—not only developable land but also agricultural and environmentally sensitive land. Agricultural land is lost to sprawl because it often is plentiful and relatively inexpensive. Development of these tracts results in sprawl's characteristic "leapfrog" pattern, where development skips over agricultural and open space, and isolated developments pop up, seemingly in the middle of nowhere. Because they are poorly protected, small areas of environmentally sensitive land, including wetlands and buffer areas, are lost to sprawl along with the larger tracts of developable land they border.

Another criticism of sprawl is its segregation of different land uses. Sprawl development often is advanced by local land-use zoning regulations. These zoning regulations typically divide an area into zoning districts, with each district allowing a single land use. In this manner, residential areas, shopping centers, strip malls, office parks, and other land uses are separated spatially from one another.

The leapfrog pattern and land-use segregation of sprawl result in the need for almost complete reliance on automobiles for transportation. The places where people live, work, shop, and play are scattered across large areas. Many of these areas are not served by public transportation. Hence, the automobile becomes virtually the only means of getting from here to there. Studies show that total vehicle miles of travel (VMT) increase with sprawl development. According to data from the Federal Highway Administration, total VMT in the United States increased by 58 percent between 1980 and 1995.

There is widespread agreement among experts that local infrastructure costs for roadways and utilities are directly related to development density, with lower development density resulting in higher infrastructure costs. The National Research Council's Transportation Research Board found that the costs for roads and utilities in compact developments were 20 to 25 percent lower than the same costs in sprawl developments. However, some scientists argue that these excess costs of infrastructure associated with sprawling development are later recouped by way of lower infrastructure costs for fill-in development.

The environmental impacts of sprawl include air and water pollution, destruction of natural resources, and flood damage. Sprawl's reliance on the automobile contributes to air pollution, including ozone, volatile organic compounds, and particulate matter. The greater number of roadways and paved surfaces associated with sprawl add contaminated urban runoff to streams, rivers, and wetlands. Sprawl further contributes to runoff and flooding problems by destroying wetlands. It ends up encouraging development on natural floodplains where people in increasing number live in harm's way. The Sierra Club reports that more than 40,486 hectares (100,000 acres) of wetlands are lost to development each year. Impervious surfaces, in addition to negatively impacting surface water and contributing to flooding, can also reduce aquifer recharge and therefore long-term water supply by increasing the overall amount of precipitation that leaves the watershed via runoff. Sprawl is energy intensive and thus contributes additional air pollution in the form of carbon dioxide, a significant greenhouse gas. (See the briefs on "Air Pollution [Outdoor]," "Global Climate Change," "Naturally Occurring and Technology-Based Disasters," "Ozone Depletion," "Surface Water Quality," and "Water Supply.")

According to a 2002 report by the Centers for Disease Control and Prevention (CDC) on the topic of urban sprawl and its health impacts, there is growing evidence that sprawling community development discourages physical activities such as walking and cycling. The research links car-dependent lifestyles with increased rates of asthma and obesity in the population. Greater reliance on cars also leads to increased risk of pedestrian injuries, car crashes, and fatalities.

Response times for police, ambulance, and fire departments to outlying suburbs often are higher than national standards, according to 1998 report by the American Farmland Trust. This potentially places residents at increased risk to their health and safety.

Evidence suggests scattered development, or "sprawlscape," can jeopardize public health in more subtle ways as well. A study published in the *Journal of Environmental Psychology* in 1991 linked the visual clutter of sprawling development with stress-related effects, such as elevated blood pressure and increased muscle tension.

While environmentalists and many land-use planners agree that sprawl is undesirable, there is less agreement among the general public. Sprawl, it seems, is in the eye of the beholder. What some see as sprawl, others view as typical suburban development—for some, the American dream. If quality of life in the United States is defined as owning a home that increases in value, living in a safe community, and having relatively low taxes, good public services, and a good quality of education, then sprawl often meets the definition. Developers, free enterprise advocates, and property rights advocates argue that sprawl is dictated by the market and that measures to stop sprawl deny property owners their rights.

▪ ADDRESSING THE ISSUES ▪

Growth is inevitable. The U.S. population is increasing by 2.7 million people per year. This growing population requires an additional 1.7 million units of housing each year. Zero growth in development is not an option. Realizing this, and having learned the lessons of sprawl, many experts, planners, and developers are turning to "smart growth" as an option in fulfilling future housing needs.

Although there is currently no single accepted definition, smart growth efforts share a number of characteristics. As described by the Urban Land Institute, smart growth is environmentally friendly and economically sound. Smart growth involves integrated regional land-use planning. Smart growth relies on existing infrastructure and includes redevelopment of infill housing and brownfields. Smart growth seeks not only to revitalize inner-city areas but also to preserve some of the natural lands in outlying areas that would otherwise be lost to development. The idea of smart growth is not to deny growth but to direct it to the best locations.

Some critics argue that there is no market for smart growth—that Americans prefer to live in sprawling suburbs. It is not entirely clear that this is the case. Studies show that Americans want to live in safe areas with a sense of community. Often, with sprawl, the sense of a cohesive community is missing. Further, the preference of the American public for the suburbs is likely to change dramatically within the next twenty to thirty years as the baby boomer generation retires. The overall aging of Americans will affect where people move and what they are looking for in their housing, neighborhoods, and communities. Experts predict that future movement will be toward urban and suburban centers, as seniors seek out safe and culturally interesting communities with easy access to shopping and other amenities. These centers do not need to have top school systems, nor will they need to be composed exclusively of one racial or socioeconomic group.

Changes in the population and its housing requirements will provide potential for improving patterns of development through smart growth—as long as public policy keeps pace with the population's changing needs. In order to meet these needs, central areas need to be made safer, more interesting, and of sufficient scale to attract people's attention. The potential for revitalization of older cities exists through brownfields redevelopment and other initiatives. However, the worst cities will not effect a comeback unless they adapt to the new reality. (See the brief on "Brownfields.")

▪ IMPORTANT POINTS FOR RESEARCHING A STORY ▪

- Smart growth requires collaboration between state and local governments, private entities, and nonprofit organizations. State governments can provide economic incentives and assistance for smart growth. Local governments have the authority and responsibility to direct growth through zoning policies. Developers and landowners need to involve local communities in the decision-making process to gain consensus on what is best for the future of the community.
- Smart growth projects can include brownfields and touch upon issues of environmental justice. Consider exploring smart growth projects from these angles. (See the briefs on "Brownfields" and "Environmental Justice and Hazardous Waste.")
- There often is an ideological clash between the desire for relatively short-term profit on the part of builders and specific landowners and the efforts of municipalities to ensure the long-term viability of the community.
- The automobile manufacturing and service industries, as well as the highway building industry, indirectly foster sprawl. Road

building and maintenance are significantly subsidized by nontransportation-related taxes (e.g., property taxes). Resources that are underpriced because of subsidies (e.g., the automobile and its infrastructure) get overused, to the detriment of efforts to control sprawl.

▪ AVOIDING PITFALLS ▪

- Even if sprawl were controlled overnight, approximately 75 to 85 percent of the current costs of development would remain. According to developers and individual rights advocates, the public is able and willing to pay, and should have the option to pay, the extra 15 to 25 percent for this type of suburban development.
- Smart growth is not antigrowth. Smart growth is a strategy to accommodate growth with existing infrastructure while preserving the environment and reversing a pattern of abandonment in older central areas.
- Smart growth does not require urban growth boundaries (UGBs). UGBs are one smart growth approach. Developed properly, with appropriate research and consideration to existing and future land-use needs, UGBs can be a positive step in redirecting growth back toward existing centers. However, UGBs are often controversial. In a number of cases, poorly planned and poorly executed UGBs have backfired, mobilizing opposition to high-density growth within the UGBs and causing developers to move to even more inappropriate locations.

▪ INFORMATION RESOURCES ▪

Local planning boards and state planning agencies can offer information on sprawl-related problems and smart growth initiatives in your area. Some states have developed plans to address the problem of sprawl and guide development decisions at the state level. For example, the state of Maryland boasts the nation's first statewide incentive program to combat sprawl. Contact your state's office of state planning to review state plans.

GOVERNMENT/ACADEMIA

- State of Maryland–Smart Growth and Neighborhood Conservation (www.op.state.md.us/smartgrowth)
  - Governor's Special Assistant for Smart Growth
    John Frece
    (410) 260-8112
    E-mail: jfrece@dnr.state.md.us
    Marty Guinane
    (410) 260-8989
    E-mail: mguinane@dnr.state.md.us
  - Maryland Department of Planning
    Tom Bass
    (410) 767-4578
    E-mail: tbass@mdp.state.md.us
- New Jersey Department of Community Affairs Office of State Planning (www.state.nj.us/osp/osphome.htm)
  101 South Broad St., P.O. Box 204, 7th Floor, Trenton, NJ 08625-0204
  (609) 292-7156; fax: (609) 292-3292
- New Jersey Planning Officials (www.njpo.org)
- New Jersey State League of Municipalities (www.njslom.com)
- Transportation Research Board (www.trb.org)
  The National Academies, 2101 Constitution Ave. NW, Washington, DC 20418
  (202) 334-2934; fax: (202) 334-2003
- U.S. Environmental Protection Agency–Development, Community and Environment Division
  (www.epa.gov/oppe/oppe)
  1200 Pennsylvania Ave. NW, Mailcode 1808, Washington, DC 20460
  (202) 260-2750

INDUSTRY/PROFESSIONAL ASSOCIATIONS

- American Road and Transportation Builders Association (www.artba.org)
- National Association of Home Builders (www.nahb.com)
  1201 15th St. NW, Washington, DC 20005

(800) 368-5242; (202) 822-0200
E-mail: info@NAHB.com

▪ NONPROFIT/CONSUMER ORGANIZATIONS

- American Farmland Trust (www.farmland.org)
  1200 18th St. NW, Suite 800, Washington, DC 20036
  (202) 331-7300; fax: (202) 659-8339
  E-mail: info@farmland.org
- American Planning Association (www.planning.org)
  1776 Massachusetts Ave. NW, Suite 400,
  Washington, DC 20036
  (202) 872-0611
- International City/County Management Association (ICMA) (www.icma.org)
  777 North Capitol St. NE, Suite 500, Washington, DC 20002
  (202) 289-4262; fax: (202) 962-3500
- National Association of Counties (www.naco.org)
  440 1st St. NW, 8th Floor, Washington, DC 20001
  (202) 661-8805
- National Association of Local Government Environmental Professionals (NALGEP) (www.nalgep.org)
  1350 New York Ave. NW, Suite 1100,
  Washington, DC 20005
  (202) 638-6254
  E-mail: nalgep@spiegel.becltd.com
- Sierra Club (www.sierraclub.org/sprawl)
  85 Second St., 2nd Floor, San Francisco, CA 94105-3441
  (415) 977-5500; fax: (415) 977-5799
  E-mail: media.team@sierraclub.org
- Smart Growth Network (www.smartgrowth.org)
- Sprawl Watch Clearinghouse (www.sprawlwatch.org)
  1100 17th St. NW, 10th Floor, Washington, DC 20036
  (202) 974-5133; fax: (202) 466-2247
  E-mail: allison@sprawlwatch.org
- Surface Transportation Policy Project (www.transact.org)
  1100 17th St. NW, 10th Floor, Washington, DC 20036
  (202) 466-2636; fax: (202) 466-2247
  E-mail: stpp@transact.org

- ULI—The Urban Land Institute (www.uli.org)
  1025 Thomas Jefferson St. NW, Suite 500 West, Washington, DC 20007
  (202) 624-7000 or (800) 321-5011; fax: (202) 624-7140

See also:

- Jackson, D. 2001. *Creating a Healthy Environment: The Impact of the Built Environment on Public Health*. Atlanta: Centers for Disease Control and Prevention.
- Ulrich, R. S., R. F. Simons, B. D. Losito, E. Fiorito, M. A. Miles, and M. Zelson. 1991. Stress recovery during exposure to natural and urban environments. *Journal of Environmental Psychology* 11:201-230.

SURFACE WATER QUALITY

▪ BACKGROUND ▪

Surface water refers to water at the surface of the earth exposed to the atmosphere. It includes oceans, lakes, rivers, streams, ponds, lagoons, bays, estuaries, and marshes. This brief will deal primarily with nonsaline (freshwater) surface water bodies. Humans, plants, and wildlife depend upon clean surface water for survival. Clean surface water is necessary for agriculture, fishing, industry, and recreation. We depend upon clean water for drinking, food preparation, hygiene, and processing waste. Clean surface water is important even in areas where it is not directly withdrawn for use. Surface water provides flow, or recharge, to many groundwater systems and can impact groundwater quality. (See the brief on "Groundwater Pollution.")

▪ IDENTIFYING THE ISSUES ▪

Sources of surface water contamination are categorized as either point or nonpoint. A point source originates from a single discharge—a waste pipe, leak, or spill. By contrast, nonpoint sources are broad and cannot be easily pinpointed. Nonpoint sources contaminate surface water when rainfall or irrigation picks up pollutants from the land surface (runoff) and carries them to the water body. Nonpoint sources include parking lots, farmland, roadways, lawns, gardens, and other similar sources within a given watershed. (A watershed is the land area that drains to a surface water body or recharges a groundwater aquifer.) Recreational boating is also considered a nonpoint source of surface water pollution.

Historically, point sources such as sewage treatment plants and industrial discharges were the primary polluters of surface water. Over the past several decades, environmental regulations and improved technology have significantly reduced the amount of contaminants discharged to surface water by point sources. Today, nonpoint sources are the largest contributors to surface water pollution. The leading nonpoint sources of surface water contamination are agriculture (see the brief on "Animal Waste Management"), urban runoff, and discharges from storm sewers. The most common pollutants from nonpoint sources are sediments (siltation), nutrients (e.g., phosphate, nitrate, ammonia), pesticides, bacteria and other pathogens, oil and grease, hazardous chemicals, and heavy metals (e.g., arsenic, cadmium, lead, mercury).

Other sources of surface water pollution include physical changes to the water body via dredging and dam construction. (See the brief on "Disposal of Dredged Materials.") These activities may result in the release of contaminants, or they may destroy existing habitat within the water body.

The sediments of many water bodies are contaminated. Sediment contamination is typically the result of numerous discharges, both past and present. Sediments may contain a variety of contaminants, including nutrients, heavy metals, organic compounds (e.g., PCBs, dioxins, petroleum hydrocarbons, polynuclear aromatic hydrocarbons), radioisotopes, and microorganisms. Sediments can be a reservoir, or sink, for certain chemicals and can contain high concentrations of some chemicals not detectable in the waters above them.

Sediment contamination is most problematic when the sediments are disturbed and some particles become resuspended in the water column. Suspended particles can be carried farther downstream, spreading the contamination, or they may be taken up by fish and other aquatic organisms. The same physical and chemical properties that make certain contaminants bind to sediments make them likely to bioconcentrate, or bioaccumulate, within the tissues of organisms exposed to them. Contaminants taken up and accumulated within fish pose health risks to the fish and to the birds, animals, and people that eat them.

The atmosphere is another important source of surface water contamination. In the Great Lakes, for example, mercury contamination of the surface water, its sediments, and fish has long been a problem. The primary sources of mercury contamination to the Great Lakes are airborne emissions from power plants, waste incinerators, and other industrial facilities. Atmospheric deposition of acidic compounds (acid rain) from power plant and industrial emissions has lowered the pH of lakes and streams in the northeastern United States and in Canada, making water undrinkable and killing fish. (See the brief on "Air Pollution [Outdoor].")

Physical changes in bays and estuaries can lead to another type of contamination—increased salinity, or salinization. For example, deeper channels created by dredging for shipping routes may draw seawater into an estuary. Increased salinity can adversely impact the estuary, nearby freshwater wetlands, and the vegetation, fish, and wildlife communities that inhabit them. Increased salinity in estuarine and wetland areas can also lead to saltwater intrusion into local surface and groundwater sources of drinking water.

Thermal pollution occurs from the release of heated waters from power stations using surface water for cooling purposes. While cooling water is typically returned without additional chemical contamination, the temperature is higher than that of the receiving water body. Increased water temperature can lead to decreased levels of dissolved oxygen in the water body, which in turn can interfere with migration and spawning of fish populations.

Natural sources also contribute to surface water contamination. Heavy storms increase siltation and turbidity. Local rock and soil types can impact the pH and concentrations of trace elements (e.g., aluminum, arsenic, iron, selenium) in surface water bodies.

▪ ADDRESSING THE ISSUES ▪

The Clean Water Act aims to make all surface water bodies safe for two primary uses: recreation and the propagation of fish and shellfish. Under the act, states and other jurisdictions may set other "designated uses" for individual surface water bodies, including drinking water supply, agricultural irrigation, and fish consumption. To provide guidance to states and other jurisdictions, the U.S. Environmental Protection Agency (EPA) develops water quality criteria. Water quality criteria may be used to set limits on the levels of pollutants in a surface water body. Water quality criteria for each pollutant vary, depending upon the designated use of the water body and the local water authority setting the standards. In many cases, water quality criteria set by the EPA are adopted as enforceable water quality standards by states and local jurisdictions.

In order to meet water quality criteria in the water body, states and other jurisdictions issue permits to point source dischargers under the National Pollutant Discharge Elimination System (NPDES) and similar state and local programs. Permit programs focus on pollution prevention—either by removing contaminants from wastewater before they are discharged or by reducing or eliminating wastewater discharges to surface water. These programs have been effective in reducing the impact of traditional point sources of surface water pollution (i.e., waste treatment plants and industrial discharges).

Over the past two decades, regulators have begun to address nonpoint sources of surface water pollution. The 1987 amendments to the Clean Water Act included a nationwide permit program to address storm water runoff from commercial and industrial facilities and municipal storm sewers. Building upon this approach, the EPA and many states have endorsed the use of watershed-based approaches for protecting and improving surface water quality. A typical project using a watershed approach looks at all possible sources of pollution to a surface water body within the area that drains to it (i.e., the watershed), develops priorities, and evaluates alternatives to address the problems. Watershed projects typically include representatives from various stakeholders within the watershed—government, industry, agriculture, public interest groups, citizens, and other interested parties.

According to regulations of the Clean Water Act (40 CFR Part 130, section 130.7), states, territories, and authorized tribes are mandated to list polluted and threatened bodies of water within their borders and develop Total Maximum Daily Loads (TMDLs). These lists must be submitted by April 1 of even-numbered years. They must identify pollutants and prioritize water bodies based on severity of pollution and how the water is to be used, for example, for fishing, swimming, or drinking water. The TMDL specifies the maximum amount of a pollutant that a body of water can contain and still meet water quality standards. It identifies the sources of pollutants from either point or nonpoint pollutant sources.

While TMDLs have been a required part of the Clean Water Act since 1972, most states did not develop them until recently. Several years ago, legal actions were taken against the EPA by civic organizations promoting the development of TMDLs.

■ IMPORTANT POINTS FOR RESEARCHING A STORY ■

- Changes in surface water quality are often linked to other environmental changes. Changes in land use, deforestation, and development can result in increased runoff and siltation. Loss of nearby wetlands, which often act as a filter, can increase contaminant loading into a surface water body. Be aware of activities within the watershed that may impact surface water quality.

- Pay attention to the effect of water quantity on water quality. When communities fail to control flooding, high waters may inundate nearby industrial facilities, causing increased surface water contamination. In one extreme example, severe floods on the Meramec River brought dioxin-contaminated soil into flooded homes in Times Beach, Missouri. After the floods, the river was also found to contain dioxin. Conversely, drought conditions are also accompanied by surface water pollution problems, as the amount of clean water to dilute contaminated discharges is reduced.
- Knowing the specific contaminants can help in tracking down potential sources. For example, Methyl *tert*-Butyl Ether (MTBE) is associated with gasoline tanks and spills; fecal contamination may be associated with leaking sewer lines or animal feeding operations; and pesticides and nitrates are typically associated with agricultural sites.
- The cost of water pollution investigations can be very high. Therefore, government agencies and the responsible parties will develop most information themselves. Find out who (if anyone) is actively investigating a site. Work with them to understand the local circumstances. Relate levels being discussed with health impact levels. Verify analyses with other experts.
- Focus on the good pollution stories as well as the bad. Many companies have taken drastic steps to clean up production waste, reducing or eliminating wastewater discharges to surface water. In many instances, waste minimization practices can increase profits. The reporter should cover such stories with input from business reporting staff.

■ AVOIDING PITFALLS ■

- The taste, smell, or color of water is not necessarily an indicator of water quality. Water may be aesthetically unpleasant and yet not actually harmful to drink. Likewise, water that to all appearances is pure could contain carcinogens in high concentrations. The only way to be certain of the water quality is to test it.

- Chemicals differ greatly in the health risks they present. Know what chemicals have been found and their concentrations. Be careful in your use of health effect terms. What are the possible health effects and under what conditions of exposure? Use more than one source of scientific information, and make sure that your source has expertise in the appropriate field.
- Laboratory reports for water analyses are highly technical and notoriously difficult to interpret. The best reports will list the contaminants tested, the limits of detection, the concentrations detected, and relevant health and environmental standards. The reports typically list all the contaminants targeted by the analysis, regardless of whether they were detected in the groundwater sample. Depending upon the contaminant, results are reported in milligrams of contaminant per liter of water (mg/l), which is equivalent to parts per million (ppm), or in micrograms of contaminant per liter of water (μg/l), which is equivalent to parts per billion (ppb). Other values are reported in units specific to the test (for example, pH, hardness, conductance, and turbidity). You may need to consult with a technical person to interpret results correctly.
- When evaluating laboratory reports, it is important to compare the detection limit—the lowest concentration of a contaminant that could be found by the analysis—with the appropriate water quality standard for each compound. If the limit of detection is higher than the water quality standard, violations of the standard could be missed.
- Bioassays are designed to identify contaminants that would result in toxicity or bioaccumulation in exposed organisms. Bioassays are expensive and time consuming and may provide equivocal results (false positives). Critics maintain bioassays are unrepresentative of actual conditions within the aquatic environment.

■ INFORMATION RESOURCES ■

■ GOVERNMENT/ACADEMIA

- Great Lakes Commission (www.glc.org)
  400 Fourth St., Ann Arbor, MI 48103
  (734) 665-9135; fax: (734) 665-4370
  E-mail: glc@glc.org

- U.S. Environmental Protection Agency—Office of Wetlands, Oceans and Watersheds (www.epa.gov/owow)
  1200 Pennsylvania Ave. NW, Washington, D.C. 20460
  (202) 260-7166; fax: (202) 260-6294
  For more information specifically on TMDLs, go to: www.epa.gov/owow/tmdl
- U.S. Geological Survey—Office of Water Quality (www.water.usgs.gov)
  Office of Media Relations, Reston, VA 20192
  (703) 648-4732

▪ INDUSTRY/PROFESSIONAL ASSOCIATIONS

- American Water Works Association (www.awwa.org)
  6666 West Quincy Ave., Denver, CO 80235
  (303) 794-7711
- Water Environment Federation (www.wef.org)
  601 Wythe Street, Alexandria, VA 22314-1994
  (703) 684-2480
- Water Quality Association (www.wqa.org)
  International Headquarters and Laboratory
  4151 Naperville Rd., Lisle, IL 60532
  (630) 505-0160; fax: (630) 505-9637

▪ NONPROFIT/CONSUMER ORGANIZATIONS

- Chesapeake Bay Foundation (www.cbf.org)
  Philip Merrill Environmental Center
  6 Herndon Ave., Annapolis, MD 21403
  (410) 268-8816
- Environmental Defense (www.scorecard.org) or (www.environmentaldefense.org)
  257 Park Ave. South, New York, NY 10010
  (212) 505-2100; fax: (212) 505-2375
- Natural Resources Defense Council (www.nrdc.org/media)
  40 West 20th St., New York, NY 10011
  (212) 727-2700; fax: (212) 727-1773
  E-mail: nrdcinfo@nrdc.org

WATER SUPPLY

▪ BACKGROUND ▪

The availability of clean water is a basic requirement for life. Water seems abundantly available on earth, where more than 70 percent of the planet's surface is covered by water. However, the amount of freshwater available for human use is, in fact, strictly limited. Less than 3 percent of the earth's water is freshwater; the remainder is seawater. Approximately two-thirds of the earth's freshwater is frozen in ice caps and glaciers. This leaves less than 1 percent of the earth's water as liquid freshwater, which is either held above ground (3 percent) in rivers, lakes, and streams or in aquifers below ground (97 percent).

The availability and sustainable use of freshwater are issues worldwide. According to the United Nations Environment Program's (UNEP) report "Global Environment Outlook 2000," approximately a third of the population in the world lives in countries with water stress, where more than 10 percent of the renewable freshwater is withdrawn for use each year. Americans are included in this UNEP total. Between 10 and 20 percent of available freshwater in the United States is withdrawn for use annually. This brief focuses on the issues of freshwater supply and use within the United States.

▪ IDENTIFYING THE ISSUES ▪

According to the U.S. Geological Survey (USGS) report *Estimated Use of Water in the United States in 1995*, a total of 341 million gallons of freshwater are withdrawn for use each day in the United States. Approximately three-quarters of this water comes from surface water sources; the rest is groundwater. Seventy-five percent of the freshwater withdrawn is returned to streams and groundwater sources after use. The remaining 25 percent is lost to consumptive uses—it is evaporated, transpired, or incorporated into a product, livestock, or a crop.

According to USGS data, most of the freshwater used in the United

States is for irrigation (39 percent) and for electric thermoelectric power (39 percent), where water is used to cool electric power plants. Twelve percent of the freshwater withdrawn is used for public potable water supply, that is, water that is drinkable. Six percent of freshwater is used by industry. Livestock, individual household use, mining, and commercial use each account for 1 percent of U.S. freshwater use.

Freshwater consumption varies significantly according to use. Thermoelectric power consumes the least amount of freshwater, using the water to cool equipment and returning more than 97 percent of the water withdrawn to its source. Farming (irrigation and livestock) is the most consumptive use, returning only 40 percent of the water withdrawn. In addition, return flow from irrigation may contain high concentrations of minerals, pesticides, and nutrients, affecting the quality of the receiving water body and making reuse difficult.

All of the uses of freshwater discussed thus far are "offstream" uses (water is withdrawn from a surface water body or groundwater aquifer and used outside of the stream). Sufficient water supply is also an issue for "instream" uses (uses that take place without water being diverted or withdrawn). Instream water uses include recreation, navigation, hydroelectric power generation, support of fish and wildlife habitat, flow of wastewater, and dilution of saline estuaries. Increasing demand for offstream uses of freshwater are, in many areas, reducing surface water flow and competing with instream needs.

Water is renewed by recharge from surface water. When all of the water supply for a community comes from renewable sources, either because the aquifer is being recharged at a rate that matches the removal rate and/or because surface water is being used—then water resource sustainability is possible. If water in the aquifer is being tapped, it will eventually be depleted, producing an additional problem of subsidence of the ground above. The water in the aquifer is the equivalent of a savings account, while the surface water is the income. A community with a sustainable water supply lives on income alone and holds its savings for contingencies, providing an inheritance for the future, if needed.

Water supply is a concern across the nation, although specific threats and concerns vary by region. In the western states, water supply is an ongoing issue due to the dry climate and the distance between many population centers and renewable sources of freshwater. In these states, increasing agricultural demand for irrigation is competing with increasing demands for potable water by growing populations. In other areas of the country, regional surface water quality problems and localized groundwater pollution threaten potable use of otherwise ample water supplies. Along the eastern seaboard, increasing population demands and water quality issues are the greatest concerns. As water withdrawals increase to meet growing population demands, saltwater intrusion is becoming an increasing threat to regional groundwater and surface water supplies along both coasts. (See the brief on "Surface Water Quality.")

Drought is increasingly a problem across the United States, even in regions previously thought to be immune from water shortages. In recent years, much of the country has experienced drier than normal conditions. According to the National Drought Monitor, states along the eastern seaboard from Maine to Georgia have had severe to extreme drought conditions throughout 2001 and into 2002. Similarly, much of the Midwest has been categorized as "abnormally dry," with large areas having moderate to severe drought conditions.

There are different kinds of droughts, for example, water-supply droughts, ecological droughts, and agricultural droughts. In every drought, different parties may be affected in different ways. The specific needs of different water uses and the ability of humans to store and transmit water may mean that while farmers are desperate and crops are dying, nearby cities may be in good shape. Conversely, the water supply to cities may be threatened (especially in areas where water sources are located far away) yet nearby farmers and ranchers may be relatively unaffected. It may be hard to make unaffected parties aware of water shortages being experienced by others.

Water shortages and competing water needs across the United States spur disputes over water rights. Most states consider surface water and groundwater to be public resources, and each state has its own laws to determine water use rights. In many western states, surface water allocation is determined on a first-use basis—those with the earliest recorded beneficial use have first rights to use the water source. In some cases, first-use rights date back to the 1800s.

There are a number of different types of water rights. Riparian water rights are given to landowners whose property abuts a surface water body. Appropriative water rights are allocated to parties who wish to use (appropriate) groundwater or surface water that is not riparian (adjacent) to their property. In most cases, appropriative rights are contingent upon continued use of the allocated water. For example, if the water allocation is not used for a period of five years, the water rights are forfeited. Prescriptive water rights are those acquired by continuously using water for a period of time. Another type of rights, reserved rights, may be claimed by the federal government to protect instream water uses, such as navigation or the protection of fish populations.

Some critics argue that current water allocation laws are outdated and that some run counter to conservation efforts. For example, under continuous use clauses, commonly referred to as "use it or lose it," an entire water allocation must be used each year or rights to the unused portion of the allocation may be forfeited back to the state. Critics maintain that such policies encourage waste and discourage conservation, as rights holders strive to use their entire water allocation in order to preserve future rights to it.

Some argue that water should be treated as private property or as a commodity. Texas, for example, treats groundwater as private property. As water has become increasingly scarce and increasingly valuable, entrepreneurs in Texas have begun to secure rights to groundwater from rural landowners, much as those in the oil business secured rights to drill for oil in the past. Environmentalists and some officials are questioning the wisdom of allowing large-scale pumping of groundwater for profit. Many fear that the sale of groundwater to the highest bidder will leave those in most need (i.e., rural towns and farmers) high and dry. (See the brief on "Cross-Border Environmental Issues [U.S.-Mexico].")

Current water shortages and disputes over water rights will only escalate as population pressures on the nation's water supply continue to grow. In addition to increasing population, there is concern that global climate change will adversely impact surface water and groundwater supplies. Effects predicted by climatologists include increased salinity in surface water and groundwater in coastal areas as ocean levels rise; increased incidence of severe weather events, increased flooding, and increased temperatures resulting in desertification of already dry areas. (See the briefs on "Global Climate Change" and "Naturally Occurring and Technology-Based Disasters.")

■ ADDRESSING THE ISSUES ■

As the population continues to grow, so will demands on the nation's already stressed water supply. Local, regional, and national efforts to conserve and manage the water supply will need to be supplemented and improved. In times of drought, most citizens comply willingly with water restrictions and conservation efforts. However, when water is plentiful, the need for water conservation is less apparent and is difficult to convey to the public. The media can help sustain public education efforts by covering stories on new technologies and efforts that support water conservation efforts.

In-home water conservation efforts include the use of water-saving appliances, including showerheads, toilets, faucets, dishwashers, washing machines, swimming pool filters, and lawn watering/irrigation systems. Installation of even just one of these devices can save tens of gallons of water per day. Water conservation tips for consumers include:

- Turning the faucet off while brushing teeth or shaving.
- Repairing leaky faucets and toilets. Even a very slow drip from a faucet can waste several gallons of water per day. A leaky toilet can waste hundreds of gallons of water per day.
- Taking short showers instead of baths and when using a tub, closing the drain before turning the water on and bathing small children together.
- Keeping drinking water cool in the refrigerator (instead of running the water at the tap until it is cool).
- Operating washing machines and dishwashers only when full.
- Using commercial car wash facilities that recycle water.
- Watering the lawn and/or garden in the early morning hours, when it is cooler and there is less water loss to evaporation.
- Switching to landscaping that requires little or no watering. This includes native plants that are accustomed to the rainfall patterns in the region.

In addition to individual efforts by residents, local governments and water supply authorities can encourage water efficiency and conservation through public education, ordinances, policies, and practices. Water supply authorities can monitor and repair leaks in the supply system, conduct water use audits, and adopt rate structures that encourage conservation. Toilet replacement rebate programs have been used successfully by a number of water supply authorities to reduce water use within their service areas. These programs offer rebates to homeowners who replace their older toilets with newer water-efficient models. Some of the larger programs have expanded to include free toilets and installation for poor households.

In areas where water is particularly scarce, municipalities and institutions have developed successful systems to reclaim or recycle wastewater. These water reclamation, or "gray water," systems reuse treated or partially treated wastewater for nonpotable uses, such as cooling water, irrigation, landscape watering, and the water supply to toilets and fire hydrants. Other water reclamation projects use treated wastewater to recharge groundwater aquifers.

Another method of replenishing groundwater stores is aquifer storage and recovery (ASR), which consists of pumping surface water (when it is available, as in periods of seasonal rain or floods) into aquifers to be stored for future use. Proponents hail ASR as a low-cost, "environmentally friendly" alternative to the development of additional reservoirs. Critics are most concerned when partially treated surface water or wastewater is pumped into ASR wells. Environmentalists and public health advocates maintain that stored water must first be treated in order to meet drinking water quality standards for the protection of private well owners.

Finally, water banking has been introduced as a strategy to reduce conflicts over water distribution and rights. Water banking is a water management strategy that allows the transfer of water from rights holders with excess allocation to users willing to pay for it. Under this system, holders of water rights can "deposit" some or all of their water allocation into the bank while retaining their rights and avoiding forfeiture for nonuse. Users pay market rates to borrow water from the bank. Proponents claim that water banking will promote water efficiency among rights holders who would gain income from the unused portion of their water allocation.

▪ IMPORTANT POINTS FOR RESEARCHING A STORY ▪

- Pay attention to the effect of water quantity on water quality. (See the brief on "Surface Water Quality.") Drought conditions are often accompanied by surface water pollution problems because the amount of clean water to dilute contaminated discharges is reduced. Conversely, flooding can increase surface water contamination. In one extreme example, severe floods on the Meramec River brought dioxin-contaminated soil into flooded homes in Times Beach, Missouri. After the floods, the river was also found to contain dioxin.

- The public is aware that rainfall is the major source of surface water flow and that lack of rainfall leads to drought and water shortages. People are perhaps less aware of the link between winter snowfall and the supply of water. Dry winters lead to water shortages in the spring or summer. This is particularly true in the dry western states that rely heavily on spring snowmelt to replenish streams. Water supply forecasts, based upon snowmelt and other factors, are available on the Internet from the U.S. Department of Agriculture's Water and Climate Center.
- Water-use data are generally expressed in million of gallons of water used per day (Mgal/d). To better visualize 1 million gallons of water, remember that a good-sized bathtub holds 50 gallons, so 1 million gallons would equal 20,000 bathtubs of water.
- A drought may take months to build to a severity where it is noticeable to the general public. Once it starts to rain again, one or two good rainstorms may not be enough to break a drought. Reservoirs may require months of normal or above-normal rainfall to fill. Groundwater levels may also require months (or years) to recover if severely lowered.

▪ AVOIDING PITFALLS ▪

- As with any topic, the water supply issue has its own jargon. Choose and use your terms carefully. "Sustainable use," "water security," and "water efficiency" are all terms used in discussing the goal of conserving freshwater supplies. Sustainable use of water falls under the wider concept of sustainable development. The goals of sustainable use focus not only on maintaining adequate supplies of clean water for human needs but also include the preservation of adequate water supplies and surface water flow for the natural environment and wildlife populations. The term "water security" is generally used in a more narrow sense to include maintaining adequate water supplies for current and future human populations. The term "water security" may also include water needed for food security. The term "water efficiency" is self-explanatory, referring to the necessary use of water with minimal waste.

▪ INFORMATION RESOURCES ▪

▪ GOVERNMENT/ACADEMIA

- National Drought Mitigation Center (http://drought.unl.edu/)
  P.O. Box 830749, Lincoln, NE 68583-0749
  (402) 472-6707; fax: (402) 472-6614
- United Nations Educational, Scientific and Cultural Organization (UNESCO) (www.unesco.org/water)
  2 United Nations Plaza, Suite 900, New York, NY 10017
  (212) 963-5995; fax: (212) 963-8014
- U.S. Bureau of Reclamation (http://www.usbr.gov/main/what/addresses.html)
  1849 C St. NW, Washington DC 20240-0001
  (202) 513-0501; fax: (202) 513-0314
- U.S. Department of Agriculture—Water and Climate Center (www.wcc.nrcs.usda.gov)
  Natural Resources Conservation Service, OOC/SNRI
  P.O. Box 2890, Room 5204-S, Washington, DC 20013
  (202) 690-2877; fax: (202) 720-4096
- U.S. Geological Survey—Office of Water Quality (www.water.usgs.gov)
  Office of Media Relations, Reston, VA 20192
  (703) 648-4732

▪ INDUSTRY/PROFESSIONAL ASSOCIATIONS

- American Water Resources Association (www.awra.org)
  4 West Federal St., P.O. Box 1626, Middleburg, VA 20118-1626
  (540) 687-8390; fax: (540) 687-8395
  E-mail: info@awra.org
- American Water Works Association (www.awwa.org)
  6666 West Quincy Ave., Denver, CO 80235
  (303) 794-7711

▪ NONPROFIT/CONSUMER ORGANIZATIONS

- Council for Environmental Education (www.c-e-e.org)
  5555 Morningside Drive, Suite 212, Houston, TX 77005
  (713) 520-1936; fax: (713) 520-8008

- National Wildlife Federation
  (www.nwf.org/backyardwildlifehabitat/greenhome.cfm)
  11100 Wildlife Center Drive, Reston, VA 20190-5362
  (703) 438-6000
- Soil and Water Conservation Society (www.swcs.org)
  7515 NE Ankeny Rd., Ankeny, IA 50021-9764
  (515) 289-2331; fax: (515) 289-1227
- World Resources Institute (www.wri.org)
  10 G St. NE, Suite 800, Washington, DC 20002
  (202) 729-7600; fax: (202) 729-7610
  E-mail: front@wri.org

ACRONYMS AND ABBREVIATIONS

AAFA	Asthma and Allergy Foundation of America
ACGIH	American Conference of Governmental Industrial Hygienists
AFBF	American Farm Bureau Federation
AFO	Animal Feeding Operations
AIA	Advance Informed Agreement
ASR	Aquifer Storage and Recovery
ATSDR	Agency for Toxic Substances and Disease Registry
BCRLF	Brownfields Cleanup Revolving Loan Fund
BECC	Border Environmental Cooperation Commission
BHC	Border Health Commission
BICC	Bonn International Center for Conversion
BLEVE	Boiling Liquid Expanding Vapor Explosion
BMP	Best Management Practices
CAFO	Concentrated Animal Feeding Operations
CBIAC	Chemical and Biological Defense Information Analysis Center
CBR	Center for Bioenvironmental Research
CDC	Centers for Disease Control
CDD	Chlorinated Dibenzo-p-dioxins
CDM	Clean Development Mechanism
CEC	Commission for Environmental Cooperation
CERCLA	Comprehensive Environmental Response Compensation and Liability Act (Superfund)
CFC	Chlorofluorocarbon
CFR	Code of Federal Regulations
CHEMTREC	Chemical Transportation Emergency Center
CIESIN	Center for International Earth Science Information Network
CITES	Convention on International Trade in Endangered Species of Wild Fauna and Flora
CLEP	Coalition to End Childhood Lead Poisoning
CNMP	Comprehensive Nutrient Management Plans
CNS	Center for Nonproliferation Studies
COP	Conference of Parties
CSEPP	Chemical Stockpile Emergency Preparedness Programs
CSGWPP	Comprehensive State Ground Water Protection Programs
CWA	Clean Water Act

DDT Dichlorodiphenyl trichloroethane
DES Diethylstilbestrol
DOT U.S. Department of Transportation
DSRT Division of Science, Research and Technology (New Jersey Department of Environmental Protection)
EDSP Endocrine Disruptors Screening Program
EOC Emergency Operations Center
EOSHI Environmental Occupational Health Sciences Institute
EPA Environmental Protection Agency
EPCRA Emergency Planning and Community Right-to-Know Act (SARA Title III)
EQIP Environmental Quality Incentives Program
ESA Endangered Specious Act
ETS Environmental Tobacco Smoke
FAC Foundation for American Communications
FAIR Food Animal Integrated Research
FAO Food and Agriculture Organization
FCCC Framework Convention on Climate Change
FDA Food and Drug Administration
FEMA Federal Emergency Management Administration
FIFRA Federal Insecticide, Fungicide and Rodenticide Act
FOIA Freedom of Information Act
FQPA Food Quality Protection Act
FWS Fish and Wildlife Service
HACCP Hazard Analysis Critical Control Point
HAP Hazardous Air Pollutants
HCF Hydrochlorofluorocarbon
HEPA High-Energy Particulate Absorption
HFC Hydrofluorocarbon
HSMRC Hazardous Substance Management Research Center
HUD Housing and Urban Development
HVAC Heating, Ventilation, and Air-Conditioning
IARC International Agency for Research on Cancer
ICDRM Institute for Crisis, Disaster and Risk Management
ICMA International City/Country Management Association
IPCC Intergovernmental Panel on Climate Change
IPEN International POP Elimination Network
IPIECA International Petroleum Industry Environmental Conservation Association
IPM Integrated Pest Management
MACT Maximum Achievable Control Technology
MCL Maximum Contaminant Levels
MG/L Milligrams of Contaminant per Liter of Water

MNA	Monitored Natural Attenuation
MOA	Memorandum of Agreement
MSDS	Material Safety Data Sheets
MTBE	Methyl *tert*-Butyl Ether
NAAQS	National Ambient Air Quality Standards
NAD BANK	North American Development Bank
NAFTA	North American Free Trade Agreement
NAS	National Academy of Sciences
NAWQA	National Water Quality Assessment Program
NBII	National Biological Information Infrastructure
NEETF	National Environmental Education and Training Foundation
NEJAC	National Environmental Justice Advisory Council
NHANES III	National Health and Nutrition Examination Survey (III)
NIOSH	National Institute for Occupational Safety and Health
NIPR	New Ideas in Pollution Regulation
NJDEP	New Jersey Department of Environmental Protection
NJIT	New Jersey Institute of Technology
NMFS	National Marine Fisheries Services
NOAEL	No Adverse Effect Level
NPDES	National Pollutant Discharge Elimination System
NRC	National Research Council
NRDC	National Resource Defense Council
ODP	Ozone Depleting Potential
ODS	Ozone Depleting Substance
OECD	Organization for Economic Cooperation and Development
OEJ	Office of Environmental Justice
OPCW	Organization for the Prohibition of Chemical Weapons
OSHA	Occupational Safety and Health Administration
OSW	Office of Solid Waste
OSWER	Office of Solid Waste and Emergency Response
PBT	Persistent Bioaccumulative Toxic
PCB	Polychlorinated biphenyl
PEL	Permissible Exposure Limit
PFC	Perfluorocarbon
POP	Persistent Organic Pollutant
PPA	Pollution Prevention Act
PPB	Parts per billion
PPM	Parts per million
PRB	Permeable Reactive Barrier
QRA	Quantitative Risk Assessment
RCRA	Resource Conservation and Recovery Act
RIP	RCRA Implementation Plan
RSV	Respiratory Syncytial Virus

SBCCOM	Soldier and Biological Chemical Command (U.S. Army)
SCBA	Self-Contained Breathing Apparatus
SEJ	Society of Environment Journalists
SEMARNAP	Secretaria de Medio Ambiente Recursos Naturales, y Pesca
SIP	State Implementation Plans
SIPI	Scientists' Institute for Public Information
SPSS	Statistical Package for the Social Sciences
TEF	Toxic Equivalence Factor
TEQ	Toxic Equivalent
TLV	Threshold Limit Value
TMDL	Total Maximum Daily Load
TOMS	Total Ozone Mapping Spectrometer
TRI	Toxic Release Inventory
UGB	Urban Growth Boundary
UMDNJ	University of Medicine and Dentistry of New Jersey
UNEP	United Nations Environment Program
UNESCO	United Nations Educational, Scientific and Cultural Organization
UNPF	United Nations Population Fund
USDA	U.S. Department of Agriculture
USDA-NRCS	U.S. Department of Agriculture–Natural Resources Conservation Service
USGS	U.S. Geological Survey
VA	Veterans Administration
VMT	Vehicle Miles of Travel
VOC	Volatile Organic Compound
WMD	Weapon of Mass Destruction
WMO	World Meteorological Organization

GLOSSARY

2,3,7,8-TCDD A form of dioxin, considered the most deadly synthetic substance known. It is one of 22 TCDDs and one of the overall families of 75 dioxins.

ACID A compound that can neutralize a base. Acids have a high concentration of hydrogen ions. An acid is a compound that has a pH of less than 7 on a scale of 0 to 14. Common acidic materials include vinegar (pH 2.2), apples (pH 3.0), tomatoes (pH 4.2), clean rain water (pH 5.6), and milk (pH 6.6). Strong acids, closer to 0 on the scale, are corrosive. Weak acids, closer to 7, are not. *See* base; pH.

ACID RAIN Any rain, snow, fog, dust, or other precipitation with a pH less than that of clean rain (pH 6.5). *See* acid; pH.

ACUTE DOSE In toxicology, a large amount of exposure or infusion received in a short time (less than a week). Acute doses of some chemicals may be hazardous to health. Acute doses are often used to test a new product or unknown chemical mixture. *See* chronic dose.

ACUTE EFFECT A reaction that occurs shortly after exposure. Sunburn is an acute effect of sunbathing; skin cancer is a chronic effect. *See* chronic effect.

AEROSOL Small particles of liquid or solid suspended in a gas. *See* soot.

AGENT (Also agent of disease) The cause of a particular effect or disease. Agents may be biological (bacteria), chemical, or physical (radiation). An agent alone or in combination with other agents can cause a disease.

AGE-SPECIFIC RATE A relative occurrence rate for a selected age group. An age-specific rate is calculated by dividing the number of events (e.g., deaths, cancer cases) in the selected age group by the total number of people in that group. For working convenience, this number is often multiplied by 100,000 or 1,000,000. For example, if there were 18 white male lung cancer deaths for the age group 55-59 during 1990 in county x, and there were 10,000 white males in county x in 1990, the age-specific rate is 18/10,000 or 180/100,000.

AGGREGATE RISK The fourth step in the quantitative risk-assessment process. The aggregate risk is the risk from exposure to a particular substance to the total population and subpopulation. *See* dose-response assessment; exposure assessment; hazard identification.

ALLERGENS Substances that trigger an immune response in sensitive individuals.

AMBIENT The surrounding environment. Ambient usually refers to the surrounding outdoor air, water, or land.

ANAEROBIC Oxygen is not present. Anaerobic conditions in bodies of water are often responsible for major fish kills. Anaerobic is sometimes confused with aerobic (oxygen is present). *See* thermal pollution.

ANIMAL BIOASSAY A test using animals to determine a chemical's effect. *See* assay.

AQUIFER An underground water source. *See* aquifer recharge; groundwater.

AQUIFER RECHARGE The process whereby water moves from the surface to aquifers under the influence of gravity.

ASBESTOSIS Scarring of the lung from inhalation of airborne asbestos fibers. This disease is often fatal.

ASSAY (Also bioassay) A test using plants, animals, or bacteria to determine a chemical's effect. Assays can determine acute or chronic effects, depending on the method used. *See* acute effect; chronic effect.

ASTHMA Chronic lung disease. Symptoms include coughing, wheezing, and difficulty breathing.

BACKGROUND LEVEL In radiation and chemistry, the concentration that naturally occurs in the environment or is added through human activities. Activities such as mining, manufacturing, disposing, and testing of chemical and radioactive products add to background levels.

BASE A compound that can neutralize an acid. Bases have a large concentration of hydroxyl (one hydrogen atom plus one oxygen atom) ions. A basic compound has a pH of more than 7 on a scale of 0 to 14. Common basic materials include blood (pH 7.4), sea water (pH 8.3), milk of magnesia (pH 10.5), ammonia (pH 11.0), and lime (pH 12.4). Strong bases, pH closer to 14, are corrosive. Weak bases, pH closer to 7, are not. *See* acid; pH.

BENIGN Noncancerous. *See* cancer; malignant.

BIOACCUMULATE (Also bioconcentrate) To build up a large amount of a substance in the body by ingesting small amounts of the substance over an extended period of time. *See* fat-soluble; food chain.

BOIAVAILABILITY The extent to which living things, as opposed to laboratory procedures, can extract toxic chemicals from soil and other material. Material that is not bioavailable is not available to cause toxic effects.

BIOCONCENTRATE *See* bioaccumulate; biomagnification.

BIODIVERSITY Numbers of plants, animals, and other organisms on earth.

BIO-INVASION Biological invasion: the introduction of nonnative species into an area, e.g., gypsy moths, foot and mouth disease.

BIOMAGNIFICATION Increase in concentration of a pollutant from one link in a food chain to another.

BIOPIRACY The process of securing patents and intellectual property rights on native resources with little or no benefit given to the source country.

BIOREMEDIATION A clean-up process in pollution events that involves providing nutrients to damaged areas. The nutrient can break down the pollutant.

BROWNFIELDS Abandoned or neglected industrial or commercial sites whose redevelopment is hindered by concerns about environmental contamination.

CANCER An uncontrolled local cell growth that can migrate to, and appear in, other parts of the body. *See* benign; malignant.

CANCER CLUSTER An abnormally high incidence of cancer in a given area. *See* cluster.

CARBAMATEM A category of pesticides that contain carbon and nitrogen.

CARCINOGEN A cancer-causing agent.

CARDIOVASCULAR DISEASE Disease pertaining to the heart and blood vessels.

CASE In epidemiology, a person with a condition (e.g., disease, birth defect) that is being studied.

CASE-CONTROL STUDY (Also retrospective study) Research that compares people who have a condition (e.g., disease, rash) with similar people who do not have the condition. *See* control group.

CATALYTIC CONVERTER A pollution exhaust-control device installed on post-1975 model cars. Using metals and metallic oxides as the effective agents, it is designed to improve combustion and lower hydrocarbon and carbon monoxide output.

CHELATION A medical procedure in which EDTA, a compound to which lead binds, is injected into the body to remove lead. It is then flushed from the blood and excreted in urine.

CHLORACNE A disfiguring skin condition caused by exposure to any one of a variety of polycyclic halogenated aromatic compounds, including, but not limited to, the dioxins, the dibenzofurans, and some of the PCBs. A virtual carpet of blackheads that can cover areas of the skin, particularly on the face. Cysts and pustules develop and must often be removed surgically. Permanent scarring is common. Most cases heal, leaving scars, in one to two years. Some persist for more than thirty years, with new eruptions occurring periodically.

CHLORINATED Containing chlorine.

CHLORINATED HYDROCARBON A compound that contains chlorine, hydrogen, and carbon. Pesticides (e.g., DDT) are often chlorinated hydrocarbons. Chlorinated hydrocarbons can bioaccumulate and are environmentally persistent. *See* bioaccumulate; environmental persistence.

CHLOROFLUOROCARBON (CFC) People-made compounds containing chlorine, fluorine, and carbon used as propellants in aerosol cans and as refrigerants and insulators. CFCs act as a greenhouse gas in the troposphere.

CHROMOSOME Gene carrier. *See* DNA; gene.

CHRONIC DOSE In toxicology, small amounts of an agent received over a long period of time (months, years). *See* acute dose.

CHRONIC EFFECT A long-term or repeated reaction that occurs after an exposure. Skin cancer is a chronic effect of sunbathing, while sunburn is an acute effect. *See* acute effect.

CLUSTER In epidemiology and statistics, an abnormally high number of events (diseases) with a common pattern in a given area. Diseases in a cluster may or may not have a common cause. *See* cancer cluster.

COGENERS Chemical compounds. *See* isomers.

COHORT STUDY (Also concurrent study, follow-up study, incidence study, longitudinal study, prospective study) Research that follows a group over time to determine how the group responds to events such as chemical exposure, living conditions, or nutrition.

COLONIAS Substandard residential subdivisions located on both sides of the U.S.-Mexico border.

COMEDONES Blackheads, often exhibited by persons who have been exposed to certain types of chemicals. *See* chloracne.

COMMUNICABLE DISEASE A contagious, infectious disease.

COMPOSTING A controlled process of degrading organic matter by microorganisms, the product of which can be used as enriched topsoil.

CONCENTRATION A relative amount of material to a given substance. For example, ten parts of benzene to a million parts air. *See* dose.

CONCURRENT STUDY *See* cohort study.

CONFOUNDING FACTOR Something that complicates or confuses the outcome of a study. For example, smoking confounds studies of occupational exposures to other agents.

CONSERVATIVE RISK ESTIMATE An estimate that ensures that risk is not understated—by overestimating risk.

CONTROL GROUP A comparison group. A group that is statistically identical to the study group except that it does not suffer from the condition (e.g., disease, chemical exposure) that is being studied. Scientifically valid studies have control groups.

CORRELATION In statistics, a number ranging from 1 to–1 that describes the extent to which two variables are related—increase or decrease together. It is a measure of the strength of the relationship between variables.

CURIE A unit used in measuring radioactivity. A curie is equal to the quantity of any radioactive material in which the number of disintegrations per second is 3.7 times 10 to the tenth power. A curie is a measure of the number of radioactive decays per unit of time. One picocurie is one trillionth of a curie. One picocurie per liter of indoor radon is usually assumed to result in 0.005 working levels under typical conditions in a building, which means that 100 picocuries per liter (pCi/l) equals 0.5 working levels.

DELANEY AMENDMENT The portion of the Food, Drug, and Cosmetic Act that prohibits adding a known carcinogen to food.

DENITRIFICATION The process of reduction of nitrate and nitrite compounds to organic nitrogen, which is recycled back to atmospheric nitrogen.

DESERTIFICATION Fertile soil loss due to deforestation of trees that causes the exposed soil to be washed away by storms.

DIFFUSION Movement of molecules of gas or vapor from a source, such as a bottle or can, to a receptor, such as the human nose and respiratory tract.

DNA (deoxyribosenucleic acid) The carrier of genetic information in cells. *See* chromosome; gene.

DOSE A measured amount. The amount of exposure of a kind that produces effects. In the case of chemical pollutants, dose is usually the amount of chemical that gels into the body. *See* concentration.

DOSE-RESPONSE A response that changes as the dose, duration of exposure, and intensity of exposure changes. For example, a few sleeping pills (a small dose) may cause drowsiness, the whole bottle (a large dose) may cause coma or death. *See* aggregate risk; exposure assessment; hazard identification.

DOSE-RESPONSE ASSESSMENT The second step in the quantitative risk-assessment process. In dose-response assessments, human and animal studies are used to determine the human health effects of varying amounts of exposure to substances. *See* animal bioassay; assay.

DRUM, 55-GALLON A standard-size industrial barrel used for storing and transporting raw materials, products, and wastes.

To convert 55-gallon drums to:

cubic feet, multiply number of drums by 7.3524

cubic meters, multiply number of drums by 0.20820.

To convert cubic feet to:

number of 55-gallon drums, divide by 7.35243.

To convert cubic meters to:

number of 55-gallon drums, divide by 0.20820.

ECOLOGY The study of the relationship between living organisms and the environment.

ECOSYSTEM Identifiable area within nature with defined boundaries between various habitat types.

EFFLUENT Outflow from a manufacturing or treatment process. Effluent is usually liquid waste products and often toxic. *See* influent.

ENDOCRINE DISRUPTERS (Also hormonally active agent) Chemicals that interfere with the functioning of the endocrine system.

ENDOCRINE MODULATORS *See* endocrine disrupters.

ENVIRONMENT In public health, everything external to a person that influences his or her health. Environment includes biological, cultural, physical, and mental factors.

ENVIRONMENTAL ESTROGENS Group of chemicals arising from external factors that mimic the effect of hormones that control female characteristics.

ENVIRONMENTAL PERSISTENCE The ability to last, or survive, in the environment. Environmentally persistent substances are long-lasting; they do not biodegrade quickly, if at all. For example, DDT is an environmentally persistent substance. *See* persistent organic pollutants.

ENVIRONMENTAL TOBACCO SMOKE (ETS) Sometimes referred to as secondhand smoke. *See* passive smoke.

EPIDEMIC A rapidly spreading disease. The occurrence in a community or a region of cases of an illness, specific health-related behavior, or other health-related events clearly in excess of what would be expected normally.

EPIDEMIOLOGY The study of diseases in society. Epidemiology includes the study of mortality, morbidity, prevalence, and distribution of diseases. Epidemiology is sometimes confused with etiology.

ESTUARY Inland marine waterway dominated by grass or grasslike plants; they lie mostly between barrier islands and beaches.

EUTROPHICATION Uncontrolled growth of plankton or algae blooms.

EXPOSURE Contact. Exposure may be oral (by mouth), dermal (through the skin), or by inhalation (breathing).

EXPOSURE ASSESSMENT The third step in the quantitative risk-assessment process. In exposure assessment, a determination is made on the concentration of substances to which humans are exposed. *See* aggregate risk; dose-response assessment; hazard identification.

EXTRAPOLATION Educated guesses regarding the impact of a substance on human health based on currently available data.

FAT-SOLUBLE Can be stored in fat (lipid) tissue. Substances that are fat-soluble are easily passed up the food chain. *See* bioaccumulate; food chain; water-soluble.

FOLLOW-UP STUDY *See* cohort study.

FOOD CHAIN A sequence of organisms where the higher form in the chain uses the lower for food. *See* bioaccumulate; fat-soluble.

FOOD WEB Interlinking food chain.

FOSSIL FUEL Coal, natural gas, oil, or any other fuel that developed from the remains of prehistoric plants and animals.

GAMMA RAYS High-energy waves often produced when a radioactive source decays. Gamma rays do not contain particles but may be emitted along with both alpha and beta particles.

GAS CHROMATOGRAPH A machine that may be used to detect very low concentrations of a gas.

GENE A code for an inherited trait. *See* chromosome; DNA.

GENETIC ENGINEERING The introduction of genes into an organism in a laboratory that endow the organism with specific desirable properties. *See* interspecies engineering; intraspecies genetic engineering.

GREENHOUSE GASES Heat-trapping gases that cause global warming. They include water vapor, carbon dioxide, methane, nitrous oxide, and halocarbons, including chlororluorocarbons.

GROUNDWATER Water that moves slowly underground in an aquifer. Once groundwater has been contaminated, it is nearly impossible to return it to its pure state. Groundwater is the main, but not the only, source of drinking water. *See* aquifer.

HABITAT Specific environment in which a species thrives and is defined by its location, climate, vegetation, and physical environment.

HALF-LIFE In radiation and chemistry, the time needed for half of the material or effect to decay, react, or dissipate. Materials and agents that have a long half-life are environmentally persistent. *See* environmental persistence.

HAZARD Exposure to the chance of loss, injury, risk, or danger. Hazard is magnitude times probability times the number of people exposed.

HAZARD IDENTIFICATION The first step in the quantitative risk-assessment process. In hazard identification, human and animal studies are used to determine whether a substance can cause human health effects. *See* aggregate risk; animal bioassay; assay; dose-response assessment; exposure assessment.

HAZARDOUS WASTE As defined by the Resource Conservation and Recovery Act (RCRA), a waste that may cause, or significantly contribute to, illness or death or that may substantially threaten human health or the environment when it is not properly controlled.

HEALTH A state of physical, mental, and social well-being.

HYDROCARBON A compound that contains only hydrogen and carbon. Hydrocarbons are found primarily in petroleum, natural gas, and coal products. *See* chlorinated hydrocarbon.

HYDROLOGICAL CYCLE The cyclical movement of water on the earth, including surface movements, evaporation, precipitation, and underground movement.

HYDROPHOBIC Chemicals that are highly soluble in fat and have little or no affinity to water; persist for a long time in the environment.

HYPOTHESIS A supposition arrived at from observation or reflection that leads to refutable predictions.

IMMUNE RESPONSE A protective action against illness. Antibody production is an immune response.

IMMUNOCOMPETENCE The ability to develop an immune response. *See* immune response.

IMPACT In ecology, the effect of human activities on an ecosystem.

INCIDENCE The number of new events (e.g., cancer cases, deaths) in a given time period. Incidence is usually calculated for a one-year time period.

INCIDENCE STUDY *See* cohort study.

INDUSTRIAL HYGIENE The study and practice of creating a safe workplace.

INFLUENT Materials that flow into a manufacturing or treatment system. Raw materials are often called influents, as opposed to effluents, which are finished products. *See* effluent.

INORGANIC SUBSTANCE Substance that does not contain carbon. Metals are inorganic chemicals.

INTEGRATED PEST MANAGEMENT (IPM) The control of crop-damaging pests through the introduction of natural predators.

INTERSPECIES GENETIC ENGINEERING Process where genetic material is removed from and combined with DNA from members of the same species. *See* genetic engineering; intraspecies genetic engineering.

INTRASPECIES GENETIC ENGINEERING Process where genetic material introduced into host organisms comes from donor of different species. *See* genetic engineering; interspecies genetic engineering.

IN VITRO Outside the body. In vitro usually refers to a test in a laboratory. *See* in vivo.

IN VIVO Inside the body. *See* in vitro.

ION An atom or molecule with an electric charge. A cation has a positive charge. An anion has a negative charge.

IONIZING RADIATION Energy that breaks a compound into ions. The high energy produced by ionizing radiation can cause severe damage to plants and animal tissue. Sources of ionizing radiation include uranium and X ray machines. *See* nonionizing radiation.

ISOMERS Two compounds are considered isomers if they have the same molecular formula (i.e., the same number and types of atoms) but different structures. *See* cogeners.

LATENCY PERIOD Delay between exposure to a disease-causing agent and the appearance of manifestations of the disease. The term may be used synonymously with induction period.

LD50 The dose needed to kill half an experimental animal population. A small LD50 indicates a highly toxic substance because only a small dose is needed to kill half the test animals. A large LD50 indicates low toxicity because a large dose is needed for the same effect.

LEAD A soft, bluish or silvery gray metal usually found in sulfite deposits in association with other minerals, particularly zinc and copper. Lead, a metal that does not biodegrade or break down into other substances, is the toxic metal present in the atmosphere in the largest concentration.

LONGITUDINAL STUDY A study of effects over time. *See* cohort study.

MALIGNANT Cancerous. *See* benign; cancer.

MAQUILADORAS Foreign-owned industrial plants.

MASS SPECTROMETER A machine that may be used to detect very low concentrations of a chemical. A mass spectrometer separates compounds by mass.

MERCURY Refined from cinnabar to form a variety of compounds, mercury is a stable-occurring toxic trace metal.

MESOTHELIOMA Cancer in the mucous membrane lining of the chest, heart, or abdomen directly related to inhalation of asbestos fibers.

METALS Chemical elements that do not break down or degrade.

MODEL A description of a process, often in the form of a mathematical equation and/or computer simulation. Models are sometimes used to predict an event. For example, a model of an oil spill can show how far a slick may spread. An air-quality model can predict where a plume may travel.

MORBIDITY Sickness. Morbidity is often confused with mortality (death).

MORTALITY Death. Mortality is often confused with morbidity (sickness).

MUTAGEN An agent that can permanently alter genetic material.

NEURONS Cells that carry nervous impulses.

NEUROTOXIN Nerve poison.

NO ADVERSE EFFECT LEVEL (NOAEL) The maximum amount of exposure to a toxic substance at which there is no detectable adverse effect on human health.

NONIONIZING RADIATION Radiation without sufficient energy to transfer large amounts of energy to individual atoms in the region through which it passes. *See* ionizing radiation.

NONPOINT SOURCE POLLUTION Pollution where the source is broad and cannot be easily pinpointed.

NUCLEAR FISSION The splitting of an atomic nucleus.

NUCLEAR MEDICINE Branch of medicine concerned with diagnostic, therapeutic, and investigative uses of radioactive materials.

OFF-GASSING Process lasting from a few days to over a month by which irritating gases and particles, such as formaldehyde, are emitted into the indoor environment by new furniture, rugs, covers, wallboard, and similar items.

ONCOLOGY Branch of medicine dealing with tumors.

ORGANIC Of, pertaining to, or derived from living organisms.

ORGANIC CHEMICAL A chemical containing carbon. Many organic chemicals are fat-soluble and can bioaccumulate. They are usually relatively insoluble in water. *See* bioaccumulate; fat-soluble; water-soluble.

ORGANOCHLORINES A category of pesticides. Organic compounds that have been chlorinated, usually with several atoms of chlorine per molecule.

ORGANOPHOSPHATES A category of pesticides that contain carbon and phosphorus. They are usually used to kill insects.

OUTCROPPING The transfer of genes from crops to wild plants through pollen transport.

PARTICULATE Minute particle. A particulate can be toxic. If inhaled, a particulate can interfere with the respiratory and other defense systems of the body.

PARTICULATE MATTER Airborne materials that can, depending on their size and composition, lodge in various areas of the human respiratory tract. A good comparison is several levels of screening with holes of increasing size. The finest particles can descend into the deepest regions of the lung; the largest particles stop within the nasal passages.

PASSIVE SMOKE Exposure of nonsmokers to smoke. *See* environmental tobacco smoke.

PATHOGEN A disease-causing microorganism.

PERMISSIBLE EXPOSURE LIMITS (PELs) Exposure limits to a chemical, as determined by OSHA, below which most individuals can work day after day with no harmful effects. This limit is legally enforceable.

PERSISTENT ORGANIC POLLUTANTS (POPs) Highly stable organic compounds used as pesticides or in industry that persist in the environment, accumulate in fatty tissue of most organisms, and are toxic to humans and wildlife.

PESTICIDE A general term covering a wide variety of chemical compounds that control unwanted plants, insects, rodents, or other pests. Pesticides include herbicides, which kill plants; insecticides, which kill insects; and fungicides, which kill microorganisms.

pH A measure of the strength of an acid or base. It is measured on a scale of 0 to 14, where 7 is considered neutral (neither acidic nor basic). Acids measure less than 7 on the scale. Bases measure greater than 7 on the scale. pH is related to the quantity of hydrogen ions present in a solution. *See* acid; base; ion.

PHARMACOLOGY The study of drugs.

PICOCURIES (pCi/l) A measurement used to assess indoor radon levels. It is usually reported as pCi per liter or pCi/l.

PLANKTON Forms of marine, organic life that gather vital energy for life through the process of photosynthesis.

POINT-SOURCE POLLUTION Discharges from a particular pipe or leak.

POPULATION The entire collection of people, houses, counties, animals, or other elements under study.

PPB (parts per billion) The occurrence relative to a base of one billion. One part per billion is 5 people out of the total world population (5 billion) or four drops of water in an Olympic-size pool (64,000 gallons). 1 ppb = 0.001 ppm = 1 nanogram/gram = 1,000 nanograms/liter.

PPM (parts per million) The occurrence relative to a base of one million. One part per million is 200 people out of the total population of the United States (200 million) or one penny in $10,000. 1 ppm = 0.0001 percent = 1 milligram/kilogram = 1 milligram/liter.

PREVALENCE A measure of how widespread a disease is in a certain population at a certain time. Prevalence is usually greater than incidence because it not only includes new cases but all old cases as well.

PROSPECTIVE STUDY *See* cohort study.

QUANTITATIVE RISK ASSESSMENT A multistep process used to evaluate chronic human health risks associated with chemical, biological, and physical substances.

RAD (radiation absorbed dose) The unit denoting the amount of absorbed radiation.

RADIATION Any variety of forms of energy generated through space. Radiation can be in the form of particles (e.g., alpha rays or beta rays) or waves (e.g., X-rays, light, microwaves, or radio waves). Ionizing radiation, such as X-rays, carries enough energy to break chemical and electrical bonds. Nonionizing radiation, such as microwaves, does not.

RADURA International symbol for radiation; used for labeling of irradiated foods.

REFUGIA Lands of nonresistant plant varieties planted between fields of Bt crops; slows development of Bt resistance in pest populations.

RELATIVE RISK (Also risk ratio) The disease rate in an exposed group compared to that in an unexposed group.

RESIN A class of organic chemicals. Resins can be mixed with other chemicals to form plastics. *See* organic chemical.

RESPIRATORY SYNCYTIAL VIRUS (RSV) A virus that is the most common cause of lower respiratory tract infections in children and is also the most common cause of pneumonia in young children. RSV can produce long-term effects such as wheezing or asthma.

RETROSPECTIVE STUDY *See* case-control study.

RIPARIAN WATER Surface or groundwater that is adjacent to a landowner's property.

RISK The chance of an injury, illness, or death caused by exposure to a hazard.

RISK ASSESSMENT A process that evaluates the risk of a hazard, estimates the population exposed to the hazard, and assesses the relative importance of the public health risk.

RISK FACTOR Correlation of causation within a risk. For example, smoking, which increases the risk of getting lung cancer, is a risk factor.

RISK RATIO *See* relative risk.

SAMPLE A portion of the population selected for study. *See* population.

SAVANNA A flat, tropical or subtropical grassland.

SOLVENT A liquid capable of dissolving a material and holding it in solution. For example, paint remover is a paint solvent.

SOOT Carbonaceous aerosol. *See* aerosol.

STATISTICAL SIGNIFICANCE An estimate of the likelihood (probability) that an observation or finding occurred by chance.

STRATOSPHERE The upper atmosphere located above the troposphere.

SUCCIMER Chelating agent used to treat lead poisoning. *See* chelation.

SURFACE WATER Water at the surface of the earth, including lakes, rivers, ponds, and streams. It is the source of much groundwater through the larger hydrologic cycle as water moves from the surface to aquifers below ground.

SYNERGISM When substances acting together have an effect greater than that of any component taken alone.

THERMAL POLLUTION Contamination caused by heat. Thermal pollution may cause an anaerobic condition in water and result in a fish kill. *See* anaerobic.

THRESHOLD The minimum amount needed for a given effect to occur. For example, an odor threshold is the smallest amount of a substance needed to produce an odor. The level of exposure below which risk is absent. The level below which no measurable harm occurs.

THRESHOLD LIMIT VALUE (TLV) The lifetime daily exposure to an airborne substance with no long-term negative effect. Occupational levels are different from public levels, since there is a greater range of threshold in the general population than in a group of workers, who are considered to be relatively healthy.

TOTAL MAXIMUM DAILY LOAD (TMDL) Maximum pollutant loading a body of water (e.g., stream or lake) can accept and still meet water quality standards.

TOXIC Poisonous.

TOXIC EQUIVALENCE FACTORS (TEFs) *See* toxic equivalents.

TOXIC EQUIVALENTS (TEQs) Method whereby dioxin or mixtures of dioxin are described relative to the toxicity of TCDD, the most toxic form of dioxin.

TOXICOLOGIST A scientist who studies how chemicals interact in a harmful way with the body.

TROPOSPHERE That part of the atmosphere within approximately 8 kilometers (4.97 miles) of the surface of the earth.

VENTILATION The active movement and distribution of air within a building.

VITAL RECORDS Governmental records of births, deaths, marriages, divorces, and so forth.

VOLATILE Able to change quickly to a gas.

WATERSHED The land area that drains to a water surface body or recharges a groundwater aquifer.

WATER-SOLUBLE Capable of being dissolved in water. Water-soluble chemicals can contaminate water supplies and aquifers. However, they do not bioaccumulate well and can pass quickly through the body. *See* aquifer; bioaccumulate; fat-soluble.

X-RAYS A form of electromagnetic waves similar to light but with a shorter wavelength (higher frequency). X-rays are a form of ionizing radiation. *See* ionizing radiation.

ABOUT THE AUTHORS

MICHAEL R. GREENBERG is professor and associate dean of the faculty of the Edward J. Bloustein School of Planning and Public Policy, Rutgers University. Greenberg studies the impact of urbanization and industrialization on public health and the environment. His books include *Urbanization and Cancer Mortality* (1983), *Hazardous Waste Sites: The Credibility Gap* (1984), *Public Health and the Environment* (1987), and *Environmental Risk and the Press* (1987). He has contributed more than 400 publications to scientific journals such as *Cancer Research*, *American Journal of Epidemiology*, and *New England Journal of Medicine* and such public interest journals as *Science*, *The Sciences*, and *Public Interest*. Most recently, he served on a National Academy of Sciences (NAS) committee that oversees destruction of the U.S. chemical weapons stockpile.

M. JANE LEWIS is an assistant professor at the School of Public Health, University of Medicine and Dentistry of New Jersey, where she teaches courses in health education, health communication, and risk communication. She has an M.A. in journalism and more than twenty years of experience in communicating health information. Her research focuses on perceptions and attitudes impacting cancer control efforts, evaluation of tobacco control communication strategies, and tobacco industry marketing practices and their effects. She is a member of the Environmental and Occupational Health Sciences Institute.

RENÉE M. ROGERS is an environmental consultant specializing in human health risk assessment. She frequently writes about environmental and public health issues for nontechnical audiences.

DAVID B. SACHSMAN holds the George R. West Jr. Chair of Excellence in Communication and Public Affairs at the University of Tennessee at Chattanooga. Previously, he chaired the journalism department at Rutgers University. He is known for his research and scholarly activities in environmental communication and environmental risk reporting.

BERNADETTE M. WEST is an assistant professor at the School of Public Health, University of Medicine and Dentistry of New Jersey. She previously served as executive director for Mid-State Health Advisory Corporation, a regional health planning agency in Lawrenceville, New Jersey. West was coauthor of the second edition of *The Reporter's Environmental Handbook*. Her other research areas include community assessment, health planning, and disabilities and violence.

INDEX